Women Activists and Civil Rights Leaders in Auto/Biographical Literature and Films

Delphine Letort · Benaouda Lebdai
Editors

Women Activists and Civil Rights Leaders in Auto/Biographical Literature and Films

palgrave
macmillan

Editors
Delphine Letort
Le Mans University
Le Mans, France

Benaouda Lebdai
Le Mans University
Le Mans, France

ISBN 978-3-319-77080-2   ISBN 978-3-319-77081-9   (eBook)
https://doi.org/10.1007/978-3-319-77081-9

Library of Congress Control Number: 2018936576

© The Editor(s) (if applicable) and The Author(s) 2018
This work is subject to copyright. All rights are solely and exclusively licensed by the Publisher, whether the whole or part of the material is concerned, specifically the rights of translation, reprinting, reuse of illustrations, recitation, broadcasting, reproduction on microfilms or in any other physical way, and transmission or information storage and retrieval, electronic adaptation, computer software, or by similar or dissimilar methodology now known or hereafter developed.
The use of general descriptive names, registered names, trademarks, service marks, etc. in this publication does not imply, even in the absence of a specific statement, that such names are exempt from the relevant protective laws and regulations and therefore free for general use.
The publisher, the authors and the editors are safe to assume that the advice and information in this book are believed to be true and accurate at the date of publication. Neither the publisher nor the authors or the editors give a warranty, express or implied, with respect to the material contained herein or for any errors or omissions that may have been made. The publisher remains neutral with regard to jurisdictional claims in published maps and institutional affiliations.

Cover credit: johnwoodcock

Printed on acid-free paper

This Palgrave Macmillan imprint is published by the registered company Springer International Publishing AG part of Springer Nature
The registered company address is: Gewerbestrasse 11, 6330 Cham, Switzerland

CONTENTS

Introduction   1
Delphine Letort and Benaouda Lebdai

Part I   The Lives of Women Activists

Winnie Madikizela Mandela: The Construction
of a South African Political Icon   13
Benaouda Lebdai

"Revoluting" or Writing? Ahdaf Soueif
and the 2011 Egyptian Revolution   33
Jacqueline Jondot

Autobiography of an Activist: Sophonisba Breckinridge,
"Champion of the Championless"   45
Anya Jabour

Lean In and *Tell Me a (True) Story:* Sheryl Sandberg's
Revision of Feminist History   65
Tanya Ann Kennedy

v

vi CONTENTS

Part II Black History in Auto/biographical Texts

The Many Lives of Ida B. Wells: Autobiography,
Historical Biography, and Documentary 91
Delphine Letort

Malcolm X: From the Autobiography to Spike Lee's
Film, Two Complementary Perspectives on the Man
and the Militant Black Leader 109
Dominique Dubois

Michelle Obama: The Voice and Embodiment
of (African) American History 123
Pierre-Marie Loizeau

Ghost Writing and Filming Biography
in *Twelve/12 Years a Slave* 139
Sylvie Charron

Part III Biographical Films and History

Biographical Motion Pictures and the Resuscitation
of "Real Lives" 153
Taïna Tuhkunen

"Negro Girl (meager)": Black Women's In/Visibility
in Contemporary Films About Slavery 171
Lisa Botshon and Melinda Plastas

Queering the Biopic? *Milk* (2008) and the Biographic Real 189
Isabelle Van Peteghem-Tréard

In Search of Purcell's Legacy: Tony Palmer's *England,
My England* (1995) 207
Nicole Cloarec

Part IV Postface

Does One Need to Be a Man to Be a Great Man?   223
Nathalie Prince

Index   227

NOTES ON CONTRIBUTORS

Lisa Botshon is Professor of English and Women's and Gender Studies at the University of Maine at Augusta. Her publications have focused on women writers, popular culture, and the middlebrow. Her current project explores women's back-to-the-land memoirs from the interwar era.

Sylvie Charron is Professor Emerita of French at the University of Maine at Farmington. She has a longstanding interest in literary voices calling for social change and expressing the human condition at the margins of society. In recent years, she focused on regional and immigrant francophone literature. She did extensive research on George Sand and translated *The Marquise and Pauline* with Sue Huseman. She also translated and analyzed *Les raisins de la galère* by Tahar Ben Jelloun (to be published) and *Canuck* by Camille Lessard-Bissonnette, which depicts the life of Franco Americans in the factories of Lewiston/Lowell at the turn of the 20th century (edited by Rhea Côté-Robbins).

Nicole Cloarec is a Senior Lecturer in English at Rennes 1 University. She is the author of a doctoral thesis on Peter Greenaway's films and a number of articles on British and English-speaking cinema. She has edited two collective volumes on letters and the insertion of written material in films and recently co-edited *Social Class on British and American Screens: Essays on Cinema and Television* (2016). Her latest research focuses on questions of transmediality, adaptation, and documentary.

ix

Dominique Dubois is currently a Professor of English Literature at Angers University. His research topic is postcolonial literature and more particularly Wilson Harris. He wrote two dissertations on Wilson Harris, the first studied the theme of the quest in the *The Guyana Quartet* and the second on the creative process at work in Harris' novels. It was published by the Presses Universitaires du Septentrion in 1998 under the title *Transcendance dans l'Oeuvre de Wilson Harris*. After his PhD, he continued his research on Harris and this led to the publication of about 10 papers on various aspects of his work. He has also published extensively on various postcolonial writers, including V. S. Naipaul, George Lamming, Olive Senior, Michael Anthony, Earl Lovelace, Margaret Atwood, and Lawrence Scott. He has also written on short-story writers such as Raymond Carver and John McGahern.

Anya Jabour is Regents Professor of History at the University of Montana, where she has taught U.S. women's history and the history of the American South since earning her Ph.D. from Rice University in 1995. Her previous books include *Marriage in the Early Republic: Elizabeth and William Wirt and the Companion Ideal* (Johns Hopkins University Press, 1998); *Scarlett's Sisters: Young Women in the Old South* (University of North Carolina Press, 2007); and *Topsy-Turvy: How the Civil War turned the World Upside Down for Southern Children* (Ivan R. Dee, 2010). Her biography of Breckinridge, *Sophonisba Breckinridge and Women's Activism in Modern America*, is forthcoming from the University of Illinois Press.

Jacqueline Jondot is a Professor at Toulouse-Jean-Jaurès University (France) and a Doctor in English Literature. She wrote a third-cycle thesis on *Orlando* by Virginia Wolf and a PhD thesis (Doctorat d'état) on Middle Eastern Arab authors who write in the English language; she has written articles on Ahdaf Soueif, Edward Atiyah, Carl Gibeily, Yasmin Zahran, Jamal Mahjoub, Fadia Faqir, Susan Abulhawa... as well as on British women writers (Virginia Woolf, Penelope Lively, Mary Shelley). She also translated *Outremer* by Nabil Saleh. Her photos of Cairene mashrabiyyas and Egyptian Revolution graffiti have been exhibited. She coordinated to an issue of *Horizons Maghrébins* on the Revolution in Egypt, including her photos of street graffiti.

Tanya Ann Kennedy is an Associate Professor at the University of Maine-Farmington. Her research and teaching interests include media

NOTES ON CONTRIBUTORS   xi

and new media studies, feminist theory, race and ethnicity, gender and globalization, and twentieth-century and contemporary US literature and culture. Her book *Historicizing Post-Discourses: Postfeminism and Postracism in U.S. Culture* is forthcoming from SUNY Press in spring 2017.

Benaouda Lebdai is a specialist in Colonial and Postcolonial Literature written in English and French. He obtained a PhD in 1987 at the University of Essex, UK, in comparative literature and has also a French doctorate on the Ghanaian novelist Ayi Kwei Armah. He has published extensively on African writers such as Chinua Achebe, Peter Abrahams, J. M. Coetzee, Nadine Gordimer, Zoë Wicomb, Winnie Mandela, Ngugi Wa Thiong' O, Ayi Kwei Armah, Rachid Boudjedra, Assia Djebar, Albert Camus, and Frantz Fanon. He published on transatlantic slave trade narratives. His critical studies deal with the complex relations between literature and history, gender, identity, migration, basing his analysis on postcolonial theory, Edward Said, Frantz Fanon, Homi Bhabha, Gayatri Spivak and on narratology, Rimmon-Kenan and Gérard Genette. He organized numerous international conferences on colonial and post-colonial literature in France, Algeria, and the USA. He is currently Professor at Le Mans University, France. He also taught Comparative African Literature at Algiers University (Algeria) and Angers University (France). His latest publication is *Autobiography as a Writing Strategy in Postcolonial Literature* (Cambridge Scholars Publishing, 2015).

Delphine Letort is a Professor in American Studies at Le Mans University, where she teaches American civilization and film studies. She has published *Du film noir au néo-noir: mythes et stéréotypes de l'Amérique 1941–2008* (Paris: L'Harmattan, 2010) and *The Spike Lee Brand: A Study of Documentary Filmmaking* (SUNY, 2015). She has written numerous articles about film adaptations, documentary filmmaking, and African American cinema in journals in France (*Revue LISA/LISA e-journal,In-Media,Transatlantica*, etc.) and abroad (*Screen,Alphaville,Media, War and Conflict*, etc.). She has co-edited several journal issues (*Documentary Filmmaking Practices: From Propaganda to Dissent;Exploring War Memories in American Documentaries*) and books (*L'Adaptation cinéma-tographique: premières pages, premiers plans*, 2014; *La Culture de l'en-gagement à l'écran*, 2015; *Social Class on British and American Screens: Essays on Cinema and Television*, 2016; *Auto/biographies historiques dans* *les arts*, 2017), a thematic issue for the *CinémAction* series (*Panorama mondial du film noir*, 2014). She serves on the advisory editorial board of *Black Camera* (Bloomington, Indiana) and is the chief editor of *Revue Lisa/Lisa e-journal* (https://lisa.revues.org/159), ISSN: 1762-6153, Presses Universitaires de Rennes (France).

Pierre-Marie Loizeau is an Associate Professor of English at the University of Angers, France. He earned his PhD in American Civilization from the University of Angers in 2000 with a dissertation entitled "American First Ladies: Their (Ir)resistible Ascent." His research focuses on White House history, the US presidency, and the role and power of First Ladies. He is a member of the AFEA (Association Française d'Études Américaines) and the SAES (Société des Anglicistes de l'Enseignement Supérieur). He is the author of *First Ladies: De la Tradition à la Modernité* (Paris: Ellipses, 2012), *Martin Van Buren: The Little Magician* (Hauppauge, New York: Nova History Publishers, 2009), *Nancy Reagan in Perspective* (Hauppauge, New York: Nova History Publishers, 2005).

Melinda Plastas teaches Women and Gender Studies at Bates College. Her interests include race and social movements, gender and militarization, and gender and tobacco capitalism. Her book *A Band of Noble Women: Race Politics in the Women's Peace Movement* was published in 2011 by Syracuse University Press.

Nathalie Prince is a Professor of Comparative Literature and French Literature at Le Mans University. She is the Director of the 3L.AM Research Center (Le Laboratoire Langues, Littératures, Linguistique des universités d'Angers et du Mans). She has published *La Littérature de jeunesse: Pour une théorie littéraire* (Armand Colin, collection «U», 2nd ed., 2015), *La Littérature fantastique* (Armand Colin, collection 128, 2015), and *Petit Musée des Horreurs: Nouvelles fantastiques, cruelles et macabres* (Robert Laffont, collection «Bouquins», 2nd ed., 2013).

Taïna Tuhkunen is a Professor of American Studies at the University of Angers. Her published work includes her PhD thesis on Sylvia Plath's poetry and prose, *Sylvia Plath: Une écriture embryonnaire* (2002), a coedited study of Stanley Kubrick's film adaptation of Vladimir Nabokov's *Lolita* (2009), and numerous articles on North American Literature and Cinema. Her most recent book *Demain sera un autre jour: Le Sud et ses héroïnes à l'écran* (*Tomorrow Is Another Day: The*

South and Its Heroines on Screen, 2013) explores representations of the American South on screen since the beginning of film history.

Isabelle Van Peteghem-Tréard teaches in Classes Préparatoires Littéraires and Cine-Sup in Nantes and is a specialist in figures of sublimation in American cinema and literature. She has published a book on Alice Walker and has written numerous articles on independent cinema (Gus Van Sant, Sofia Coppola, Debra Granik).

LIST OF FIGURES

Winnie Madikizela Mandela: The Construction of a South African Political Icon

Fig. 1 Nelson and Winnie Mandela met in the early 1960s and agreed to a marriage based on a "political pact". © Photofest. Photographer: David Messenbring — 20

Lean In **and** *Tell Me a (True) Story***: Sheryl Sandberg's Revision of Feminist History**

Fig. 1 Sheryl Sandberg embodies the philosophy of *Lean In* (2013). © Penguin Random House LLC — 66

Fig. 2 Lilly Ledbetter exhibits her working-class background. © Penguin Random House LLC — 67

Fig. 3 Unite Here Local 26, a union of employees at the Hilton DoubleTree Suites hotel in Boston created leaflets to appeal for Sandberg's support. © UNITE HERE Local 26 — 84

*Malcolm X***: From the Autobiography to Spike Lee's Film, Two Complementary Perspectives on the Man and the Militant Black Leader**

Fig. 1 Spike Lee focuses on Malcolm X's public figure and political message. © Warner Bros./Photofest — 110

Michelle Obama: The Voice and Embodiment of (African) American History

Fig. 1 Michelle Obama on *The Ellen DeGeneres Show*, an "ordinary" woman with an "extraordinary" destiny. © NBC/Photofest — 126

xvi   LIST OF FIGURES

Ghost Writing and Filming Biography in *Twelve/12 Years a Slave*
Fig. 1   The fiddle appears as a recurrent trope to illustrate
Northup's emotions. © Fox Searchlight Picture/Photofest   146

"Negro Girl (meager)": Black Women's In/Visibility in Contemporary Films About Slavery
Fig. 1   *Belle* (Gugu Mbatha-Raw) appears on equal footing with
her half-cousin (Sarah Gadon). © Fox Searchlight
Pictures/Photofest   181

Queering the Biopic? *Milk* (2008) and the Biographic Real
Fig. 1   Gus Van Sant's celebratory portrait of pioneering gay
activist Harvey Milk Sean Penn shows him earning his place in
history. © Focus Features/Photofest Photographer: Phil Bray   192

Introduction

Delphine Letort and Benaouda Lebdai

Literature scholar Philippe Lejeune has pioneered academic studies into the genre of autobiography, which he defines as a "retrospective prose narrative produced by a real person concerning his own existence, focusing on his individual life, in particular on the development of his personality" (Lejeune 1989: 5). Autobiographical writers often retrace their own lives in an attempt to understand the events that shaped their lives, delving into the intimate reasoning behind some of their vital decisions. Whether such accounts are truthful or not arouses debates about their authenticity, which however undermines their testimonial values. Jean Starobinski contends that the psychological dimension of autobiographies may overshadow their historical value, for writers use their own lives to reflect on broader issues. He thereby differentiates the journal and its emphasis on the narrator's internal dilemmas from the memoir which spotlights historical facts (Starobinski 1970: 3). Literature scholars have long contested the literary values of autobiographical writing,

---

D. Letort (✉) · B. Lebdai
Le Mans University, Le Mans, France
e-mail: delphine.letort@univ-lemans.fr

B. Lebdai
e-mail: benaouda.lebdai@univ-lemans.fr

© The Author(s) 2018
D. Letort and B. Lebdai (eds.), *Women Activists and Civil Rights Leaders in Auto/Biographical Literature and Films*,
https://doi.org/10.1007/978-3-319-77081-9_1

whose creative power and narrative originality are limited to the facts of one's life. However, autobiographies also rely on narratives and storytelling to convey one's individual perception of oneself—even if this image construction results in mythmaking. While some life narratives replicate dominant cultural models, others offer conscious reflections on the practice of writing about oneself and resist "master narratives" (Lyotard 1979).

The "biographical turn" transformed inquiring methods in the humanities and social sciences in the 1970s, renewing interest in individual lives and stories as a way of understanding the processes of historical and social change. Autobiographies provide historians with a unique lens through which one can access the past and a prism which enables readers to understand how individuals negotiated their life trajectories in the context of past events. *Autobiography as a Writing Strategy in Postcolonial Literature* comprises several chapters about the use of autobiography as a path of resistance and a liberating experience in postcolonial literature while participating in the rehabilitation of autobiographies as literary texts (Lebdai 2015: 1–2). The postcolonial angle also highlights the political intent of the genre: many civil rights activists have turned to autobiographical writing to gain a voice in a collective narrative and resist the grand narrative which, according to Lyotard, represses individual creativity and rejects difference. Instead, Lyotard argues for an abundance of little narratives which acknowledge diversity and difference in postmodern society (Lyotard 1979).[1] Postcolonial leaders have used their own life stories to challenge and question the authority of grand narratives, leveling criticism at their claim for universal values by calling attention to their failings. These historical figures have empowered autobiographical writing by endowing the genre with a political agenda. Feminist writers Angela Davis, Assata Shakur, and Elaine Brown have chronicled their experience of the Black Power movement in autobiographies that interweave their personal stories with communal engagements,

---

[1] "Instead of the grand narrative, Lyotard argues for a multiplicity of little narratives which resist and challenge the dominant narratives, the fragmented quality of the former protecting them from being incorporated into any of the latter. The little narrative is the antithesis of the grand narrative, representing flexibility and constantly reinventing itself, free from the weight of tradition and the restrictions of preconceived ideologies" (Du Toit 2011: 88).

INTRODUCTION 3

thereby demonstrating that their individual choices could not be severed from the collective (Perkins 2000). Their first-person narratives reinforce their agency by carving out space for their voices, and articulate an engagement with history that cannot be reduced to the personal. Homi Bhabha aptly underlines the political importance of women's autobiographical voices which make visible "the traumatic ambivalences of a personal, psychic history to the wider disjunctions of political existence" (Bhabha 1994: 15). Postcolonial scholars examine the "unhomely moments" in female autobiographies and draw attention to "domestic space as the space of normalizing," hoping to make visible what should be hidden from sight. This view pervades the writing by civil rights activists whose political awareness emerges from living in the interstices of society.

Women Activists and Civil Rights Leaders in Auto/Biographical Literature and Cinema argues that the recognition of autobiography as activism has paved the way for the biographical turn by highlighting "the capacity of an individual life to reflect broad historical change" (Caine 2010: 5). Some historians lament the focus on private life that undermines the "grand narratives" of the past and neglects the importance of historical process by shifting attention away from political developments as well as social and economic dynamics. We posit that life writing—in the form of autobiographies translating the subjective perspective of their author or biographies transcribed by different authors—is a source of artistic creativity that enables us to take a fresh look at history. This creative input may flourish through the introduction of fictional elements in biographies and autobiographies, paving the way for the construction of historical characters and narrative arcs that generate the so-called "reality effect"—identified as "an *effet de réel* which is created by irrelevant details mentioned in the historical text" (Ankersmit 1994: 139–140). Drawing on historian and literary scholar Hayden White's tropology of *Metahistory* (White 1974), Joanny Moulin remarks that every form of historiography is "bound to demonstrate some form of 'fictionality', be it only because it cannot avoid a degree of 'emplotment'" (Moulin 2016). The writing of historical biography draws on the same stylistic and narrative processes as fiction, dramatizing the events in a narrative that endows historical characters with subjectivity while underlining personality traits revealed by their political stances. The focus on historical leaders foregrounds the relationship between the individual and the collective, showing that collective movements influence individual choices.

By focalizing on the creation of historical leaders, some of them being civil rights activists, this book renews the study of auto/biographies and allows for a renewed understanding of recent or past history because "all personal literature contains a mixture of historical and non-historical elements" (Gengembre 2006: 99). Sociologist Pierre Bourdieu contends that the value of the biographical endeavor resides in its power to reflect the social forces at play; in other words, biography should illuminate a life trajectory through an analysis of the public and the personal as expressive of the social forces at play (Bourdieu 1986: 69–72).

Women Activists and Civil Rights Leaders in Auto/Biographical Literature and Cinema lies at this crossroads between the personal and the political, the fictional and the documentary, through expanding on the notions of political auto/biography. The articles gathered in this edited collection broaden the traditional approach to auto/biography by including a variety of sources that range from literary and historical works to filmic representations. The individual lens provided by auto/biography opens a window into the collective past, offering opportunities for research on the interweaving of public and personal narratives. This book is divided into three parts that explore and analyze the construction of historical characters as acting subjects who relate their lives themselves or whose lives are narrated by others, using the intricacies of their intimate lives to examine their political convictions and their ideological stances. Contributors explore a diversity of autobiographies and biographies that underline the role of charismatic individuals and the impact of events that represented turning points in their lives. They ponder the historical and political values of testimonials and the weight of memory as regards historical truths and personal authenticity in two literary genres that make the personal public—autobiography and biography.

The first part is comprised of four chapters dealing with autobiographies written by female activists who aim to gain a political voice through writing about how their personal life intertwines with the social and political constraints of their environment. Benaouda Lebdai opens this part by retracing Winnie Madikizela Mandela's life journey through two autobiographies *Part of Soul Went with Him* (1984) and *491 Days: Prisoner 1323/69* (2013), which provide valuable information about the personal struggle the woman faced as Nelson Mandela's spouse. Benaouda Lebdai digs intimate details from her first-hand account narratives and contributes to portraying subtle hidden facets to her character, thus drawing attention to character traits which various media-fueled controversies have overshadowed. Jacqueline Jondot reads Egyptian writer Ahdaf Soueif's *Cairo, My City, Our Revolution* (2012) as an activist's autobiographical attempt to consciously address the impact of a collective historical moment (the Arab Spring) on her personal and family stories. Soueif's attachment to Cairo accounts for her political commitment, for she contends that the future of the individual is tied to that of the country. Ahdaf Soueif positions herself as an activist writer whose autobiographical writing reflects an endeavor to gather pieces of a collective story which the revolution has shattered. Historian Anya Jabour reconstructs the narrative of Sophonisba Preston Breckinridge (1866–1948), a woman activist whose name has vanished from historical records although she committed her life to promoting policies aimed at amelioration of the conditions of the disadvantaged—including women, children, workers, immigrants, African Americans. Anya Jabour writes from autobiographical fragments that were never published, thereby confining the memories of the woman's activism to the forgotten histories of the past. Breckinridge's influence behind every reform of the Progressive and New Deal eras nonetheless proved determinant in defining standards for the first generation of public welfare workers. Her writing provides an original prism through which to examine the contradictions of the post-civil war period, an experience that the white southern woman would rather not comment on considering her father's rigid racial stance. In the following article, Tanya Ann Kennedy explores how Sheryl Sandberg's and Lilly Ledbetter's memoirs serve a different political agenda. Sandberg makes use of her personal experience as a successful businesswoman to promote what she defines as postfeminist leadership. The author questions the ideological ethics that permeates Sandberg's narrative, which she argues distorts the history of feminism into an individualistic project that foregrounds women's responsibility for their own careers and downplays the impact of structural barriers.

The second part focuses on the interplay between autobiographical texts and films. Delphine Letort's article serves as a transition, delving into the life of anti-lynching crusader Ida B. Wells through various biographical works, including William Greaves' biographical television documentary. Comparing these texts with Wells' autobiographical writing, Delphine Letort spotlights how the historical context impacted the activist's personal life journey and professional career, calling attention to gender prejudices that Wells struggled against. She also interrogates the place of the African American activist in collective memory through various biographical documents that denote different ideological perceptions of the past. Dominique Dubois looks back at the adaptation of *Malcolm X* (Spike Lee, 1992), noting that Spike Lee appropriates the African American leader's autobiography penned by Alex Haley. Although Malcolm X's status as an iconic figure may limit the filmmaker's creative input, Spike Lee often deviates from the autobiography to follow a personal agenda that Dubois aims to decipher. Through a close examination of two biographies devoted to Michelle Obama, Pierre-Marie Loizeau assesses the collective impact of her success as First Lady noting that the authors retrace the family stories of her ancestors to celebrate the woman as an icon of American values. Growing up in a middle-class environment with a strong work ethic, Michelle Obama is portrayed as the embodiment of African American achievement. The part ends with a chapter by Sylvie Charron who questions the notion of authorship through a close analysis of *Twelve Years a Slave* (1853), a book that is presented as Solomon Northup's autobiography although David Wilson wrote the narrative, inserting his mediating voice into the slave narrative. Sylvie Carron identifies literary traces of Wilson's intervention in the narrative, thereby imposing his own perspective on the slave's account, and points out visual details that indicate another interpretive layer in the filmic adaptation of *12 Years a Slave* (Steve McQueen, 2013), suggesting further distance from the original source text.

The third chapter of the collection deals with biographical films which, as products of an entertainment industry geared to making profits, glorify the heroes of dominant society in a hagiographic mode.[2] Autobiographies and memoirs offer an array of primary sources for directors and screenwriters who draw inspiration from them, whereas biographies provide complementary information on historical contexts and figures. The historical biopic is situated at the crossroads between two writing modes about history and subject; it foregrounds the character whose personal path it aims to capture through delving into intimate details of daily life, while also incorporating numerous historical elements in the diegetic world to create an authenticity effect.

---

[2] William H. Epstein explains that "biographical narrative of whatever kind has traditionally been an ally of the dominant structure of socioeconomic authority, as have the film industry, in general, and the industrial, technical, and aesthetic practices of biopics, in particular" (Epstein 2011: 2).

INTRODUCTION   7

Film scholar Taïna Tuhkunen articulates a theoretical reflection on the evolution of a genre that favors the creation of exceptional, emblematic individuals capable of reincarnating entire eras or value systems. Analyzing the influence of "Jesus movies," she observes that biopics exploit the salvation narrative to relate the life of exceptional individuals and cult figures on screen. Referring to *Lincoln* (Steven Spielberg, 2012), Taïna Tuhkunen calls attention to lighting and *mise-en-scène* effects that contribute to the mythification of historical figures by connecting their life stories with larger, collective, grand narratives. Analyzing the role of secondary female characters in biopics, Lisa Botshon and Melinda Plastas spotlight the gendered treatment of black women in *12 Years a Slave*, which they compare with British period drama *Belle* (Amma Asante, 2013). Arguing that the suffering of black women is used to propel Solomon Northup's narrative of escape, the authors contend that *Belle* complexifies the representation of slavery through borrowing the conventions of heritage films. The authors argue that Amma Asante eschews the voyeuristic violence that bears on the representation of the past in *12 Years a Slave*. Furthering the study of biopics that reassess the legacy of minority activists, Isabelle Van Peteghem-Tréard uses psychoanalysis to analyze *Milk* (Gus Van Sant, 2008), a hagiographic film about San Francisco's first gay political activist to hold public office. The author explores Van Sant's creative input in a formulaic genre with tight conventions, which the director appropriates to celebrate the queer 1970s through the figure of Harvey Milk. The film nonetheless downplays the significance of the individual and places a collective movement at the center of the narrative, shedding light on political processes rather than individual characters (Erhart 2017: 261). In the last article of this collection, Nicole Cloarec examines Tony Palmer's *England, My England* (1995), a biopic that retraces the life of English composer Henry Purcell, who died 300 years before (1695) without leaving any diary about his own life. The director engages with an enigmatic figure whose inner life and opinions he can only imagine through listening to his music. Nicole Cloarec's title "In Search of Purcell's Legacy" emphasizes the director's aesthetic creativity which seems to be directly inspired from Purcell's musical style.

By interweaving various forms of auto/biographical writing to better understand the collective impact of historical leaders, this book brings a broad range of disciplinary and interdisciplinary approaches to this genre. Literature scholar Nathalie Prince artfully questions the notion of gender in the postface by suggesting that history might be seen as a woman to be subdued and dominated for a man to achieve greatness. She nonetheless concludes that Machiavelli's feminization of history may limit our understanding of women's roles as active agents, a pre-conceived idea which the book aims to challenge by giving voice to civil rights activists whose stories biographies and autobiographies (written and filmed) actualize in the present.

WORKS CITED

Ankersmit, Frank R. "History and Tropology." *The Rise and Fall of Metaphor.* Berkeley, Los Angeles and Oxford: University of California Press, 1994.

Bhabha, Homi K. *The Location of Culture.* London and New York: Routledge, 1994.

Bingham, Dennis. *Whose Lives Are They Anyway? The Biopic as Contemporary Film Genre.* Piscataway: Rutgers University Press, 2010.

Bourdieu, Pierre. "L'illusion Biographique." *Actes RSS* 62/63, Juin 1986, 69–72. https://doi.org/10.3406/arss.1986.2317.

Caine, Barbara. *Biography and History.* Basingstoke, UK: Palgrave Macmillan, 2010.

Custen, George F. *Bio/Pics, How Hollywood Constructed Public History.* New Brunswick, NJ: Rutgers University Press, 1992.

Du Toit, Angélique. "Grand Narrative, Metanarrative." In Stuart Sim (ed.), *The Lyotard Dictionary.* Edinburgh: Edinburgh University Press, 2011, 86–88.

Epstein, William H. "Introduction: Biopics and American National Identity— Invented Lives, Imagined Communities." *a/b: Auto/Biography Studies*, vol. 26, no. 1 (2011): 1–33. https://muse.jhu.edu/. Accessed on March 17, 2018.

Erhart, Julia G. "Toward a New LGBT Biopic: Politics and Reflexivity in Gus Van Sant's *Milk* (2008)." In William H. Epstein and R. Barton Palmer (eds.), *Invented Lives, Imagined Communities: The Biopic and American National Identity.* Albany: State University of New York, 2017, 261–280.

Gengembre, Gérard. *Le Roman historique.* Paris: Klincksieck, 2006.

Lebdai, Benaouda (ed.). *Autobiography as a Writing Strategy in Postcolonial Literature.* Cambridge: Cambridge Scholars Publishing, 2015.

Lejeune, Philippe. "The Autobiographical Pact." In Paul John Eakin (ed.), *On Autobiography*, trans. Katherine Leary. Minneapolis: University of Minnesota, 1989.

Lejeune, Philippe. *Le Pacte autobiographique.* Paris: Seuil, 1996.

Lejeune, Philippe. *Signes de vie, Le pacte autobiographique 2.* Paris: Seuil, 2005.

Lukács, Georg. *The Historical Novel*, trans. Hannah and Stanley Mitchell. Lincoln: University of Nebraska Press, 1983.

Lyotard, Jean-François. *La Condition postmoderne: rapport sur le savoir.* Paris: Les Editions de Minuit, 1979.

Moulin, Joanny. "Biophoty: The Biofilm in Biography Theory." *Revue LISA/ LISA e-journal,* vol. XIV, no. 2, 2016. http://lisa.revues.org/8959, https:// doi.org/10.4000/lisa.8959. Accessed on June 6, 2017.

Perkins, Margo V. *Autobiography as Activism: Three Black Women of the Sixties.* Jackson: University Press of Mississippi, 2000.

Sim, Stuart (ed.). *The Lyotard Dictionary.* Edinburgh: Edinburgh University Press, 2011.

Starobinski, Jean. "Le style de l'autobiographie." *Poétique,* no. 3 (1970): 257–265.

Touzin, Marie-Madeleine. *L'Écriture autobiographique.* Paris: Bertrand Lacoste, 1993.

White, Hayden. *Metahistory: The Historical Imagination in Nineteenth-Century Europe.* Baltimore, MD: Johns Hopkins University Press, 1974.

PART I

The Lives of Women Activists

Winnie Madikizela Mandela: The Construction of a South African Political Icon

Benaouda Lebdai

An emblematic figure in South African history, Winnie Madikizela Mandela (hereafter referred to as Winnie Mandela) is one of the rare African National Congress (ANC) historical figures still alive. Her two autobiographies, *Part of My Soul Went with Him* (1984) and *491 Days: Prisoner Number 1323/69* (2013),[1] provide valuable historical testimonies about her growing up within the turmoil of South African history, enhancing her image as an adamant anti-apartheid resistant. This essay retraces the construction of the woman's image as a political icon, using her autobiographical writing to shed light on the events that have prompted Winnie Mandela to take political action. She has authored two

---

[1] *Part of My Soul Went with Him* is hereafter referred to as *POS* and *491 Days: Prisoner Number 1323/69* as *491PN*. Winnie Mandela refers to her first autobiography (*POS*) and Winnie Madikizela Mandela refers to her second work (*491PN*).

B. Lebdai (✉)
Le Mans University, Le Mans, France
e-mail: benaouda.lebdai@univ-lemans.fr

© The Author(s) 2018
D. Letort and B. Lebdai (eds.), *Women Activists and Civil Rights Leaders in Auto/Biographical Literature and Films*,
https://doi.org/10.1007/978-3-319-77081-9_2

books that portray a woman who developed her charisma independently of her husband Nelson Mandela, showing how her political views matured and her personal political consciousness evolved. If her life and actions have aroused public criticism, including rumors which gave rise to various fantasies and journalistic comments about her, I will eschew these controversies by focusing on the struggles of black South African women, whose efforts have all too often been neglected and relegated to passive contributions within the national storytelling of the struggle against apartheid. This analysis will show that Winnie Mandela is indeed a black South African anti-apartheid militant, a character who has always had "an exceptional grasp of the popular mood" (Krog 1999: 369)[2] and of black women, in particular. Both autobiographies ensure that she remains "a powerful political figure in her own right" (Krog 1999: 378), underlining that her life path has been determined by the political choices she made in times of national crisis.

UNPLANNED PUBLICATIONS

Retracing the genealogy of both publications enables us to understand the complex relationship between Winnie Mandela and the political context of her life. Critical history acknowledges that life storytelling participates in the construction of a public personality. Invited to speak about herself during apartheid by the white anti-apartheid militant Anne Benjamin, Winnie Mandela was propelled to the forefront of international and national news as a significant figure in Soweto. Anne Benjamin convinced her to comment on her role as the leader of a struggle which her husband Nelson Mandela had been compelled to abandon while imprisoned at Robben Island. Anne Benjamin proposed to record her testimonial in secret, because blacks were not allowed to speak in public, let alone write and publish, in apartheid South Africa. Winnie Mandela's secret recordings were then transcribed and adapted by Mary Benson, her white anti-apartheid militant friend, into an autobiographical book entitled *Part of My Soul Went with Him*. Personal letters exchanged with Nelson Mandela and other testimonies by various militants were included in the book, which shows the impact she already had on those militants and on women prisoners. Anne Benjamin made her reveal the

---

[2]Antjie Krog is a poet and an anti-apartheid campaigner; she published her accounts of the Truth and Reconciliation Commission in *Country of My Skull*.

events which nurtured her political development, and which ushered her into the struggle against a discriminatory political system imposed by the Pretoria government. The transcripts of the recording were smuggled out and the book version was published in New York in 1984.

Her diary *491 Days: Prisoner Number 1323/69* also has great significance for the writing of South African history in connection with Winnie Mandela's own epic political story. The story surround the publication process is worth a reminder. Winnie Mandela wrote a secret diary while in prison from May 1969 to September 1970. She succeeded in giving the pages to her solicitor David Soggot, an Englishman, who smuggled them out of prison and hid them in his London residence. His wife Greta Soggot discovered the manuscript in the attic of their house forty years later. She then traveled to Johannesburg and returned the forgotten pages to Winnie Mandela. Reading the manuscript was a traumatic shock for Winnie Mandela, bringing back "horrifying memories" of her imprisonment in the 1970s (fourth cover page, *491PN*). She later added in the introduction to the published version: "I was afraid. There are memories you keep in a part of your brain; it is part of those things that hurt so much you do not want to remember" (*491PN* 232). Winnie Mandela's two daughters urged her to publish the diary and the letters she had both sent to and received from Nelson Mandela when he was a captive at Robben Island. The published diary sold out within three days in South Africa in December 2013.

Literary critic and autobiography specialist Philippe Lejeune contends that an autobiography is a "retrospective story written in prose in which a living person gives of his/her own existence and his/her personality."[3] *Part of My Soul Went with Him* and *491 Days: Prisoner Number 1323/69* correspond to this definition insofar as the narrator abides by the "autobiographical pact" defined by Lejeune. While "the character does not have a name as he/she is 'I'" (Lejeune 1996: 26) in autobiographies, the genre allows the narrator to assert his/her identity as the author. Winnie Mandela's texts disclose views that help characterize her as an individual; yet the first book also includes various letters which convey another perception of the woman and therefore complete her portrayal. It appears that Winnie Mandela used autobiographical writing to gain a voice that was subdued in apartheid South Africa.

---

[3] My translation of "un récit rétrospectif en prose qu'une personne réelle fait de sa propre existence *et* de sa personnalité" (Lejeune 1996: 14).

Winnie Mandela's Family Background

Both autobiographies are far from being mere political pamphlets. *Part of My Soul Went with Him* shows the impact of history on her own life narrative, and that of her own people, those who live in poverty in the townships and the Bantustan. Her childhood and teenage years memories are interwoven with the history of South Africa, highlighting the impact of apartheid on her intimate life. Her autobiography discloses private feelings that underpin political actions, leading her to be perceived as the "Mother of the Nation." Interestingly, the reader discovers that she became a politically aware subject when a child, realizing that blacks were always inferior to whites whatever the level of their education:

> I became aware at an early stage that the Whites felt superior to us. And I could see how shabby my father looked in comparison to the white teachers. That hurts your pride when you are a child; you tell yourself: If they failed in those nine Xhosa wars, I am one of them, and I will start from where those Xhosas left off and get my land back. (*POS* 28)

These lines also show that Winnie Mandela's sense of community devotion originated from her childhood experience. Her love for her father, whom she wanted to protect because of the historical circumstances, nurtured a strong feeling of responsibility. As a history teacher, he would not tell the same history as Afrikaners who declared that they set foot on virgin land when they disembarked at Cape Region in 1652. Her father glorified those South African heroes whom Afrikaners never mentioned; he related the Xhosa wars against the whites, knowing that all the black tribes fought the whites, including the Zulu with King Chaka. Winnie remembers:

> We had textbooks, naturally written by white men, and they had their interpretation, why there were nine 'Kaffir' wars. Then he would put the textbook aside and say: 'Now, this is what the book says, but the truth is: these white people invaded our country and stole the land from our grandfathers'... My father taught us other songs which dealt with events in the history of our people. They were songs from tribesmen, by traditional composers. (*POS* 30–31)

Her father's political education consisted in revisiting black history. Philippe Lejeune observes that "social and political history have their place" in autobiographies (Lejeune 1996: 15), which both Winnie

Mandela's texts emphasize by referring to everyday conversations with her father and her paternal grandmother Makhulu. Both discussed historical facts in front of her, feeding her growing awareness of South African racial reality. They brought her a realistic picture of the tribes where white people were called *Aba Nyephi*—a phrase that implied that whites illegally enjoyed the wealth of a country whose lands they stole from her ancestors on their arrival. Winnie Mandela always heard her grandmother warn children against stealing: "You must not behave like an Aba Nyephi!" (Meer 1993: 126). Her autobiography shows that in everyday life moral education and politics were intertwined and the memory of such details had great importance in Winnie's political awareness of the history of South Africa: she was not brought up in denial of a tragic reality that had serious consequences on the life of the tribe.

In terms of family influence the autobiography also points out the influence of her relationship with her mother who died when she was eleven. Their relationship was fraught with tension: her mother's overt preference for boys over girls led her to pray day and night for a boy when she was pregnant. Winnie suffered from that rejection and decided to challenge her mother: "I will prove to her that a girl is as much of value to a parent as a son" (*POS* 29). Winnie Mandela consequently developed awareness of gender inequalities within the black community, and this deeply rooted experience planted the seeds of feminism in her life. Her successful studies were also a response to her craving for liberty and independence, and knowledge. Winnie Mandela also suffered from her paternal aunts' disdain regarding physical features (her straight hair and greenish eyes) which indicate her mixed blood genealogy, as her mother was half Xhosa, half English. Winnie Mandela never "boasted" about her European genealogy and claimed her "Africanity" instead—a source of pride and self-esteem in her tribe.

Autobiographies shed light on events the autodiegetic narrator chooses to tell. By focusing on her moral and political education, Winnie Mandela self-consciously displays the elements that paved the way for her political choices.

An Intimate and Political Struggle

Part of My Soul Went with Him underlines Winnie Mandela's primary political education, which foretells her involvement in political organizations and social actions. She joined the Society of Young Africa when she was a secondary school student in Transkei. When she moved to Johannesburg, she registered with the Convention where she became familiar with ANC literature and the names of its leaders, including Nelson Mandela. During her internship at Baragwanath Hospital, she subscribed to the South African Congress of Trade Unions. Winnie Mandela insists on these commitments as they obliterate the idea that Nelson Mandela introduced her to politics. She uses her autobiographies to explain that her political convictions were rooted in her family background.

In Soweto, she was shocked by the poverty of single black women, hence her protest against such a precarious and disastrous human situation due to apartheid. Dr. Nthatho Motlana recalls that Winnie Mandela would press him to visit sick women in the middle of the night: "You would find her touring the townships, looking for destitute old ladies with nobody to look after them, waking me up in the middle of the night to say, there is that lady in such and such a place, who needs medical treatment" (*POS* 35). Her first job as a social worker testifies to her personal character and her political ideas where the other is important. Later she joined the ANC and met such leading black women as Albertina Sisulu, Florence Matomela, Frances Baard, Kate Molale, Hilda Bernstein, Ruth Mopati, and Lilian Ngoyi—the organizer of the resistance campaigns after 1952. Winnie reckons that Nelson Mandela's secretary Ruth Mopati taught her ideological concepts whereas Mary Benson, the editor of her autobiography, contributed to her political training. Winnie Mandela the "subaltern," to use Gayatri Spivak's term to define the colonized, had an intuitive political education, but she learnt how to lead a struggle with other committed white, black, and Indian women. Her autobiography reveals the training power of meetings that strengthened her political convictions and reinforced her will to revolt. She launched her first public political action under the ANC with the Defiance Campaign. She was among the women who led Anti Pass Campaign demonstrations and burnt their passes in front of Soweto police stations.[4]

---

[4]Under the banner of the ANC, Winnie Mandela organized the Defiance Campaign along with women in the township of Soweto. They burnt their passes as a protest against discrimination. The Pass Laws (1952) made it compulsory for all black people to have passes with them at all times. This internal pass was a means to control the movements of black people in white areas.

Nevertheless, Winnie Mandela's testimonies are by no means a denial of Nelson Mandela's influence and impact on her political life. Her political awareness blossomed with him, which is implied by the very title of her autobiography *Part of My Soul Went with Him*. Her title expresses her extreme distress as a spouse whose husband was imprisoned. In *Long Walk to Freedom*, Nelson Mandela reveals that he detected her strong personality at first sight: "Her spirit, her passion, her youth, her courage, her willfulness—I felt all of these things the moment I first saw her" (*LWTF* 251). Her life after her marriage was also enmeshed with politics; she knew right from the beginning that marrying Nelson Mandela was marrying "the struggle, the liberation of her people" (*POS* 41). The history of the ANC turned out to merge with her own story—*Herstory*. Her autobiography demonstrates that without her passion for freedom, without her positive sense of the march of history, without her knowledge of Xhosa culture, without her own hope for a fair and nonracial society, she would not have entered into such a risky marriage, as she explains:

> So there never was any kind of life that I can recall as family life, a young bride's life, where you sit with your husband and dream dreams of what life might have been, even if we knew that it would never be like that. (*POS* 50)

The choice of being a couple struggling politically against apartheid was a tacit agreement, "a marriage pact" that extended to a "political pact." Nelson Mandela divorced his first wife Evelyn Mase because she wanted a black middle-class life, making him choose between politics and herself. He chose politics and the liberty of South African people. Winnie's love and political convictions gave him that married life he was looking for; however, he explains in his own autobiography that he "never promised her gold and diamonds as the wife of a freedom fighter is often like a widow" (*LWTF* 251–253) (Fig. 1).

Winnie Mandela's autobiography shows that she felt drained by the anguish of not being up to the role she had inherited after his imprisonment. Her sudden public exposure frightened her. The whole narrative portrays a sensitive woman shouting out her despair. Her autobiography actually gave her an unexpected opportunity to talk about her anxieties, which she could not do in public speeches. The paradox is that in the townships she tried to transmit her strength, an

Fig. 1 Nelson and Winnie Mandela met in the early 1960s and agreed to a marriage based on a "political pact". © Photofest. Photographer: David Messenbring

attitude that allowed her to control extremely difficult moments, as she confesses:

> Solitude, loneliness, is worse than fear—the most wretchedly painful illness the body and mind could be subjected to. When you suddenly realize that you are stripped of a man of such formidable nature, of whom you are just a shadow, you find yourself absolutely naked. He was a pillar of my strength I fumbled along and tried to adjust. It was extremely difficult. (*POS* 75)

Both autobiographies show that she embraced the role of an active witness of the history of South Africa in the making, from the point of view of an insider of her own community. Building on the interferences between history and culture, history and memory, the autobiographies shed light on an autodiegetic character: Winnie Mandela embodies an epic character in the anti-apartheid struggle. The township woman transformed into a heroine in the face of brutality targeting the black population—including the Soweto uprising and the tragic massacre of pupils in 1976 by the police who shot 575 black children and teenagers because they did not want to study in Afrikaans as a language of teaching. The pupils were demanding to be taught in English which would open more possibilities in terms of jobs. Winnie Mandela wrote that the uprising was due to "the anger of young Blacks in South Africa against the injustices of the regime *which* had reached boiling point... with slogans attacking Bantu Education and demanding the release of Mandela, Sisulu and other political prisoners" (*POS* 109). Beyond Winnie's story, the text calls attention to the struggle for equality of all black people. Winnie Mandela's account of her life sheds light on the human tragedy that was taking place in all the townships of South Africa, behind closed doors. Her first autobiography put her in the forefront of the anti-apartheid struggle in terms of international visibility, as an active spokeswoman for Nelson Mandela and therefore as a leader of the struggle.[5]

Henceforth, anti-apartheid militants across the world transformed Winnie's "autobiographical pact" into a "struggle pact." Winnie Mandela's text challenges the ongoing theoretical debate about autobiographies, which are deemed narcissistic and therefore negatively perceived because

---

[5] In the French translation of her autobiography, the then French President's wife, Danielle Mitterrand, wrote in her foreword that all young French people should read about Winnie Mandela's struggle in order to be aware of what was going on under the apartheid regime.

of "the myth of the I" and the hateful egotist "I" (Lejeune 1971: 105). However, her writing contradicts such a view of autobiographical texts, because in this specific case the first personal pronoun is imbued with positive meaning as it has allowed Winnie to assert her personality and her personal political position. Inscribing her name on the front cover of a book has therefore become an act of defiance, and her will to exist as a militant writer has confirmed her in her role as a leader of the struggle against the apartheid regime.

Another point is worth stressing, which is breaking a taboo within her Xhosa tribe where the "we" of the community was more important than the individual "I." Winnie Mandela, by standing up as an individual, challenged that tradition. She endorsed then a dual revolt as a woman speaking against apartheid and against African tribes' mentality.[6] The best testimony of such a dual struggle is the use of "I" and "myself" throughout *Part of My Soul Went with Him*, which opens with a violent scene in which Pretoria police break into her house in the middle of the night. She describes the scene as a violation of her inner self:

> It was the night of 16 May 1977. I was doing an assignment in sociology and, because I was working, I used to do my assignments at night—it took me right up to 2 a.m. There was a deadline. I had to submit something the following day. So I finished it at about half past two. I had been hearing strange noises outside. But then it's such a usual part of my life, that kind of thing. I've always known that I'm never alone wherever I am … At about four o'clock in the morning I heard a great noise outside—It seemed as if a hail of stones were dropped on my house and it sounded as if they were falling inside the wall. (*POS* 2)

Repetition of the personal and possessive pronoun is accentuated throughout the autobiography, which demonstrates her yearning for self-assertion in a violent context. All the chapters start with "I" or "My," an indicator of a political and cultural revolution. *Part of My Soul Went with Him* becomes a paradigm for the narrow relation between "Autobiography" and "History" (Lejeune 1996: 15). Winnie Mandela inscribes herself in an historical narrative as she is in the process of herself writing a page on contemporary South Africa history. For the first time,

---

[6]Three years after the publication of her autobiography, Winnie Mandela received the United Nations Prize for Human Rights (in December 1988).

the repressive acts of the Pretoria regime are told from the point of view of a woman who recalls her detention in Pretoria Central Prison and her banishment at Brandfort. Her trials and the accusations of violation of the law are also given through detailed accounts. In parallel, she recalls the sufferings of other women prisoners. She gives her vision of Nelson Mandela's various trials and recalls the Soweto revolts. Official documents from the police and judiciary related to Winnie Mandela's arrests are included in an appendix to the book, providing evidence of the veracity of her stories as a militant.

The most impressive chapter of the autobiography, in terms of emotions, may be the opening one entitled "My little Siberia." She denounces the harsh reality of her banishment and the extreme violence of her deportation to Brandfort, where the Afrikaner police forbade the black population from approaching her or from speaking to her. Local children were even forbidden to play with her daughter Zindji. It was a shocking episode of her life, which was also reported in Nelson Mandela's autobiography as a tragedy for Winnie (*LWTF* 509). Despite the harassment and her loneliness, her narrative tone is nevertheless ironic and witty. She declares, for example, that "once a Black is told by a white man that something is bad, then it must be good and vice versa" (*POS* 5). Her life under house arrest at Brandfort was tumultuous because her struggle never stopped; she had decided to be a nuisance to the local police. She organized political "happenings" in front of both whites and blacks, who were surprised and impressed by such a daring black woman. For example, she depicts with gravity and humor that she went into the shops instead of waiting outside to be served, as was the law—blacks were not allowed to enter shops and mix with whites. Brandfort police did not know how to deal with Winnie Mandela's acts of defiance; she disregarded the apartheid laws through systematic disobedience. Through individual acts of courage, Winnie Mandela aimed to awaken a sense of revolt among the blacks of Brandfort. She describes the disastrous living conditions of her brothers and sisters, underlining that, although life in Soweto was extremely difficult, it was even worse at Brandfort:

> The situation in the ghetto of Brandfort is terrible—people are starving... It was the first time I'd seen the type of poverty I've encountered here... For the first time I saw with my own eyes families where the evening meal— the only meal—is comprised of mealie-pap and saline solution, ordinary salted water... almost every weekend we bury babies. Last weekend

we had six funerals, this week there will be three, all children under two... The health of people is deteriorating. (*POS* 9–11)

Her autobiography provides a description of the extreme poverty of black women in South Africa, a country rich with gold and diamonds. Winnie Mandela helped her community to organize itself and helped cure the children. She demanded from the authorities premises for black youth, but most of the time they did not respond. Her writing conveys her sense of humor, which has become her survival weapon: "So far there is no law against dreaming!" (*POS* 14)

Her account further shows the absurdity of apartheid, which required her to ask the police for authorization to go to church. However, she objected to the whites' power to interfere in religious questions: "That's going too far, giving them the religious powers they think they have" (*POS* 18). Religion and the Bible were used as tools to humiliate prisoners. In prison she was told: "There is the Bible, ask your God to release you from jail!" (*POS* 96). At Brandfort, her health deteriorated so much that her lawyer tried to have her admitted to the only hospital of the town. The Board of Doctors decided that a letter on her part should be written and signed in case the operation went wrong. She refused: "I would rather die in the ghetto than apply for permission to be operated on in a white operating theatre... I refused to stay" (*POS* 15). In front of her obstinacy, her lawyer moved her to Johannesburg General Hospital as an emergency in an ambulance with a high-security escort. Her political convictions show that her struggle was constant, at the risk of her own life. These personal memories highlight a cruel image of apartheid compared with many official reports of the same events, as produced in the appendix.

Winnie Mandela relates that she was constantly and repeatedly harassed, taken to police stations, or imprisoned. With great economy of words, in realistic cinematic style, which shows her talent as a storyteller, she describes the inhumanity of the apartheid system. When she writes about one of her various arrest scenes, which the police report differently of course, she conveys her feeling of violation of her intimacy and private life. She expresses concern for her two daughters who did not understand the violence of the police:

> Detention means that midnight knock when all about you is quiet. It means those blinding torches shone simultaneously through every window of your house before the door is kicked open. It means the exclusive

right the Security Branch have to read each and every letter in the house. It means paging through each and every book on your shelves, lifting carpets, looking under beds, lifting sleeping children from mattresses and looking under the sheets. It means tasting your sugar, your mealie-meal and every spice on your kitchen shelf. Unpacking all your clothing and going through each pocket. Ultimately it means your seizure at dawn, dragged away from little children screaming and clinging to your skirt, imploring the white man dragging Mummy away, to leave her alone. (*POS* 91)

Not only does she denounce the brutality of interrogations, humiliations, and physical torture, but she also dwells on the horror of confinement, which leads to a state of madness in her prison diary *491 Days: Prisoner 1323/69*:

Being held incommunicado was the most cruel thing the Nationalists ever did. I'd communicate with ants; anything that has life. If I had lice I would have even nursed them. That's what this solitary confinement does; there is no worse punishment than that. I think you can stand imprisonment of 27 years. You are mixing with other prisoners, you get your three meals a day, the only thing you have lost is your freedom of movement. Your mind isn't incarcerated that's all but with solitary confinement you are not allowed to read, you are not allowed to do anything, you have just yourself. (*491DP* 57)

The narrative highlights her capacity for survival and verbal reaction toward the wardens, the doctors, and the police of the prison. Whenever she could, she wrote about the harsh moments of the day on scraps of paper. When the psychiatrist Dr. Morgan told her on May 28, 1970, that he came to see whether she had been agitated lately, she replied scathingly, cleverly, and politically:

Yes—certainly—my problems are solitary confinement and the political ones do not belong to a psychiatrist's diary. In fact, the person who needs your interview is the one who subjects human beings to solitary confinement for over a year. (*491DP* 32)

The psychiatrist was just continuing the police interrogation. The subterfuge was obvious to her, especially when he asked her whether she considered herself the messenger of God: "Do you feel you are chosen by God for the role you are playing amongst your people? Do you hear God's voice sometimes telling you to lead your people?" (*491DP* 33) These constant visits in her cell were an indication of the political importance Pretoria was granting Winnie Mandela; she wrote about the day when they suggested she "call upon the ANC forces at the border to retreat and put down their arms" (*491DP* 95). The police told her that if she did that she would be freed from prison. In any case the police were always trying to destabilize her by treating her as a real threat for the whites, which explains the psychological pressure stepped up on her.

Nonetheless, her diary shows the implicit reckoning of the power she had built up over Soweto people. In a country where illiteracy in the townships was high, the details concerning her prison experiences were not known; instead, derogatory rumors were spread by the Afrikaner Secret Service in the townships about her supposedly intense sexual life while her husband was in Robben Island. In order to disqualify her political activities, Nelson Mandela was also told by his "friendly" wardens that his wife was being unfaithful and taking advantage of her situation to act for herself—not for him or the ANC. She quotes the Secret Service agent Swanepoel whose task was to brainwash her:

> If I had a wife like you, I would do exactly what Nelson has done and go and seek protection in prison. He ran away from you. What kind of woman holds meetings up till four o'clock in the morning with other people's husbands? You are the only woman who does this kind of thing. (*491DP* 95)

The autobiography shows the psychological perversity of a system that aimed at breaking her sanity and undermining her political struggle. In any case, she became conscious of the importance of political ideas as she wrote: "When they send me into exile, it's not me as an individual they are sending. They think that with me they can also ban the political ideas... I couldn't think of greater honour" (*491DP* 1).

WINNIE MANDELA'S POLITICAL IDEAS

Winnie Mandela's autobiographical story is embedded in women's collective story. Indeed, the female section of the prison fort of Johannesburg praised her generosity: "Winnie was a pillar to most of us political detainees, and very sympathetic to the other prisoners" (*POS* 112). As President of the Women's League within the ANC, her commitment was rooted within her strong relationships with the eldest sisters of the ANC with whom she developed a great sense of organization. She reckoned that they were of great help at a time when she was involuntarily put at the forefront of the struggle: "The difficult part was finding myself with a spotlight on me. I wasn't ready for that. I was ready to deputize for Nelson. Before, even if I battled to put my own ideas across in a meeting, it was Mandela speaking. And suddenly he was not there" (*POS* 77). Her responsibility was growing and the people of Soweto were relying on her. As the Orlando West Branch of the ANC's Women's League became involved with the women's movement against the pass laws, she felt she had to show leadership on behalf of all the angry women by confronting the Afrikaner police. Nelson Mandela tells about her courage and her sense of abnegation in *Long Way to Freedom*: "she never had had to be worried about where her next meal was coming from" (*LWTF* 258). His own autobiography points out character traits that pervade her writing; he remarks that she gave up all the little privileges she could have enjoyed as a middle-class black woman in favor of her political convictions.

She was the financial provider of the family and her life conditions worsened when she lost her job at the hospital because of her political involvement in the anti-Pass Laws demonstrations: "After I was arrested, I lost my job" (*POS* 51). Her dismissal pushed her definitely into real-politics and the struggle became her life. Organizing disobedience actions and sit-ins led to the hellish cycle of arrests, trials, imprisonments, banishments, underground life, hidings, and most distressing fear of not seeing her two daughters grow up. She denounced the cruel absurdity of the apartheid system: Winnie Mandela never had the pleasure of taking her daughters to school because a Pretoria law forbade her to set foot in schools. She wrote with bitter irony that her house was "like an operational area, an extension of the police station, with the police going in and out" (*POS* 17).

Winnie Mandela led a dual struggle: while she was the spokeswoman for Nelson Mandela, she also had to consolidate her personal political position, not to be solely "a carbon copy of Nelson" (*LWTF* 73). Her autobiography enhances that dilemma, precisely because she was growing into a political figure. Her struggle for the liberation of black women, who were doubly discriminated by the whites and by the blacks of the townships, was part her agenda. Her political analysis sharpened:

Looking at our struggle in this country, the black woman has had to struggle a great deal, not only from a political angle. One has had to fight the male domination in a much more complex sense. We have the cultural clash where a black woman must emerge as a politician against the traditional background of a woman's place being at home! Of course most cultures are like that. But with us it's not only pronounced by law, we are permanent minors by law. So for a woman to emerge as an individual, as a politician in this context, it is not very easy. (*POS 73*)

She explains that her gender caused her to be even more discriminated against and humiliated. Nevertheless, she managed to resist black and white male chauvinism. She uses the term "cultural clash" to underline the cultural revolution she was engaged in against men of her own community and against white Afrikaner men.

THE POLITICAL FIGURE

Winnie Mandela's life was neither a fairy tale nor an epic story, but the life of a black South African woman under the apartheid regime, with its horror and its negation of human rights. Her autobiography implicitly suggests that she wished for a family life that she never had, making choices in light of specific circumstances that placed her in the limelight. Both texts illustrate her psychological and political evolution as a politically "angry" woman, convinced that her rights to liberty, justice, and equality justify her fight.

Although she harbored doubts about her ability to lead, she delivered speeches to persuade township women to go on strike: "I must tell the truth, I made pronouncements on platforms and said things I hadn't tested myself on. I was a social worker, I was a mother" (*POS* 125). She transcended her limitations to become the leading voice of the ANC, imposing her direct style and frank speech in front of the ANC male-dominated board. She was able to reorient the movement after Nelson Mandela's arrest at a moment when inner tension was rife. From prison, her husband portrayed her as "a determined person" in *Long Walk to Freedom* (*LWTF* 258) and praised her talent as an orator. In her autobiography, Winnie Mandela recalls the moment when she clarified the political position of the ANC during the Soweto uprising. She then confirmed her ideological maturity by defining political strategies for the future of the movement:

It was never the policy of the ANC to be violent. All that this people's organisation is doing is responding to the violence of the system. Our great leader, Chief Lutuli, said "when a man attacks my Kraal, I must take my pear and defend my family"… A non-violent organisation was forced to take up the spear and defend the honour of the black man against an enemy which had been waging war since the arrival of Jan Van Riebeek in 1652. We are determined to fight to the bitter end for the liberation of our people. I am afraid that the white regime will have to decide whether to give in, when they realize they are fighting a futile battle. It is their decision whether they want to give in violently or sensibly and save our country. (*POS* 124)

She was drawing the political line of the ANC in an effort to avoid a disastrous bloodbath. Over the years, she proved that she had acquired a remarkable insight into internal ANC politics. To unite all the forces, she addressed the Students' Union leader Steve Biko, who had created the Black Consciousness movement which was in favor of an armed struggle against the whites. She publicly honored him, qualifying him as a "national idol for whom she has the greatest admiration" (*POS* 119), but she warned his Black Consciousness movement that it would be a mistake to exclude the whites from the peace process. She made it clear that the ANC was the historical representative political party for all anti-apartheid black and white militants. She reiterated then the decisions of the Party: "We never look at people as black and white; it is the enemy who compels us to use those terms. The umbrella organization of the ANC embodies everyone who is fighting side by side with us against oppression" (*POS* 118).

Her 1980s' speeches showed that she had become confident and gained a national voice. She could deliver her views on the specific situation of South Africa when almost all the ANC leaders were either in jail or in exile. She was then in a position to warn the Pretoria regime:

In the present political structure there is no room for dialogue any more. Not at all. That chapter was closed by the government on 12 June 1964, when they jailed the leadership. Dialogue can only take place on the release of all our leaders in prison, all the banned peoples and the return of all our exiled leaders. That's the only way one can shape the country's future. Anything else is a sheer waste of time… The leadership would have to be involved in an entirely new kind of political thinking; perhaps a completely new basis for dialogue and negotiation. (*POS* 126)

She made such propositions as early as 1984, during the peak years of apartheid, when nobody believed in a peaceful solution. Historical events made her right ten years later, when negotiations started between Nelson Mandela and Peter Botha who was responsible for his release from prison.

Winnie Mandela's autobiography and diary are the life stories of a resistant, a militant, and a politician who pointed out the right direction, culturally and politically, through eloquent storytelling. *Part of My Soul Went with Him* is an orature (told and transcribed), conveying her personal vision of historical facts; the text ultimately underlines the significance of autobiographies as personal testimonies of political and social debates. They are tools of struggle and contribute to a deeper understanding of South African history. In the apartheid context, Winnie Mandela's first autobiography was a political act and its very publication represented an act of rebellion against an unfair judiciary system. Her writings show her commitment to women and to Xhosa culture, which she honored through her public appearances dressed in traditional African costumes. Her costumes were the symbol of her resistance (*Unbuntu* in Xhosa). She was the only black South African woman who was forbidden to wear traditional African costumes, which transformed her into an icon.[7] Winnie Mandela succeeded in transforming a traditional costume into an anti-apartheid weapon.

CONCLUSION

Winnie Mandela's autobiographies contributed to making her a national historical icon, portraying her as the advocate for all suffering black women of the townships. Both texts ensure that she will remain "a powerful political figure in her own right" (Krog 1999: 378), one of the purposes of this type of autobiographical writing.

Today her every move and word are reported and analyzed by journalists. She is still very critical of the current situation in post-apartheid South African political life. In the epilogue of *491 Days: Prisoner 1323/69*, she writes: "Right now, people like myself who come from

---

[7] Indeed, during Nelson Mandela's trial, Winnie Mandela decided to wear Xhosa traditional costumes as a form of resistance and protest. The police then forbade her from coming to court dressed in her traditional costume (*POS* 76).

that era become petrified when we see us sliding and becoming more and more like our oppressive masters. To me, that is exactly what is happening and that is what scares me" (*491PN* 239). For many black South African women in the townships, she remains the model of resistance and she still embodies hope.

Nevertheless, the death of the young Stompie Seipei in January 1989 cast a shadow on Winnie Mandela's life as a revolutionary woman.[8] Winnie Mandela was accused of having ordered the murder of Stompie Seipei, suspected of being an informer and a spy for the Afrikaner police. Her bodyguards claim that they beat him to death to obey orders that she allegedly gave them. This tragedy has sullied her reputation, even if she denies all allegations made against her. Her trial took place in February 1990 in Rand Supreme Court in Johannesburg. For Nelson Mandela, the Afrikaner state was continuing to discredit his wife. In his own autobiography *Long Walk to Freedom* he writes in her defense:

> After three and half months, the court found her guilty of kidnapping charges and being an accessory to assault. The Judge, however, acknowledged that she had not taken part in any assault herself... As far as I am concerned, verdict or no verdict, her innocence was not in doubt. (*LWTF* 711)

In post-apartheid South Africa, Winnie Mandela was invited by Edmond Tutu to attend the hearings on human rights violations at the 1996 Truth and Reconciliation Commission. She apologized for the first time about what happened to the man and his family. The journalist Rich Mkhondo reports how Stompie Seipei's mother reacted to her apology: "It was the first time she'd apologized... Bishop Tutu had to actually ask her to do it publicly... Mrs Seipei, whose son was supposedly killed by some members of the football club actually came forward to hug and kiss Winnie."[9] Here again, this gesture by Stompie's mother redeemed Winnie in the eyes of the Soweto women she had been defending all her life.

---

[8] The body of Stompie Seipei was found on January 6, 1989 (Krog 1999: 375).

[9] Rich Mkhondo in "Facing the Past: Truth and Winnie Mandela," http://www.pbs.org/newshour/bb/africa/July-dec97/mandela_12-4.htlm, accessed on June 25, 2017.

WORKS CITED

Krog, Antjie. *Country of My Skull*. London: Vintage Books, 1999.

Lejeune, Philippe. *L'Autobiographie en France*. Paris: Colin, 1971.

———. *Le Pacte autobiographique*. Paris: Seuil, 1996.

Madikizela Mandela, Winnie. *491 Days: Prisoner 1323/69*. Johannesburg: Picador Africa, 2013.

Mandela, Nelson. *Long Walk to Freedom*. London: Hachette Digital, 2013 [1994].

Mandela, Winnie. *Part of My Soul Went with Him*. New York: W. W. Norton, 1984.

Meer, Fatima. *Plus haut que l'espoir, une biographie de Nelson Mandela*. Paris: Présence Africaine, 1993.

Mkhondo, Rich. "Truth and Winnie Mandela." *Online Newshour*, December 4, 1997, 1–7.

———. "Facing the Past: Truth and Winnie Mandela." http://www.pbs.org/newshour/bb/africa/July-dec97/mandela_12-4.htlm. Accessed on November 22, 2017.

Njabulo, Ndebele. *The Cry of Winnie Mandela*. Claremont: Ayebia, 2004.

"Revoluting" or Writing? Ahdaf Soueif and the 2011 Egyptian Revolution

Jacqueline Jondot

The January 25, Revolution that took place in Egypt in 2011 was one of the uprisings known as the Arab Spring, when a wave of protests and demonstrations were sparked in several countries in North Africa and the Middle East, starting with Tunisia in December 2010. Protestors were denouncing dictatorship, human rights violations, corruption, extreme poverty, unemployment, etc. While the Arab Spring represented a period of elation and hopefulness after several regimes were ousted, it was followed by violent responses from diverse parties; civil wars are still raging at the time of writing in Libya and Syria and human rights violations are happening in an attempt to repress rebellion across the region. The Arab Spring nonetheless generated great hopes and interest. Many essays were published, a number of them in the immediate wake of the events, by those who had taken part and felt they had to bear witness to such unexpected events. It was no surprise that acclaimed novelist and political and literary commentator Ahdaf Soueif took part in what was first known as the January 25 Revolution in Egypt and wrote about it.

J. Jondot (✉)
Université Toulouse-Jean Jaurès, Toulouse, France
e-mail: jjondot@wanadoo.fr

© The Author(s) 2018
D. Letort and B. Lebdai (eds.), *Women Activists and Civil Rights Leaders in Auto/Biographical Literature and Films*,
https://doi.org/10.1007/978-3-319-77081-9_3

Born in a family of activists (Soueif 2012: 24–25), Soueif is critical of both Arab and Western policies when they jar with justice and truth. As the author of numerous essays published in both English and Egyptian newspapers[1] which appeared in an edited book *Mezzaterra: Fragments from the Common Ground* (Soueif 2004), she initiated the Palestinian Festival of Literature "with the aim of showcasing and supporting cultural life in Palestine, breaking the cultural siege imposed on Palestinians by the Israeli military occupation and strengthening cultural links between Palestine and the rest of the world," in order "to reaffirm, in the words of Edward Said [whom she greatly admired], 'the power of culture over the culture of power'."[2] Soueif regularly stood up against the Mubarak regime and the National Democratic Party, protesting against undemocratic, self-serving policies that cause poverty, social injustice and threaten essential freedoms. As an intellectual, she helps "articulate and politicize [the] demands [of the people]."[3]

It is therefore not surprising that she took part in what was first known as the January 25 Revolution in Egypt and wrote about it. Her book, *Cairo, My City, Our Revolution* was written during and soon after the outbreak and first tribulations of the Revolution.[4] As both a writer and an activist, she was faced with a dilemma: "I wanted more to act the revolution than to write it" (Soueif 2012: xiii). The book was published shortly after the first phase of the Revolution and commented on the events leading up to its beginning. The book makes an attempt to articulate activism and to come to terms with her role as an activist in critical times. Soueif attempts to define a literary strategy that allows her to convey events as they unfold, while finding the right balance to give them a more universal dimension. On August 17, 2012, she wrote that "In times of crisis, fiction has to take a back seat":

> The novelist, like the activist, is also a citizen of the world and bears the responsibility of this citizenship. The question is, then, can you honour your responsibility as a citizen of the world and fulfill your responsibility

---

[1] http://ahdafsoueif.com/ and https://www.theguardian.com/profile/ahdafsoueif.

[2] http://palfest.org/about, accessed on November 22, 2017.

[3] https://www.theguardian.com/books/2016/jan/23/arab-spring-five-years-on-writers-look-back, accessed on November 22, 2017.

[4] This article refers to the 2012 edition of the book. A revised edition was published later as *Cairo, Memoir of a City Transformed* (London: Bloomsbury, 2014).

to your art? [...] In Egypt, in the decade of slow, simmering discontent before the revolution, novelists produced texts of critique, of dystopia, of nightmare. Now, we all seem to have given up—for the moment—on fiction. [...] Attempts at fiction right now would be too simple. The immediate truth is too glaring to allow a more subtle truth to take form. For reality has to take time to be processed, to transform into fiction. [...] You, the novelist, can't grab one of them [stories] and run away and lock yourself up with it and surrender to it and wait and work for the transformation to happen—because you, the citizen, need to be present, there, on the ground, marching, supporting, talking, instigating, articulating. Your talent—at the time of crisis—is to tell the stories as they are, to help them to achieve power as reality not as fiction.[5]

Ahdaf Soueif voices the discontent of Egyptians and their hopes, recalling the long years of failure to make their claims heard. As she perambulates Cairo, she records its "ruined condition" (Soueif 2012: 13), its disintegration (2012: 43) under the current regime, which she considers as a metaphor for Egyptian society as a whole: "degraded and bruised and robbed and exploited and mocked and slapped about" (2012: 45). Her mapping of the city coincides with a list of violations of civil rights under the "Forces of Darkness" (2012: 66) which have been "de-developing Egypt for thirty years" (2012: 123). She denounces the deficiencies of the education system which favors teachers' enrichment to the detriment of the students (2012: 15) and the ejection of Egyptians from their museums which are reserved for foreigners (2012: 58), since both restrict access to personal and social improvement as well as fostering unemployment (2012: 19). Behind the violation of these basic rights looms the corruption of the regime at all levels, a regime that intends to privatize the public space for its own benefit: "The regime had been planning to sell Tahrir. They'd been planning to sell the central public space in our capital to a hotel chain, to a foreign hotel chain" (2012: 11). Such property scandals concerned, among other public services, hospitals thereby endangering public health (2012: 16). The right to a proper health system is not only denied to Egyptians, they are also subjected to organ trafficking (2012: 44). This is one of the numerous types of violence perpetrated on the people of Egypt by the regime.

[5] https://langaa-rpcig.net/+In-times-of-crisis-fiction-has-to+.html, accessed on November 22, 2017.

State violence is one of the worst offenses ("Your security, your police—killed our brothers," 2012: 17) as the regime uses coercion by diverting the army and police for its own protection (2012: 20). Egyptians undergo arbitrary arrests (2012: 23, 65, 146), torture (2012: 31, 44), military trials for civilians (2012: 65, 72–73) while the judiciary also is corrupt (2012: 24). The list of state violence is endless. A shroud of silence lies over all these infringements as Egyptian citizens cannot speak freely and are kept in the dark. They are denied freedom of expression and the right to information ("Egyptian state TV is lying so shamefully," 2012: 130)—even foreign reporters are muzzled (2012: 26, 150–151). When the Revolution began, the regime was in denial and pursued its vicious policies using snipers (2012: 27, 28) and *baltagis* (thugs) (2012: 28, 36, 37).[6]

The first claims of the demonstrators on Midan el-Tahrir[7] were to reclaim the essential rights that had been trampled on for decades by the regime: "They marched for bread and they marched for freedom, for social justice and for human dignity" (Soueif 2012: 46). "Dignity" (2012: 59) and "humanity" (2012: 174) are recurrent terms in the narrative proposed by Ahdaf Soueif. But, above all, she focuses on the civil movements and the civic spirit around Tahrir: "As well as housing the symbols of military and political power, Tahrir is home to the civic spirit of Egypt" (2012: 11). In the footsteps of the demonstrators' aspirations, she shifts responsibility for the organization of Egyptian society from the unworthy, "uncivic" government to the people on Tahrir who spearheaded proposals to right the regime's wrongs. The demonstrators became the creators of an ideal city. Insistence on the term "city" is important as it refers not only to the city as town but also to the city as political organization. The polysemy of city is echoed in that of the word *Masr*: "'Masr' is Egypt, and 'Masr' is also what Egyptians call

---

[6]http://english.ahram.org.eg/NewsContent/1/64/15715/Egypt/Politics-/Who-are-Egypts-thugs-.aspx, accessed on November 22, 2017.

[7]I prefer the Arabic word *midan* because, like piazza, it does not tie you down to a shape but describes an open urban space in a central position in a city. The space we call Midan el-Tahrir, the central point of Greater Cairo, is neither a square nor a circle but more like a massive curved rectangle covering about 45,000 square meters and connecting downtown and old Cairo to the east, with the river and Giza and the newer districts to the west; its southern boundary is the Mugamma 3 building and its northern boundary is the 6 October Flyover. Six main roads lead out of its center and a further six out of the larger space surrounding it (Soueif 2012: 10–11).

Cairo" (2012: 9). The city, epitomized by the *midan*, a microcosm of the country, became the laboratory for a new society, which explains why Ahdaf Soueif writes "they've demolished our small city" (2012: 108) when the new regime recovered Tahrir, meaning that the protestors' attempt at reforming society had failed. The recurrence of the word "citizen" throughout the text reveals the collective effort at shaping a new society based on legality and the restoration of civil rights. Ahdaf Soueif presents Egyptians as actors in their society despite the regime's will to suppress them. The microcosm on Tahrir experimented with alternative civil structures: education (2012: 20), culture (the young protesters protect the museum when the National Democratic Party building is on fire because "it's their Museum and they have to protect it," 2012: 27), an organized health system (2012: 27–28, 31, 33), the safety of each citizen (2012: 37), free communication (2012: 27) in respect of the diversity of Egypt ("a great and varied body of citizens," 2012: 179). Regaining space allowed the protestors to become responsible for building the new state: "In Tahrir Square and on the streets of Egypt the people of Egypt have reclaimed their humanity. Now they will reclaim their state…" (2012: 178–179).

If Ahdaf Soueif's book were a mere record of violations of civil rights and of counterproposals to improve Egyptian society, it would merely be one among many essays or testimonies about the situation in Egypt before the Revolution. Ahdaf Soueif is a well-known commentator who repeatedly gave her testimony on several TV or radio channels (Soueif 2012: 140). However, her book is more than just another document. Its title, *Cairo: My City, Our Revolution*, unveils a design that weaves personal ("my") and collective ("our"). The close relationship—not to say identity—that she establishes between the city and the revolution, in the same way as Cairo is Egypt, shows that "my" and "our" are not opposed but they overlap.

If "I" and "my" prevail in the preface ("I signed a contract to write a book about Cairo; my Cairo. […] In February 2011, I was in Tahrir," Soueif 2012: xiii), they very quickly blend into a first person plural: "This story is told in my own chosen order, but it is very much the story of our revolution" (2012: xiii). The constant shift from singular to plural is recurrent throughout the book. If the "I" is Ahdaf Soueif's, the "we" is more complex, as it may mean Ahdaf Soueif's family ("We—myself and two beautiful young women [my two nieces, Salma and Mariam]," 2012: 6–5) or the people of Egypt ("We, the citizens," 2012: 67).

The family "we" is subdivided into a generational "we" as Ahdaf Soueif's generation is present alongside a younger generation of the family. She shifts from one "we" to the other, often in the same paragraph, merging her own and her family's experience with that of Egyptians as a whole. The two maps of Cairo included in the book are a mixture of both objective, official and subjective, personal geographies, the latter expressed in the handwritten names of places and the inclusion of very personal indications: "our house" and "the hospital where I was born" (2012: 2). The handwriting superimposes, or rather imposes, a personal mapping over the city, which competes with the official one.

This personal map coincides with Ahdaf Soueif's "novel of formation." The book includes aspects of the "novel of formation" as the author conjures up numerous memories of her childhood in different places in Cairo, with different members of her family who played a part in her awakening to the realities of her country. The author gives details of her own initiation, but she also stages herself as an initiator for her sons and her nieces (Soueif 2012: 20). The personal elements that she records belong to the present and to the past. As she perambulates the city while marching and protesting, she comes across important locations of her family's story in/with the city. For instance, the hospital where she was born is "at mid-point between my mother's family home in Ataba and the flat in Zamalek that we were to move into" (2012: 77). She focuses on different places linked to different episodes of her education (2012: 29–30), but each of them is put in a social, political, or historical context ("Ataba [...] was always connected with bustle and commerce, and Abdeen [...] was the royal and then presidential palace," 2012: 29), linking the personal and the collective. Her personal memories often coincide with the story of the political involvement of her family (2012: 48–49), therefore with her own growing awareness of politics in Egypt. Her rare and fleeting nostalgic spells concur with the fear of a threat on some symbolic part of the city, though she never dwells lengthily on the past unless it can serve to stimulate the spirit of resistance (2012: 151–152). Besides, Cairo is also a space of domestic activities: "At home I find a mountain of laundry on the kitchen floor" (2012: 85); "I go home and hang out some more washing. More phone calls" (2012: 92); "Nahla's car smells of mangoes. [...] Which reminds me that I have to go and collect our fruit as well" (2012: 105). Ahdaf Soueif mentions these domestic chores as evidence that she belongs to the daily life of the city, that she is not an outside observer. She derives her legitimacy to speak of "my city" from her sharing in the menial tasks of its population in the same way as relating her different ages to the political history of the city seen from the standpoint of her protesting family.

Ahdaf Soueif's personal involvement in the Revolution, as she takes part in most demonstrations and speaks on numerous media, is rooted in her family's experience of political activism and protest. Her "I" is the product of a family "we"; all its members across generations are active in the Revolution: "Like so many 'politically engaged' Egyptian families it's now in its third generation of activists [...]. We, the older revolutionaries, have been trying since '72 to take Tahrir. They [the third generation] are doing it. [...] We follow them and pledge what's left of our lives to their effort" (2012: 24–25). All the members of the family are present in the book and on Tahrir: sons, nieces and nephews, brothers and sisters, father, aunts. The younger generation is united in one family entity, "our children" (2012: 116), regardless of the branch from which they descend yet without losing their individuality: each youngster's personal skills are put to the service of the Revolution: "Ahmad Seif is running the amazing team at HLMC and they're at the heart of the practical and legal support for the revolution. Mona is doing her brilliant lab work and her brilliant communication work. That just leaves Sanaa, seventeen, [...] who's also in the Midan with her friends: taking notes, collecting information" (2012: 131). This pattern applies to the wished-for new society, all marching towards the same goal jointly and severally.

There exists a mutual transgenerational respect. The youngsters claim that: "we've learned from you [...] and we're building on what you've accomplished" (Soueif 2012: 48). However, the older generation acts as watchdogs ("My parents' generation warn us," 2012: 53) while admiring the achievements of the young generation, the *shabab*:

> The shabab of Egypt decided they would no longer allow their lives to be stolen, and in every district in the country they got up and walked into the hearts of their cities. [...] We followed them and we marveled at them and we stood shoulder to shoulder with them and every so often [...] we'd grab one of them and hug them and shake their hand and thank them. (2012: 46)

The *shabab* taking hold of the Revolution is not only a continuation of the opposition undertaken by their parents' generation ("The Midan [el-Tahrir] has been our Holy Grail for forty years," 2012: 10), considered now as an "establishment opposition" (2012: 47), but also a reversal of roles as the children's generation creates a future for their parents ("What manner of homeland, what manner of future am I leaving my future?" 2012: 46). This is probably where the Revolution actually takes place, shifting from parents' repetitive circular pattern of failures to disruption brought about in that order by the *shabab*.[8]

The *shabab* are semantically at the junction between personal and collective, between family and Egypt, as Ahdaf Soueif uses the term for both her own relatives and all young Egyptians. Therefore, the family "we" shifts to a collective "we", including all the generations of Egyptians ("families of four generations are walking into Tahrir," Soueif 2012: 52). This complex "we" is far more interesting than a mere opposition between "we" and "they": "'We' are a people fighting for what's right, and 'they' are a faction fighting for a sliver of gain" (2012: 186) The complex "we" allows Ahdaf Soueif to be part of the Revolution at all levels, as an individual belonging to all the different groups: family, older generation, or Egyptian citizens.

The author draws a parallel between her experience rooted in her family's story and young Egyptians who have inherited a revolutionary, or at least a resistance culture, going back to the French expedition: "Boulac rose against the French in 1798" (Soueif 2012: 136) and the uprising of Orabi (2012: 9) or of Nasser (2012: 9). The collective "we" includes "every sector in civil society—judges, lawyers, farmers, teachers, pensioners, journalists, tax collectors" (2012: 24); interestingly, Ahdaf Soueif moves from "sector" to individuals (judges, lawyers, etc.) and not actual sectors (law, agriculture, education, etc.), this time shifting the focus from the collective to the individual. Although she views the collective drive, she insists on the personal involvement of each of the million protestors: "We had come together, as individuals, millions of us, in a great cooperative effort" (2012: 7); "There's been something different, something very special, about the quality of the attention the Egyptian revolution has attracted: it's been personal" (2012: 183).

From the personal to the collective and back to the personal, Ahdaf Soueif inextricably binds the fate of each individual and that of the country. She ties their individual fate to their fate as citizens. Her "we" means

---

[8] This refers to the oxymoronic definition of the term *revolution*, which is both a repetitive circular, therefore endless, movement and disruption.

herself as Ahdaf Soueif and herself as citizen ("We, the citizens," Soueif 2012: 67), as exemplified in the first pages of the book: "Me, I was in India [...]. I did an interview [...]: We've been watching what's been happening in Tunisia and we've been very excited by it" (2012: 7–8). She moves from her own personal standpoint ("Me, I was") to her citizen engagement ("we've been"). She does not speak on behalf of Egyptians, but from within the Egyptian community. Her concluding sentence "Our story continues..." (2012: 194), which comes after the testimonies of the young members of her family, means as much.

But how does she manage "to 'revolute' and write at the same time" (Soueif 2012: xiv)? How does she manage to conciliate the paradox of immediacy and distance, of the position of the protestor and that of the commentator? The difficulty appears in her numerous metatextual attempts at defining her text: "This is not a record of an event that's over; it's an attempt [...] to make you part of an event that we're still living" (2012: 63); "an intervention, rather than just a record" (2012: xiv).

To write immediacy, she chooses the form of the diary. The 18 days of the Revolution are recorded from day to day and also from hour to hour: "Friday 28 January, 5.00 p.m." (Soueif 2012: 5), "Tuesday 1 February" (2012: 51), "7.00 p.m. [...] 9.00 p.m." (2012: 134). But, the diary is interrupted in the middle of February 1 by a section entitled "An Interruption. Eight Months Later: October 2011" (2012: 61) which corresponds to the time of publishing; the preface is dated October 2011 (2012: xiv). Ahdaf Soueif uses the same sentence to end the last entry of the diary section and to begin the embedded section ("And now, of course, we know what happened next," 2012: 63) taking up where she has left her narrative "It is not possible to say what will happen next" (2012: 59, 63) This embedded section raises the reader's expectation as to comments on the preceding section. Yet, Ahdaf Soueif soon returns to diary form ("23 July 2011," 2012: 74) which seems more suitable to convey the heat of the moment. The activist finds it difficult to distance herself from the emotion of the ongoing Revolution. The strategy that consists in embedding the events following the fall of the regime corresponds more to a desire to protect herself from disillusion than to comment upon the events ("This book is part of my fight, my attempt to hold our revolution safe in my mind and my heart," 2012: 184), all the more so as this section of the book ends on doubts: "And the thought is starting to take hold that maybe even elections will not lead to where we want to go" (2012: 118).

Following a linear chronology would probably lead her to own up to part failure of the Revolution, and to end on a pessimistic note despite vowing at the beginning that "I would not write an elegy for my city" (Soueif 2012: xiii). What she shapes is a myth,[9] the myth of the first 18 days: "Tahrir is a myth that creates a reality in which we've long believed [...] a myth fed with belief and sacrifice" (2012: 190). Making a myth out of this period turns her personal testimony into collective memory. The power and value of the myth spring from the collective "we" that she fabricates throughout the book. Each individual is appointed a role in the new society created on Tahrir during the 18 days. The poet's role is to give shape to the narrative of the collective aspirations and achievements so that the experience can be passed down to following generations and to the world at large in a spirit consistent with the "civic spirit" of Tahrir: "This is a national epic that will be taught in schools for generations to come" (2012: 145). Her desire to preserve the spirit of Tahrir goes together with her wish to convey the spirit of Tahrir outside Tahrir. In the same way as she pictures Tahrir as an open space as opposed to the regime represented by its iconic building, the monolithic Mugamma 3 ("the government decided to consolidate all its departments that the citizen directly dealt with in one central building," 2012: 11), she wants the spirit to carry on and she carries it over through the appended testimonies of her family members in the epilogue. It is impossible for her to accept the failure of the Revolution, therefore she cannot wrap up her narrative as if the hopes raised by the 18 days were lost. The appendage is followed by her open conclusion, "Our story continues..." (2012: 194). The suspension points relate to the numerous references made to her reader and the appeal that she makes for the reader to supply the present as the time of reading: "You, my reader, are better placed to answer this than I. From where we are now we can only guess" (2012: 68). She confers on the readers the responsibility of not accepting a possible failure of the Revolution but of pursuing the fight. "Our Revolution" includes Ahdaf Soueif, her family, the other protestors, and also the readers she draws into her struggle by constantly calling on them.

[9] See Jacqueline Jondot, "The Geography of the Creation of a Myth," *Creativity and Revolution. Proceedings of the Eleventh International Symposium on Comparative Literature* (Cairo: Cairo University, Department of English Language and Literature, 2014).

If Tahrir is an open space, her narrative is also an open text, because of its structure and its appeal to its readers. Ahdaf Soueif the activist outranks Ahdaf Soueif the writer. She reconsiders the place and role of the writer, whom she views no longer as a witness looking from his/her own individual experience at unfolding events, but as an agent called upon to have an active role in the collective building of the new city—that is to say, a poet, a true creator.

WORKS CITED

Jondot, Jacqueline. "The Geography of the Creation of a Myth." *Creativity and Revolution. Proceedings of the Eleventh International Symposium on Comparative Literature.* Cairo: Cairo University, The Department of English Language and Literature, 2014.

Soueif, Ahdaf. *Mezzaterra: Fragments from the Common Ground.* London: Bloomsbury, 2004.

Soueif, Ahdaf. *Cairo: My City, Our Revolution.* London: Bloomsbury, 2012.

Autobiography of an Activist: Sophonisba Breckinridge, "Champion of the Championless"

Anya Jabour

In 1912 the *Woman's Journal*, the official organ of the largest woman suffrage organization in the U.S., published a biographical profile under the headline "A Woman Who Helps," promising to tell "the story of a southern woman who is [...] a champion of the championless." The subject of the story was Sophonisba Preston Breckinridge (1866–1948), whose "many-sided work" on behalf of women, children, workers, immigrants, blacks, and other disadvantaged groups made her the ideal individual to represent the wide range of women's activism in modern America.[1] By the time the *Woman's Journal* published its biographical profile of Breckinridge, she already had established a national reputation as both a social justice activist and a social work educator. Born and raised in Lexington, Kentucky, Breckinridge spent her adult life in Chicago,

---

[1] "A Woman Who Helps: The Story of a Southern Woman Who Is a Power in Chicago—Her Many-Sided Work—A Champion of the Championless," *Woman's Journal*, May 18, 1912.

A. Jabour (✉)
University of Montana, Missoula, MT, USA
e-mail: anya.jabour@mso.umt.edu

© The Author(s) 2018
D. Letort and B. Lebdai (eds.), *Women Activists and Civil Rights Leaders in Auto/Biographical Literature and Films*,
https://doi.org/10.1007/978-3-319-77081-9_4

46   A. JABOUR

where she earned advanced degrees in economics, political science, and law; joined the community of women reformers based at Hull House; and established the University of Chicago's School of Social Service Administration, the first school of social work affiliated with a major research university (Fitzpatrick 1990; Goan 2003: 45–73; Johnson 2008; Klotter 1986; Muncy 1990). At the same time that she helped to professionalize social work and thereby create new career opportunities for educated women, Breckinridge was active in virtually every reform of the Progressive and New Deal eras, including legal aid for immigrants, civil rights for blacks, labor legislation for workers, equal rights for women, and juvenile courts for youth. An indefatigable advocate for the nation's dispossessed, Breckinridge pressured local, state, and federal officials to fund programs and pass legislation to benefit the poor, the elderly, and the disabled. As a member of an advisory committee for the Social Security Act of 1935, the basis for the modern welfare state, Breckinridge literally set the standards for professional education and civil service for the first generation of public welfare workers (Jabour 2012: 22–37).

Breckinridge's influence extended beyond national boundaries. A co-founder of the U.S. chapter of the Women's International League for Peace and Freedom, Breckinridge called on European governments to establish an international community, uphold national self-determination, enforce international law, defend human rights, and ensure lasting peace—a set of goals that ultimately informed both the League of Nations and the United Nations. As the first American woman to represent the U.S. at an international diplomatic conference, she promoted the Good Neighbor Policy, which established a new framework for U.S.–Latin American relations in the 1930s. Finally, as a participant in both European social work circles and Pan-American child welfare conferences, she exemplified transnational feminism and advanced human rights (Branscombe 1948: 433–446). In 1945, near the end of her life, Breckinridge wrote her own account of how she became "a champion of the championless." Breckinridge's unfinished autobiography offers an extended meditation on why and how she became "a woman who helps" (*SPB*).[2]

---

[2] *Autobiography of Sophonisba P. Breckinridge*, Sophonisba P. Breckinridge Papers (Chicago, IL: Special Collections Resource Center, Regenstein Library, University of Chicago). Although the extant autobiography extends to 1905 and includes Breckinridge's graduate study at the University of Chicago, this essay addresses only the period from childhood through college.

Although she published extensively in her lifetime, Breckinridge did not finish her memoirs before her death. The extant manuscript consists of an assortment of fragmentary reminiscences, some typed and some hand-written, most unnumbered and out of order, and all much-amended, on approximately 150 sheets of paper, a mix of bond and yellow-lined pages.[3]

The unfinished autobiography offers unique insights into how Breckinridge thought about herself and how she wished to present herself to the world. Because Breckinridge approached this writing project in her characteristic fashion—double-checking details and correcting minor errors—it is factually accurate. However, like all memoirs, it is a selective account, and the materials that Breckinridge chose to include and exclude, as well as how she chose to present those materials, are revealing (Jabour 2014, 2015).

Breckinridge did not initially set out to write her autobiography. Rather, she intended to pen a biography of her father, Confederate veteran and Democratic Congressman W.C.P. Breckinridge. Yet despite years of research resulting in the accumulation of file after file of information about her father—and other famous male ancestors—she found herself unable to write the volume she intended. Instead, she wrote about herself. In doing so, despite nagging self-doubt and reflexive self-criticism, she scribed her own story and inscribed herself into history. In her final writing project, Breckinridge attempted to impose order on her memories and to take stock of her long life. In one version of the introduction, Breckinridge wrote: "What I hope to do in the following pages is … to review my own life which has now extended beyond the fourscore milestone" (*SPB*).

Breckinridge's review of her own life represents a genre of women's autobiography that allows future scholars to examine women's experiences and perspectives. Breckinridge's unfinished narrative prefigures contemporary feminist biography in interesting ways. She contemplated, but ultimately rejected, writing yet another story about a "Great White Man," instead choosing to write her own story. She placed her individual experience in historical context. And she insisted on calling attention to the interconnectedness of the personal and the political (Alpern 1992).

---

[3] An edited and annotated version of the autobiography, accompanied by an interpretive essay, is forthcoming; see Anya Jabour, "Sophonisba Preston Breckinridge: Memoirs of a Southern Feminist," in Giselle Roberts and Melissa Walker (eds.), *Southern Women in the Progressive Era: A Reader* (Columbia, SC: University of South Carolina Press, 2019).

48   A. JABOUR

Most importantly, however, Breckinridge chose to craft her memoirs as the autobiography of an activist. In her eighties, when Breckinridge looked back on her youth, she highlighted the family traditions, parental examples, and childhood experiences that she believed predisposed her toward a life of social activism. She also sketched the rough outlines of her particular interests: assisting immigrants, the poor, and the disabled; feminism and pacifism; and African American equality. With the benefit of hindsight, Breckinridge anticipated her adult activism in her account of her early years.

Family Legacy and Parental Influence

When she came into the world on Easter Sunday, April 1, 1866, Sophonisba Preston Breckinridge was the newest member of one of Kentucky's greatest dynasties, which claimed not only distinguished bloodlines but also a record of public service that spanned numerous generations. As a child, Breckinridge knew that she would have to work hard to live up to the example set by illustrious relatives on both sides of the family. As an adult, she took pains to emphasize how much her ancestry and family shaped her life. Explaining her rationale in beginning her own life story with her family heritage, she noted: "I do this because they meant so much not only in the way of my inheritance but because they meant so much in my conscious experience" (*SPB*). Breckinridge's father, lawyer and politician W.C.P. Breckinridge, constantly urged his daughter to carry on the family tradition of higher learning and public service. "The [Breckinridge] name has been connected with good intellectual work for some generations—for over a century," he counseled. "You must preserve this connection for the next generation" (Klotter 1986: ix, 317). Like many "new women" of her generation who went on to become pioneering professionals and social reformers (including several of her own family members), Breckinridge enjoyed a close relationship with her father.[4] W.C.P. also nurtured his daughter's intellectual ambitions by teaching her the alphabet from his law books, rewarding her for perfect reports in school, and providing her with the opportunity to attend college.

---

[4]Reflecting both family traditions of public service and shifting expectations for "new" women, several of Nisba's contemporary kinswomen pursued careers as teachers and reformers (Censer 2003; Frankfort 1977).

While Breckinridge's father may have prompted her to follow in his footsteps by pursuing a career in public service, her mother's example also had a profound effect on her life course. Married at seventeen, Issa Breckinridge gave birth to seven children in rapid succession, losing two children to infant maladies and damaging her own health. Her mother's nonstop childbearing, chronic health problems, and early death may well have led Breckinridge to reject marriage and motherhood at an early age. As Breckinridge repeatedly pointed out in her memoirs, family life was hazardous to women's health. "There was no doctrine of birth control or spaced child bearing prevalent at that time," she noted. "I was only 15 months old when Desha was born and he was only 15 months when Campbell came and then after the same interval Little Issa. There were babies and babies to come." Small wonder, then, that, as Breckinridge commented, "My mother was very frail" (*SPB*).

Awareness of her parents' marital difficulties may also have contributed to Breckinridge's resolution to remain single for life. Breckinridge's mother offered a vivid reminder of the drawbacks of "woman's sphere" and domestic life. Not only did she die young, but she also lived with the knowledge that her husband had carried on a long-term affair with a much younger woman, conceiving a child with his mistress while his wife lay on her deathbed.[5] Thus, it is not surprising that Breckinridge's memoirs suggest that she never seriously considered marriage. Although she mentioned two suitors in her memoirs, she provided no details about youthful romance. Like other women of her generation who remained single and devoted their lives to activism rather than to domesticity, Breckinridge may have felt pressure to include references to heterosexual romance in her memoirs to deflect potential criticism of her enduring and intimate relationships with women, particularly her forty-five year partnership with fellow educator and activist Edith Abbott. During Breckinridge's lifetime, ideas about female sexuality were in transition. By the time she wrote her memoirs, an earlier positive assessment of women's "romantic friendships" had been replaced by a negative stigma about lesbianism. To avoid having her lifetime of activism discredited by critics who linked lesbianism and feminism, Breckinridge may then

[5]For the scandal, see "Falls Like Lucifer," *Atchison Daily Globe*, March 21, 1894, p. 3; and "Says She Tempted Him," *North American*, March 22, 1894, p. 1; (a retrospective) Frank Cipriani, "Madeline Pollard and Cong. Breckinridge: The Story of a Famous $50,000 Love Suit," *Chicago Tribune*, April 7, 1940, p. F3.

50 A. JABOUR

have found it useful to establish a claim to heterosexuality early in her memoirs (*SPB*; Barry 1992: 23–35, esp., pp. 23–24). Rather than depict her coming of age as a southern belle, Breckinridge chose to highlight experiences that prompted her to become "a woman who helps" and encounters that prepared her for her "many-sided work" as a social justice advocate.

IMMIGRANTS, THE POOR, AND THE DISABLED

Breckinridge's childhood memories—at least those she chose to include in her autobiography—revolve around illustrative anecdotes that demonstrated her early interest in serving others. An encounter with a missionary to China, for instance, inspired Breckinridge to donate all her savings—her reward for "perfect reports" at school—to alleviate the suffering of others. "I had quite a little sum saved," recounted Breckinridge, "when a lady who had been a Missionary to China came to stay with us. She gave such an account of the poverty of the Chinese Children that I gave her my savings" (*SPB*).

Breckinridge probably included this story in her autobiography because it so succinctly established her early interest in assisting the poor. As an adult, Breckinridge would become a tireless advocate for the dispossessed, whether by lobbying on behalf of a living wage, designing the nation's first "mothers' pensions" for single mothers, or helping to establish the welfare state.[6] Breckinridge may also have included this particular anecdote because it hinted at both her devotion to the welfare of American immigrants and her participation in international welfare movements. In addition to publishing sympathetic accounts of immigrants, Breckinridge would establish Chicago's Immigrant Protective League, which provided newcomers with both practical assistance and legal advice. She also would become one of the most committed internationalists of the early twentieth century, participating in numerous conferences and organizations in both Europe and Latin America throughout the 1910s, 1920s, and 1930s (Breckinridge 1921; Branscombe 1948: 436–441).

---

[6]"Will Ask Parties for Living Wage," *Chicago Tribune*, June 14, 1912, p. 7; S.P. Breckinridge, "Neglected Widowhood in the Juvenile Court," *American Journal of Sociology*, vol. 16, no. 1 (July 1910): 53–87; Joanne L. Goodwin, *Gender and the Politics of Welfare Reform: Mothers' Pensions in Chicago, 1911–1929* (Chicago and London: University of Chicago Press, 1997), 91–94, 97–104.

While still a schoolgirl, Breckinridge had another lesson in helping the less fortunate—and avoiding snap judgments. In a segment of her memoirs titled "The Man Who Begged" she related a memorable incident when her father gave a five-dollar bill—a substantial sum—to "a forlorn looking man":

> I was surprised at my father's giving a beggar such a very large sum, and asked him how he happened to do this, and he gave me the following reason. This apparently down-and-out man was an ex-confederate soldier. Clever and witty and of good substantial family, he was one of the casualties of the war in that when he was seriously wounded and the pain seemed unendurable, he was given opiates and became the victim of the morphine habit. There was in those days no psychiatric treatment, any more than an occupational provision; and, he, like others, lived on the affectionate but inadequate and uncertain contributions of the older members of the company or regiment or unit to which they found it least humiliating to appeal. (*SPB*)

From this experience, Breckinridge learned to consider each individual's circumstances, rather than blaming the poor for their plight. The encounter also opened her eyes to the negative consequences of there being "no psychiatric treatment," and no "occupational provision" for physically or mentally incapacitated people. Both of these insights would inform her later work on behalf of the poor and the disabled. As an adult, Breckinridge not only encouraged her students to conduct research on vocational opportunities for individuals with disabilities but also personally served on advisory committees on services for disabled children administered by the U.S. Children's Bureau under the Social Security Act of 1935 (Hathway 1928; Lenroot 1948: 428–429).

Pacifism and Feminism

When she wrote her memoirs, Breckinridge suggested that her childhood experiences made her especially attuned to the needs of disadvantaged individuals; she also indicated that growing up in a border state in the immediate aftermath of the Civil War fostered her commitment to pacifism. Breckinridge grew up hearing stories about her ancestors' political leadership and distinguished bloodlines. Many of these stories revolved around the secession crisis and "the bitter cleavages of opinion characteristic of many families of the border states" (*SPB*). Her mother's entire family had been "ardent advocate[s] of the Confederate Cause," but the Civil

War had divided the Breckinridge clan. Breckinridge's grandfather, Robert Jefferson Breckinridge (1800–1871), was a Presbyterian minister and an outspoken anti-slavery advocate. Two of his sons served in the Union Army; two others, including Breckinridge's father, joined the Confederate Army. "It is difficult to imagine the family strains in the face of such varied and difficult problems" (*SPB*), she reflected in her autobiography.

Decades later, Breckinridge insisted that her childhood awareness of war's destructiveness inspired her lifelong pacifism. Witnessing firsthand the "resentment," "confusion," "hatred," "domestic tragedy," "deprivation," and "distorted social relationships" created by the Civil War, she recalled, convinced her early on of the "futility" of war. Although, like most Confederate children, she originally learned that "the object of resentment and hatred was the enemy," she soon became convinced "that not the enemy but war itself is the source of wrong!" Instead of defending "states' rights," as so many southern whites did, Breckinridge instead, as an adult, came to advocate "an indestructible union of indestructible states" dedicated to ensuring all countries, groups, and individuals "full enjoyment of community rights" and lasting peace. Despite vicious red-baiting throughout her career, Breckinridge never wavered in her pacifism, remaining an outspoken opponent of militarism throughout both world wars.[7]

Breckinridge's memoirs also suggest that her youthful experiences foreshadowed her future feminist commitments. Eager for his precocious daughter to continue her education, W.C.P. convinced the trustees of Kentucky Agricultural and Mechanical College (now the University of Kentucky) to admit women, and fourteen-year-old Nisba enrolled in 1880 (Klotter 1986: 195). Although A&M allowed women to attend classes, it by no means treated them as equals. Female students could only earn certificates, not diplomas, and there was significant resistance to their presence on campus. Although Breckinridge excelled in her coursework—including English, mathematics, German, and geography— she did not obtain a degree from the future University of Kentucky.

In her recollections, Breckinridge indicated that her experience at A&M made her a determined advocate for women's equality. While she always had "cared a great deal about grades," she now had an additional reason to do well in her coursework: to prove women's intellectual

---

[7] "Some Ways to Peace," January 24, 1936, Speech and Article Files, *Sophonisba Preston Breckinridge Papers*, Library of Congress, Washington, DC, microfilm edition (hereafter *SPBP*).

capacity. Her father had convinced the trustees to admit women, she explained, so that "I cared about grades because it pleased my Father to have me make good grades and justified his position with reference to the treatment of women" (*SPB*). However, Breckinridge's account of her competition with the men in her class for top grades and, even more, her account of an altercation with a mathematics professor "who did not like girls in his class," indicated that she also had something to prove. In her memoirs, she related, with relish, an occasion on which she turned the tables on the sexist instructor:

> At the University of Kentucky I had an instructor, the brother of the president who did not like girls in his class, and one day he gave me a really difficult problem which I could not solve. That night, in my sleep it came to me but I said nothing to him. I thought that he would try again to humiliate me, and that was a day when the trustees were likely to drop in. Sure enough, the committee of trustees dropped in and sure enough he gave me the unsolved problem of the day before. I was so pleased that I probably looked a little triumphant and put my problem on the board and then explained to the visitors about the equation. I was maliciously complacent and he was really quite upset. He knew that nobody could have helped me, and at last he said, "How did you do it[.]" And I said politely ["]I suppose I knew that you thought I couldn't do it and so would give it to me. At any rate it came to me in my sleep. I am glad you gave me another chance.["] (*SPB*)

Dissatisfied with A&M, in 1884 Breckinridge persuaded her parents to allow her to go North to attend Wellesley College. She later observed that "the great charm that Wellesley had for me was that it was made or established for me or the likes of me" (*SPB*). Indeed, Wellesley College was an ideal place for an intelligent woman in Victorian America to develop confidence in her abilities and find a context for her ambitions. In this "Adamless Eden," a women's college with an all-female faculty, students and teachers alike forged strong personal and professional bonds that fostered female achievement and social reform. Breckinridge did not exaggerate when she described Wellesley as her "natural sphere" (*SPB*; Palmieri 1995).

Attending Wellesley reinforced Breckinridge's commitment to public service, provided her with role models of female independence, and prepared her for a lifetime dedicated to higher education. As a group, the college's all-female faculty prepared their students for professional careers and public service. Several faculty members—including those

54   A. JABOUR

Breckinridge especially admired—were active in social reform movements, including the woman suffrage movement.[8] Attending Wellesley thus helped prepare Breckinridge to become both a self-supporting professional and one of the most well-known feminist activists in twentieth-century America. In addition to conducting pioneering studies of women's wage work, political activity, and social reform, Breckinridge served as vice-president of the National American Woman Suffrage Association and successfully campaigned to eliminate involuntary pelvic exams for suspected prostitutes in Chicago.[9]

RACE RELATIONS AND CIVIL RIGHTS

Leaving home to pursue higher education at Wellesley also profoundly reshaped Breckinridge's ideas about race relations, paving the way for her to become a civil rights advocate. As she explained in her memoirs, attending the only one of the Seven Sisters women's colleges to admit black students provided her with the opportunity of "working through the problem of racial relationships" (*SPB*). In her recollections of life before Wellesley, however, Breckinridge gave little indication that she needed to reevaluate her ideas about race. Rather, her decision to frame her life story as the autobiography of an activist, together with her desire to present her father in a positive light, led Breckinridge to elide, obfuscate, and misrepresent her childhood training in white supremacy.

While many children of Confederate veterans grew up learning to revere the Lost Cause and its fallen soldiers, in her autobiography Breckinridge chose to interpret the Civil War differently. According to her, at the end of the war, her father gracefully conceded the Confederacy's defeat and committed himself to "a new union which the arbitrament [*sic*] of war had determined was 'one and indissoluble.' Being both brave and honest," she concluded her account of her father's military service, "he accepted the verdict of the Confederate failure and made his contribution to the building of a new nation" (*SPB*).[10]

---

[8]Class History, Class of 1888 Records; Wellesley Annals, "Wellesley in 1884–1885," p. 3; Wellesley Annals, "Wellesley in 1886–1887," Wellesley College Archives, Wellesley, MA; Palmieri, *In Adamless Eden*, 1995, 38–39, 163, 178–180.

[9]Breckinridge (1933); Jane Addams to SPB, March 21, May 7, and August 11, 1912; SPB to Jane Addams, April 17, 1912; Anna Howard Shaw to Jane Addams, August 16, 1912, *Jane Adams Papers Project* (microfilm); Jabour (2013): 143–166.

[10]On Southern children and the memory of the Civil War, see Jabour (2010): Chap. 6.

As Breckinridge well knew, however, her father was a much more enthusiastic supporter of the Confederacy than she chose to record for posterity. Letters he wrote to his daughter while she attended Wellesley, for instance, indicated that he held periodic reunions of his old unit and regarded his service in the Confederate Army as a valuable lesson about "the wrestle of life."[11] Moreover, the documents Breckinridge herself collected about her father's political career demonstrated that her father was not only loyal to the "Lost Cause," but also that he was an advocate of white supremacy. Indeed, W.C.P. Breckinridge achieved political success by playing on local whites' resentments over so-called "radical" Reconstruction, touting the South's right to self-rule, and allying himself with the "Redeemers," who reclaimed white Democrats' political dominance in the post-Reconstruction era. As W.C.P. Breckinridge put it: "We want a white man's State and we intend to have it" (Klotter 1986: 147).[12]

Rather than emphasizing her father's nostalgia for the "Lost Cause" of the Southern Confederacy and his continuing commitment to white supremacy, however, Breckinridge chose to depict her father as a racial liberal. As Breckinridge liked to point out, her father "was always for fair play"; he supported public schools for African Americans, and he espoused blacks' rights to give testimony against whites. But—as Breckinridge certainly knew from her research into her father's career— W.C.P. Breckinridge also characterized African Americans as "savages" incapable of self-government. According to him, although African Americans were entitled to "fairness, justice, and protection," the "Teutonic race" was destined to "dominate the world." Nonetheless, in her memoirs, Breckinridge emphasized the ways in which her father supported African American rights, rather than the ways in which he upheld white supremacy.[13]

---

[11] W.C.P. Breckinridge to SPB, May 10, 1885; see also W.C.P. Breckinridge to SPB, June 1, September 4, 1891 (*SPBP*).

[12] See also W.C.P. Breckinridge, "Who Were the Confederate Dead?," address at the unveiling of the Confederate monument at Hopkinsville, Kentucky, May 19, 1887, and other materials in Miscellany: Speeches and Articles by and about Breckinridge Family (*SPBP*).

[13] *SPB*; W.C.P. Breckinridge, "Who Were the Confederate Dead?," address at the unveiling of the Confederate monument at Hopkinsville, Kentucky, May 19, 1887, quotations pp. 3, 16, and 28–29, copy in Miscellany: Speeches and Articles by and about Breckinridge Family (*SPBP*).

Breckinridge selectively included information about her father's record on race to cast him in a favorable light; she also scrupulously avoided discussing local race relations in her autobiography. Given the racial tensions that characterized the South during Breckinridge's childhood and adolescence, this is a telling omission—one that reveals how important it was for her to tailor her memoirs to match her adult career as a civil rights activist rather than to reflect her childhood training in upholding racial hierarchies. Breckinridge was born in the heyday of Radical Reconstruction, when southern whites fought to maintain white supremacy in both legal and extralegal ways. In Breckinridge's hometown, the city council, at her father's suggestion, held elections early, before the Fifteenth Amendment went into effect, to preempt blacks from participating. W.C.P. Breckinridge later defended local officials who prevented African Americans from casting a ballot on the basis that new laws required all voters to pay a "capitation tax," Kentucky's version of the notorious "poll tax" that robbed newly enfranchised blacks of their potential political power. He also defended suspected Klansmen accused of brutalizing local blacks. Because Breckinridge collected clippings about her father's career at the same time that she was working on her autobiography, there is no doubt that, by the time she wrote her memoirs, she was familiar with her father's record on race. Therefore, she deliberately omitted this information from her autobiography.[14]

Although, given her silence on the matter, it is impossible to know how much young Breckinridge knew about these events at the time, it stretches credulity to assume that she was entirely ignorant of the tense race relations that prevailed in her hometown during her childhood. Racial violence was endemic during Breckinridge's childhood. In the post–Civil War South, public lynchings served both as grisly reminders of the importance of maintaining racial segregation and as community rituals for enacting and reinforcing white supremacy. Some white southerners, hoping to maintain a social order based on white dominance and black subordination by "raising racists," even encouraged their children to view lynchings as a lesson in race relations (DuRocher 2011). Even if her parents were among those who attempted to shield their children from knowledge of racial violence, Breckinridge could have read about incidents of

---

[14]Clippings and transcripts, *Lexington Daily Press*, July 8, 1871; *Lexington Dollar Weekly*, July 22, 1871; *Kentucky Gazette*, February 15, 1873; *Courier Journal*, February 17, 1873; Council Proceedings, January 14, 1870, January 4, 1872, and June 6, 1872; all in Miscellany: Speeches and Articles by and about Breckinridge Family (*SPBP*).

racial violence for herself in the newspapers. For instance, when she was eleven years old, three black men were summarily executed in Lexington in January 1878 on suspicion of having information about the recent murder of a white man. Responding to criticism from the *New York Times*, local newspaper editors defended lynching as a necessary response to African Americans' alleged lawlessness, as well as to the purported sexual danger they posed to white women. Even if her family did not discuss this case around the dinner table, it seems likely that Breckinridge would have learned about these highly publicized deaths, which took place in her own hometown (Wright 1996: 53, 64–65, 77, 82, 97).

Prevailing concern about white supremacy also shaped the Breckinridge children's experience in the public schools, where their aunt, Mary Desha, taught. In Lexington, whites maintained racial hierarchies by funding and maintaining a racially segregated public school system for the city's African American population. Whether Breckinridge knew about the racial politics of segregated schools at the time or not, she certainly was well acquainted with the reality of racial segregation.[15]

Despite her father's participation in the disfranchisement of African American citizens, her likely exposure to racial violence, and her own experiences in segregated schools, Breckinridge scrupulously avoided any discussion of local race relations in her autobiography. Indeed, she did not even mention that several African Americans worked in the Breckinridge home as domestic servants. Instead, Breckinridge created a narrative in which she imbibed racial liberalism from her father.[16]

---

[15] Public schools for blacks in Kentucky were first established in 1874, maintained by taxes on black residents. In 1881, in response to threats of a federal lawsuit to integrate the schools, white Kentuckians instead agreed to equalize the funds for maintaining the racially segregated school system. See *Kentucky Historic Schools Survey*, 18–19.

[16] She did this not only in her own writing, but also in the newspaper clippings that she chose to preserve. A typical newspaper story on Breckinridge remarked: "Perhaps the most interesting characteristic of Miss Breckinridge's work is a singular freedom from prejudice—where one might expect to find her in bondage, she is not only free, but willing and even eager to preach the gospel of freedom. In spite of being a Southern woman, for example, she has no prejudice on the race problem, and has recently been active in forming the Chicago League for the Advancement of the Colored People. Those who knew her father, the late Colonel Breckinridge, remember that he, too, was distinguished in this way, that he organized public schools for Negroes in Lexington immediately after the war, and later, while still a young man, he was defeated in his first political campaign because he advocated the admission of negro testimony—a most advanced and radical demand for a Southern lawyer to make." See clipping, "Sophonisba Preston Breckinridge," April 16, 1911, Miscellany, 1873–1917 (*SPBP*).

58   A. JABOUR

Although Breckinridge carefully avoided discussing race relations in her hometown, her older sister wrote her own memoirs, which offer some revealing details about the Breckinridge children's childhood training in white supremacy. Breckinridge's sister Ella later claimed of her childhood: "There was no race problem in Lexington in the days of which I write." She went on to detail the "pleasant relations" between the Breckinridge family and their African American servants: Easter, the parlor maid; her husband Tom, the coachman; "Aunt Mandy," the cook; Adelaide, the laundress; and Clacy, the children's nurse, who, Ella explained, had been awarded to Issa "as a first present to the hour-old baby," and subsequently "nursed my Mother through every illness, received every one of her children into our arms, loved, scolded, and disciplined every one of us... and would gladly have died for any one of us." Throughout Ella's reminiscences, African Americans appear only in subservient roles, providing prompt and efficient service under all circumstances, as when, Ella recalled, "Adelaide the laundress [who] expected to keep busy every day in the week" accepted it as "a matter of course for us and for the girls who were visiting us to throw over the rail of the upstairs back veranda an armful of crumpled muslin dresses saying, 'Please press them right away, Adelaide, and send them up.'" [17]

Ella's comments make it clear that the Breckinridge family, like many other white families in the post–Civil War South, adhered to a code of "racial etiquette" that upheld white supremacy. For instance, white parents trained their offspring to display their own racial superiority and reinforce blacks' servility by referring to adult African Americans by their given names, rather than by a title and surname, while at the same time requiring blacks to use titles when referring or speaking to whites of any age. This pattern is clear in Ella's reminiscences; Breckinridge also displayed this linguistic hierarchy in fragmentary, handwritten reminiscences about her family's African American servants—reminiscences she chose not to include in later, typed drafts of her autobiography (Ritterhouse 2006: Chaps. 1 and 2).

Instead, Breckinridge carefully avoided the subject of race relations until she began to discuss her experiences at Wellesley College. In this way, Breckinridge was able to present her experiences with

---

[17] Eleanor Breckinridge Chalkley, "Magic Casements," Part I, pp. 12, 20, 33, 39–41, 49. Mss. Autobiography, ca. 1940s, transcript by James C. Klotter, Special Collections (Lexington, Kentucky: University of Kentucky, King Library).

African Americans as part of her coming-of-age story as an advocate for equality—without criticizing her father. Indeed, her description of her initial arrival on campus again credited her father with racial liberalism: "On that first day when my Father and Mother and I arrived... as we approached the entrance of Wellesley a handsome handsomely dressed couple of the Negro race with an attractive daughter approached the door[.] Mrs. Stone asked my Father 'will you let Nisba go to school with a Negro?' To which my father replied 'she got on all right with the boys [at A&M]; I think that she will get on all right with the colored.'" (*SPB*). Although in this passage Breckinridge presented her father as unconcerned about his daughter's attending classes with African Americans, in one of his first letters to his daughter while she was away at school, he cautioned her to treat her black classmates with "forbearance." Although he opined that it would be impossible to regard African Americans as equals, he concluded, "to a gentleman or lady there need be no personal embarrassment."[18]

Despite her efforts to conceal her father's racist attitudes, her early lessons in white supremacy, as well as the ways that attending college challenged these familiar beliefs, are evident in Breckinridge's account of the first time she shared a meal with African Americans. When Wellesley College President Alice Freeman invited an African American choir from Fisk University to dine with the students and faculty, Breckinridge was in a quandary. Wellesley protocol called for students to serve each other— and guests—at the dinner table. For Breckinridge, who was accustomed to being served by African American servants, this was a reversal of familiar racial dynamics. Moreover, sharing a meal symbolized social equality. Although white family members necessarily shared household space with black domestic workers, white southern parents taught their children to maintain physical separation and social superiority by dining separately from (and prior to) African Americans. Caught between her childhood training and her desire to please the college president, Breckinridge recalled that although "I found no difficulty in serving them... my own food I could not swallow" (*SPB*).

Two years later, a debate surrounding the Junior Promenade revealed how much Breckinridge's attitudes about racial equality had changed. In her three years at Wellesley, Breckinridge had become friendly with fellow classics student Ella Smith, one of Wellesley's few African American

---

[18]W.C.P. Breckinridge to SPB, October 3, 1884 (*SPBP*).

students. Smith wanted to invite guests to attend the Junior Promenade, but several white students objected, arguing that educational equality did not necessitate social equality. Breckinridge, with President Freeman's backing, "insisted that every experience at Wellesley was educational" and convinced her classmates to admit Smith's guests to the event. In her autobiography, Breckinridge indicated that the Junior Promenade was a decisive turning point in her life, one that cemented her commitment to racial equality and set her on a path to become a civil rights advocate (*SPB*; Johnson 2008: 104; Fitzpatrick 1990: 8).

In later years, Breckinridge helped found the Chicago Urban League, a civil rights organization, as well as a chapter of the National Association for the Advancement of Colored People. She insisted on extending social services to African Americans and helped ensure their inclusion in public welfare legislation. And she used her Kentucky connection to promote a federal anti-lynching bill, both by writing to Kentucky-elected officials and by planting pro–civil rights editorials in the newspaper her brother Desha edited, the *Lexington Herald* (Fitzpatrick 1990: 180–182; Jabour 2015: 158; Stehno 1988: 485–503).

Thoroughly committed to the cause of African American equality by the time she penned her memoirs in the mid-1940s, Breckinridge deliberately omitted information about her racially charged childhood—especially the racism espoused by her beloved father—to focus on the experiences that led her to embrace African American rights. Her decision set her apart from later Southern white civil rights activists, such as Lillian Smith, who published her revealing account of her own training in racial etiquette the year after Breckinridge's death (Smith 1949).

Conclusion

When Breckinridge approached "the fourscore milestone" and set out "to review my own life" (*SPB*), she framed her account of her early life—from childhood through college—as the autobiography of an activist. She used her memoirs to explain her life course, making meaning out of her memories by emphasizing the ways in which her family heritage and youthful experiences prepared her for a lifetime of activism. She also highlighted her early interest in the issues—poverty, disability, and immigration; world peace and women's rights; and African American equality—that would define the remainder of her long life. Because she intended her memoirs to serve as an explanation of how she became an advocate for social justice, Breckinridge also omitted information—such as her childhood training in white supremacy—that did not align with her adult commitments. Breckinridge died before completing her account, which perhaps is part of the reason that a woman who was nationally and internationally renowned in her own time is now largely forgotten. Nonetheless, Breckinridge's memoirs offer valuable insights into both the coming-of-age experiences and the self-image of a Southern-born Progressive reformer. Breckinridge's unfinished autobiography is not a complete account of her life, but it is a compelling and carefully constructed narrative about how she became "a champion of the championless" (*SPB*).

Works Cited

Autobiography of Sophonisba P. Breckinridge (*SPB*), Special Collections Resource Center, Regenstein Library, University of Chicago.

Sophonisba P. Breckinridge Papers (*SPBP*), Special Collections Resource Center, Regenstein Library, University of Chicago.

"A Woman Who Helps: The Story of a Southern Woman Who Is a Power in Chicago—Her Many-Sided Work—A Champion of the Championless." *Woman's Journal* (May 18, 1912).

Alpern, Sara et al. (eds.). *The Challenge of Feminist Biography: Writing the Lives of Modern American Women*. Urbana and Chicago: University of Illinois Press, 1992.

Barry, Kathleen. "Toward a Theory of Women's Biography: From the Life of Susan B. Anthony." In Teresa Iles (ed.), *All Sides of the Subject: Women and Biography*. New York and London: Teachers College Press, 1992, 23–35.

Branscombe, Martha. "A Friend of International Welfare." *Social Service Review*, vol. 22, no. 4 (December 1948): 436–441.

Breckinridge, Sophonisba P. "Neglected Widowhood in the Juvenile Court." *American Journal of Sociology*, vol. 16, no. 1 (July 1910): 53–87.

Breckinridge, Sophonisba P. *New Homes for Old*. New York and London: Harper & Bros., 1921.

Breckinridge, Sophonisba P. *Women in the Twentieth Century*. New York and London: McGraw Hill, 1933.

Brown, Victoria Bissell. *The Education of Jane Addams*. Philadelphia: University of Pennsylvania Press, 2004.

Censer, Jane Turner. *The Reconstruction of Southern White Womanhood, 1865–1895*. Baton Rouge and London: Louisiana State University Press, 2003.

Conrad, Susan Phinney. *Perish the Thought: Intellectual Women in Romantic America, 1830–1860*. New York: Oxford University Press, 1976.

62   A. JABOUR

DuRocher, Kristina. *Raising Racists: The Socialization of White Children in the Jim Crow South.* Lexington: University Press of Kentucky, 2011.

Faderman, Lillian. *To Believe in Women: What Lesbians Have Done for America—A History.* Boston: Houghton Mifflin, 1999.

Fitzpatrick, Ellen. *Endless Crusade: Women Social Scientists and Progressive Reform.* New York and Oxford: Oxford University Press, 1990.

Frankfort, Roberta. *College Women: Domesticity and Career in Turn-of-the-Century America.* New York: New York University Press, 1977.

Goan, Melanie Beals. *Mary Breckinridge: The Frontier Nursing Service and Rural Health in Appalachia.* Chapel Hill and London: University of North Carolina Press, 1998.

Goan, Melanie Beals. "Establishing Their Place in the Dynasty: Sophonisba and Mary Breckinridge's Paths to Public Service." *Register of the Kentucky Historical Society,* vol. 101, no. 1/2 (Winter/Spring 2003): 45–73.

Goodwin, Joanne L. *Gender and the Politics of Welfare Reform: Mothers' Pensions in Chicago, 1911–1929.* Chicago and London: University of Chicago Press, 1997.

Hathway, Marion. *The Young Cripple and His Job.* Chicago: University of Chicago Press, 1928.

Hay, Melba Porter. *Madeline McDowell Breckinridge and the Battle for a New South.* Lexington: University Press of Kentucky, 2009.

Jabour, Anya. *Topsy-Turvy: How the Civil War Turned the World Upside Down for Southern Children.* Chicago: Ivan R. Dee, 2010.

Jabour, Anya. "Relationship and Leadership: Sophonisba Breckinridge and Women in Social Work." *Affilia,* vol. 27, no. 1 (February 2012): 22–37.

Jabour, Anya. "Prostitution Politics and Feminist Activism: Sophonisba Breckinridge and the Morals Court in Prohibition-Era Chicago." *Journal of Women's History,* vol. 25, no. 3 (Fall 2013): 143–166.

Jabour, Anya. "Duty and Destiny: A Progressive Reformer's Coming of Age in the Gilded Age." In James Marten (ed.), *Children and Youth During the Gilded Age and Progressive Era.* New York: New York University Press, 2014, 230–251.

Jabour, Anya. "Sophonisba Breckinridge (1866–1948): Homegrown Heroine." In Melissa A. McEuen and Thomas H. Appleton (eds.), *Kentucky Women: Their Lives and Times.* Athens, GA: University of Georgia Press, 2015, 140–167.

Johnson, Joan Marie. *Southern Women at the Seven Sister Colleges: Feminist Values and Social Activism, 1875–1915.* Athens and London: University of Georgia Press, 2008.

Klotter, James C. *The Breckinridges of Kentucky.* Lexington: University of Kentucky, 1986.

Knight, Louise W. *Jane Addams: Spirit in Action.* New York: W. W. Norton, 2010.

Lenroot, Katherine F. "Friend of Children and the Children's Bureau." *Social Service Review*, vol. 22, no. 4 (December 1948): 427–430.

Muncy, Robyn. "Gender and Professionalization in the Origins of the U.S. Welfare State: The Careers of Sophonisba Breckinridge and Edith Abbott, 1890–1935." *Journal of Policy History*, vol. 2, no. 3 (July 1990): 290–315.

Palmieri, Patricia Ann. "Patterns of Achievement of Single Academic Women at Wellesley College, 1880–1920." *Frontiers: A Journal of Women Studies*, vol. 5, no. 1 (Spring 1980): 63–67.

Palmieri, Patricia Ann. *In Adamless Eden: The Community of Women Faculty at Wellesley.* New Haven and London: Yale University Press, 1995.

Ritterhouse, Jennifer. *Growing Up Jim Crow: How Black and White Southern Children Learned Race.* Chapel Hill and London: University of North Carolina Press, 2006.

Roberts, Giselle and Melissa Walker (eds.). *Women of the South: The Progressive Era.* Forthcoming.

Sklar, Kathryn Kish. *Florence Kelley and the Nation's Work: The Rise of Women's Political Culture, 1830–1900.* New Haven and London: Yale University Press, 1995.

Smith, Lillian. *Killers of the Dream.* New York: W. W. Norton, 1949.

Stehno, Sandra M. "Public Responsibility for Dependent Black Children: The Advocacy of Edith Abbott and Sophonisba Breckinridge." *Social Service Review*, vol. 62, no. 3 (September 1988): 485–503.

Taylor, Amy Murrell. *The Divided Family in Civil War America.* Chapel Hill and London: University of North Carolina Press, 2005.

Welter, Barbara. *Dimity Convictions: The American Woman in the Nineteenth Century.* Athens, GA: Ohio University Press, 1976.

Wright, George C. *Racial Violence in Kentucky, 1865–1940: Lynchings, Mob Rule, and Legal Lynchings.* Baton Rouge, LA: Louisiana State University Press, 1996.

Lean In and *Tell Me a (True) Story*: Sheryl Sandberg's Revision of Feminist History

Tanya Ann Kennedy

The images reproduced here are the book covers for two memoirs published in 2012 and 2013, Sheryl Sandberg's *Lean In* (Fig. 1) and Lilly Ledbetter's *Grace and Grit* (Fig. 2). Looking at the two covers the viewer sees that one is more confident of its subject's reception. On the first cover, Facebook COO Sandberg smiles out at the viewer. As she leans slightly forward, her face emerges from a neutral background only a shade darker than the soft white sweater she wears. This soft focus on Sandberg's face obscures her corporate power and economic status, while showing us that she needs no accessorizing details to locate her within a specific occupation, no tools to define her trade. With a few alterations, she could be an advertisement for a commodity, feminine and cosmetic. The other cover tries harder to visually portray its title, to juxtapose grace and grit. The picture is awkwardly posed and the frame seems crowded with accessories to better identify Ledbetter for book buyers. Instead of wearing the coveralls that she routinely donned for work, she is professionally dressed and made up, the large wrench in her hand the accessory

---

T. A. Kennedy (✉)
University of Maine, Farmington, ME, USA
e-mail: tanya.kennedy@maine.edu

© The Author(s) 2018
D. Letort and B. Lebdai (eds.), *Women Activists and Civil Rights Leaders in Auto/Biographical Literature and Films*,
https://doi.org/10.1007/978-3-319-77081-9_5

Fig. 1 Sheryl Sandberg embodies the philosophy of *Lean In* (2013). © Penguin Random House LLC

indicating that hers is a blue-collar story. The steel wrench coordinates with the hard and dark background, a wall of tires and brick that convey the nature of her work and the oppressiveness of her story.

The first book is a "sort of feminist manifesto" that Sandberg hopes will "reignite a revolution," encouraging women to lean in to their work as a way of creating more women leaders; the second book is the

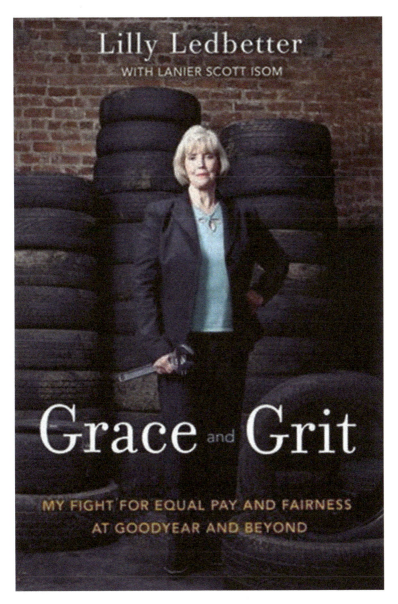

Fig. 2 Lilly Ledbetter exhibits her working-class background. © Penguin Random House LLC

story of working-class Ledbetter's isolated decades-long struggle against Goodyear Tire Co. The first is a bestselling story of leadership linked to an online social movement of the same name, while the second records the bitter experiences of pay inequity and a hostile work environment, ending in a crushing defeat at the U.S. Supreme Court. These differences between the two books are important because the two stories are essentially about the same subject: leaning in. However, Ledbetter's story will likely not appear as a "lean in" story on Sandberg's Lean In website dedicated to women's inspirational stories of workplace ambition and success.

In this chapter, because of its dominance in popular culture, I focus on Sandberg's story to examine the feminist implications of *Lean In*'s structuring of the link between self and history. As G. Thomas Couser has argued, "genres encode or reinforce particular values in ways that may shape culture and history" (Couser 2005: 145–146). Sandberg's memoir not only uses her personal experience to model workplace success, but also seeks to establish her as a feminist leader. However, the book does not neatly fit into the genre of memoir nor is it political in the way that we expect manifestos to be political. This restructuring of genres is of particular interest to feminists concerned with the values encoded in Lean In as a movement. Sandberg's appropriation of the feminist manifesto for apolitical ends, her appropriation of feminist history to produce herself as feminist subject, undoes previous formulations of the link between the personal and political that has been central to feminist politics. This undoing is an attempt to bury feminist social justice activism in service of advancing corporate authority in the public sphere. Thus, I want to return at the end of this chapter to Ledbetter's "lean in" story—*because that's exactly what it is*—as a framing device for reconsidering the feminist values encoded in Sandberg's linking of self to history.

There are two salient contexts for examining *Lean In* as a memoir in which the author attempts to link her personal story to a social movement and to authorize herself as a leader through the device of the personal: the first is Facebook as a dominant form of automedia, a concept that life-writing theorists have developed to describe how media technologies "expand the field of self-representation" (Smith and Watson 2001: 168), and how its architecture structures Sandberg's linking of the personal and the historical; the second is feminist history as represented in Sandberg's memoir.

The Choice Architecture of Lean In Feminism

While social-networking sites often appear to be user controlled, Facebook maintains a "choice architecture" that coaxes users into viewing particular features of identity as more intrinsic to self than other features. For example, a user's taste in movies, television shows, and music become an integral part of the authentic self, because Facebook's profile page design highlights the disclosure of these tastes as significant and ignores other features of identity. "Choice architecture," a phrase first used by Richard Thaler and Cass Sunstein, describes how organizations "influence decisionmaking by structuring choice so that the costs associated with an institution's desired behavior is significantly lower than the behavior desired by the individual *ceteris paribus* (all other things being equal)" (Marichal 2012: 38). In fact, as several theorists have pointed out, while Facebook's founder Mark Zuckerberg has imagined Facebook as a medium for social connection, the rules of the site and its structure reflect his own beliefs about identity and representation. In 2011, Zuckerberg introduced the Timeline feature into Facebook's platform, stating "Millions of people curate stories of their lives on Facebook every day and have no way to share them once they fall off your profile page… [Timeline is] the story of your life and a completely new way to express yourself… Timeline lets you tell the whole story of your life on a single page" (Zuckerberg 2011). As Van Dijck notes, Timeline organizes user data into a narrative biography and automatically begins to summarize previous years' events, selecting only some previous "highlights" from the past to present to readers (Van Dijck 2013: 200). Timeline as a "narrative biography" offers up personal data as history since only those historical pieces of data that come into the user's view offline will exist in Timeline and become part of the social network.

Zuckerberg insists that Facebook's interface is a new way of expressing identity, but his own views about self-representation align with the conventions of Lejeune's "autobiographical pact," which relies on the singularity and authenticity of identity (Lejeune 1988: 14). In 2010, Zuckerberg told David Kirkpatrick, "You have one identity. The days of you having a different image for your work friends or co-workers and for the other people you know are probably coming to an end pretty quickly. […] Having two identities for yourself is an example of a lack of integrity" (Kirkpatrick 2010: 199). In that same interview, Zuckerberg argues that Facebook's success is dependent on a kind of autohegemony:

"We always thought people would share more if we didn't let them do whatever they wanted, because it gave them some order" (Kirkpatrick 2010: 100). Zuckerberg has built Facebook on the idea that sharing our identity with others is key to our sense of our selves, but that Facebook needs to build avenues for self-disclosure that limit the range of expression. Moreover, Timeline is assumed to be a chronological retelling of our authentic selves without regard to other narrative orderings. In this particular coding of the self, the individual Timeline gives the illusion of constructing an historical self, but it lacks those events not uploaded by the user. What's missing from Timeline might be as important to the structuring of the historical self as what is included; the structuring historical absence of feminism in her own Timeline is what Sandberg must account for in order to reframe her memoir as history.

Sandberg agrees with Zuckerberg about the transparency of the self, telling Kirkpatrick: "You can't be on Facebook without being your authentic self" (Kirkpatrick 2010: 208). As Laurie McNeill argues, while social media have been examined as reconfiguring the relationality of the self, "Insisting on identity as singular and 'authentic,' Facebook fails to question the limitations of that concept or its foundations (who determines 'authenticity'? Who has access to it?), and instead reproduces its ideologies" (McNeill 2012: 68). Sandberg's self-history in *Lean In* models this version of identity, and, as I discuss later, this concern for creating a medium for the true expression of self links the social projects of Facebook and Lean In.

POST-FEMINIST MEMOIR AS FEMINIST HISTORY

Sandberg's insistence on the transparency of self-expression is in stark contrast to Ann Snitow's thoughts on her editing of *The Feminist Memoir Project*, a collection of personal stories from U.S. feminists who came to political consciousness in the 1960s (Snitow 2010). For many feminists, experience has been both a foundational category and a site of political and epistemological conflict. In the 1960s, to U.S. second-wave feminists the slogan the "personal is political" represented sharing one's personal experience as a way of organizing that experience into political action. It also represents how feminist political issues are deeply rooted in women's personal lives. From domestic violence and sexual assault to reproductive justice, feminists fought to change the framing of these issues as individual problems. Moreover, as Rosalyn Baxandall argues, "The idea of CR [consciousness raising] was that women, rather than doctors, psychologists, and religious leaders, were the experts about their own experiences and that feminist theory and practice should arise from experiences of women's daily life" (Baxandall 2008: 414).

Discussing her editing of the memoirs, Snitow writes of the difficulty of assembling a coherent history of the movement from the many pieces she collected for the project. For her, the fragmented collection of pieces demonstrates the "unstable" relation of memory to history as memory establishes identity through a "selective, simplifying, distorting work" (Snitow 2010: 143). Memory is a significant but faulty hinge connecting the self to history. Adding to Couser's contention that life writing encodes particular values in how it links the self to history, Snitow points out that the "mechanism of memory" is filled with "politically charged choices," arguing that the history of feminism and women's contributions to institution and coalition building is often "actively misremembered" in histories of the 1960s (Snitow 2010: 144). Feminists in the memoir project actively engage in a shaping of historical values by attempting to rework memory into history, because such relations, however unstable, are the means through which the activists are able to secure a place for the women's movement in U.S. history. The feminist memoir project comes together "fused by the political desire" that "memory might serve as a fountain of sustained future action" (Snitow 2010: 143); it is a project—not elegiac—but forward looking (Snitow 2010: 142–144).

Sandberg's recollection of feminist history through personal storytelling avoids this difficult work of interrogating the processes of "active misremembering," of seeking the political in the personal to forge a "sustained future action." Instead, in order to invert its key insight that the "personal is political," Sandberg establishes feminism's historical absence by refusing to discuss the feminist politics women coming of age in the 1980s and 1990s experienced. The purpose of placing feminism in the distant past seems to be twofold: (1) to depoliticize her own history and (2) to center her own Timeline as a history of feminism marked by its absence. A few examples demonstrate how she manages to write herself into history as a feminist leader while writing the feminist movement out of the political near past and present. By taking her personal story and universalizing it as a broader generational narrative, Sandberg creates a choice architecture that connects women to Lean In feminism, erasing other possible pasts and, thus, other possible feminist futures.[1]

Through the strategic use of "we" Sandberg universalizes her own experience into a generational narrative about the death of feminism. In the first chapter, "Internalizing the Revolution," she places feminism in the distant historical past: "We stand on the shoulders of the women who came before us, women who had to fight for the rights that we now take for granted" (Sandberg 2013: 4). Later, she states, "I headed into college believing that the feminists of the sixties and seventies had done the hard work of achieving equality for my generation" (Sandberg 2013: 141). In "The Leadership Ambition Gap," Sandberg details the heroic work ethic and educational achievements of her mother and grandmother and her family's social consciousness; she discusses her mother's decision to be a stay-at-home parent in the 1970s, and her parents' commitment to having gender-neutral expectations of their children (Sandberg 2013: 13–14). Sandberg generalizes from this experience that "My generation was raised in an era of increasing equality, a trend *we thought* would continue. In retrospect, *we* were naïve and idealistic" (Sandberg 2013: 14). Throughout the book, she continues this universalization of her own experience: "My generation grew up watching our mothers do the child care and housework while our fathers earned the wages" (Sandberg 2013: 119). By telling a generational story of feminism, Sandberg uses her personal experience to create a normative barrier between past and present so that the absence of other feminist voices in the text is naturalized.

When she tells readers about working for Larry Summers in the Treasury Department during the Clinton administrations, she never mentions some of the most controversial feminist issues of her generation, including the sexual and reproductive politics represented by Clinton's pro-choice stance, Hillary Clinton's career and mothering "choices," the continuing focus on sexual harassment, the rollback of *Roe v. Wade* by the Supreme Court, and the Welfare Reform Act.[2]

---

[1] Portions of the following have been previously printed in my book *Historicizing Post-Discourses: Postracialism and Postfeminism in U.S. Culture.*

[2] In 1989 the U.S. Supreme Court, in Webster v Reproductive Health Services, upheld states' rights to regulate women's right to abortion. In 1991 the Senate held televised hearings on Anita Hill's sexual harassment allegations against Supreme Court nominee Clarence Thomas. In 1996, against strong feminist opposition Clinton passed the Personal Responsibility and Work Opportunity Reconciliation Act. These national controversies

In 1992, the year after Sandberg graduated from Harvard, Yale undergrad Rebecca Walker penned "Becoming the Third Wave" to call women to action in the wake of Anita Hill's testimony before the Clarence Thomas confirmation hearings. It was a call to political action that provided a framework for young feminist activists to organize. Sandberg deliberately sweeps innumerable feminist leaders, organizations, and conflicts from the feminist table. Instead, what Sandberg notices is that "with each passing year, fewer and fewer of my colleagues were women. More and more often, I was the only woman in the room" (Sandberg 2013: 6). While the historical consequences of the anti-feminist backlash ushered in by the Reagan administration and continuing into the 1990s might have been an important element of most feminist memoirs, Sandberg argues that it is women's bad choices that prevent them from sharing the room with her (Faludi 1991). She does not connect her own ideologies to feminism's absence in her life, not even in the memory work that a memoir would seem to entail. Sandberg imagines and attempts to fix the hinge between "unstable" memory and collective histories and futures by deliberately reframing feminism as narrowly concerned with elite women's success.

Instead of exploring the feminist politics of her generation and the sexism that fueled the dominant politics of the era, she fuses together memory and history into a persuasive enunciation that universalizes her vision of the world. She states that her anti-feminism was due to "childish" immaturity and not ideology. She uses selected quotes from well-known second-wave feminists to legitimate her focus on psychological and behavioral makeovers for women as the "commonsense solution" to women's underrepresentation in power. Sandberg tells readers, "One of my favorite quotes comes from author Alice Walker, who observed, "The most common way people give up their power is by thinking they don't have any" (Sandberg 2013: 63). She uses Walker to close a chapter. Thus, the words are not analyzed in context, but ripped from their attachment to Walker's radical politics. In taking up Walker's voice, Sandberg reinforces her own power but does not engage with Walker's ideas. Walker's version of power is about creation and indigenous

---

occurred simultaneously with the first uses of the term "third wave" to describe the emergence of a new generation of feminists. For a critical examination of this generational model of feminist history, see *Third Wave Feminism: A Critical Exploration.*

women's wisdom that extends beyond the self and the current political and economic systems; her version of power always challenges leaders to recognize power from below. It is not compatible with Sandberg's feminism. Sandberg quotes Walker because it creates the feminist affect that the invocation of a "we" demands. In doing so, she also trades on Walker's black womanism as the signature of the revolutionary.

But why does Sandberg need to produce herself as a feminist subject, given that her life story is about having been successful without a feminist politics? If it is true, as Sidonie Smith and Julia Watson argue, that "whatever claims to experience we make must be made within a rhetorical framework that is recognizable to the audience" (Smith and Watson 2001: 33), then Sandberg cannot tell her personal story without feminism as the identifiable historical narrative that structures the conditions for her own power even in its absence from her Timeline. As Mary Hawkesworth points out in "Feminists versus Feminization":

> Feminism's death by report erases the social-justice activism of women around the globe while covering the traces of erasure [...]. Those who would expunge feminist activism from public perception and memory seek to construct fictive versions of the present and past that will become embedded in culture as shared memory. In so doing, they also shape the future by producing new generations who assent to these cultural fictions. (Hawkesworth 2007: 174)

In producing her historical fiction, Sandberg frames feminism so that it appears in *her* Timeline when it comes to her perception; this is not a problem of the instability of memory or the limitedness of perception, but a desire to use the personal Timeline as a mode for leaving feminist resistance out of the choice architecture of Lean In. Sandberg displaces feminism in order to situate herself as the catalyst for a revival of this movement that she first has to bury. This revived movement avoids the kind of messy entanglements with hierarchy, difference, and memory itself that inform Snitow's attempt to create feminist history by piecing together different and sometimes irreconcilable perspectives. It also unifies a vision of the past for the present that omits questions of racial and economic justice that continue to be central for feminist activists. In this way, she is able to avoid any questions about how her own anti-feminism might have contributed to the oppression and subordination of women *and* contributed to her own success in white, male-dominated workplaces.

RESTRUCTURING THE SELF: MAKING OVER FEMINISM

The feminist future Sandberg imagines for women is one that urges them to interface with citizenship through self-improvement. As Wendy Parkins has argued in "Bad Girls, Bad Reputations: Feminist Ethics and Postfeminism," this is a characteristic of postfeminists who attempt to transform feminism into an apolitical project of individualism:

> Postfeminism assumes that the women's movement took care of oppressive institutions, and that it is up to individual women to make personal choices that simply reinforce those fundamental societal changes. Put this way, 'feminist' practices become matters of personal style or individual choice and any emphasis on organized intervention is regarded as naïve and even oppressive to women. (Parkins 1999: 377)

Sandberg's book performs a similar feat, taking the "personal is political" message of second-wave feminism and inverting it.

Contemporary theorists such as Nikolas Rose have argued that contemporary governance operates, in part, through the self-improvement mandate as part of good citizenship. In *Governing the Soul*, Rose observes that contemporary culture has produced a field of experts

> who are not experts in a field of knowledge but in the field of the self: psychologists, social workers, personnel managers, probation officers, counselors, and therapists... have based their claim to social authority upon their capacity to understand the psychological aspects of the person and act upon them, or to advise others what to do. The multiplying powers of these "engineers of the human soul" seem to manifest something profoundly novel in the relations of authority over the self. (Rose 1990: 2–3)

While these authorities over the self have multiplied in social service and government fields, nowhere is this model of expertise more prevalent than in media, including women's memoir and popular literature and reality television makeover shows (Roberts 2007: 240). The choice architecture of social media is strikingly similar to the limited choices offered the makeover victim of reality television. Martin Roberts, in "The Fashion Police," argues that the persuasive design of such shows is a good example of Rose's argument because it requires women to freely choose a new, postfeminist image *for themselves*, albeit within the prescribed guidelines. This is most clearly on view in the sequences in which the subject is provisionally "released" into retail stores to begin shopping for her new wardrobe under the watchful eye of the experts. The point, repeated *ad nauseam*, is that she has to learn to make the "right" choices *herself*. As the frequent interventions that are necessary make clear, this contradictory objective is by no means easy to achieve, but it remains the object of the exercise because it enables the subject's transformation to be presented as a *self-transformation*, freely accepted and undertaken, rather than a form of social discipline. (Roberts 2007: 241)

Palmer calls this a form of "soft domination" wherein citizens are encouraged to imagine their true selves through the "illusion of choice" (Palmer 2003: 128). Sandberg, however, focuses on the citizen as worker, leveraging the choice architecture of social media to more closely align feminism with the ends of the corporation. Facebook and Lean In offer a limited set of narratives for the self while assuring us that these narratives are manifestations of our true selves.

In Sandberg's postfeminist lexicon, "choice" is a key term resonating with feminist meaning that she uses to describe every action and decision. And, while Sandberg gestures toward the idea of respecting women's choices, she is most interested in addressing an audience willing to engage in the self-disciplining "adjustment or difference that we can make" that is "under our own control" (Sandberg 2013: 9). Women must make adjustments at work and at home. To help women understand how to make the right choices, Sandberg accumulates a long list of mistakes that she has—with "disappointment"—watched women make:

> We hold ourselves back in ways both big and small, by lacking self-confidence, by not raising our hands, and by pulling back when we should be leaning in. We internalize the negative messages we get throughout our lives – the messages that say it's wrong to be outspoken, aggressive, more powerful than men. We lower… we continue… We compromise… This is not a list of things other women have done. I have made every mistake on this list. At times, I still do. (Sandberg 2013: 8)

The message is clear: women have choices, but they are continuously making the wrong ones. The new feminism can empower us to make the right ones.

Through her anecdotes, her gendered mode of address, and self-deprecation Sandberg is able to construct a gendered intimacy that she represents as more authentic and useful than the legal protections of the state. Sometimes she lapses into third person, constructing a hypothetical woman and telling us a story about the deluded protagonist. This image of the woman who makes bad choices is a strategy that lets readers know what parts of ourselves should be rejected in order not to "disappoint" Sandberg, the compassionate expert. Take, for example, her discussion of the prohibition against asking prospective employees—especially women—about their plans for children. Sandberg mentions these limitations that anti-discrimination laws place on her twice (Sandberg 2013: 96, 144). In her imaginings the discourse in the office should take place outside the boundaries of normative laws that *prevent* authorities from validating women's choices. Instead of addressing the law, Sandberg suggests that it is possible for managers to speak to women as women outside the normative legal structures designed to manage barriers to women's advancement.

Women's choice to address sexism in the workplace is a bad choice. While Sandberg wants to start a conversation about women and ambition, she does not argue that women should take more initiative in fighting discrimination or in activism for change in family and workplace laws. In fact, the existence of these laws themselves suggests that the state's attempt to regulate employment discrimination is actually an impediment to women's progress rather than a form of redress. In Sandberg's narrative, such discrimination may exist but the solution is "those of us who are different have to teach others *how* we want to be treated."

The heightened language that Sandberg uses, including the repetition of words such as "true," "real," "choices," and "power" as well as "revolution," depoliticizes these terms and appropriates them for the workplace and are words now attached to a restructuring of women's selves. As Kate Losse, former speechwriter for Zuckerberg, argues in "Feminism's Tipping Point: Who Wins from Leaning In?" Sandberg has taken up her boss's practice of blurring the political and the corporate. Losse claims that Zuckerberg wants to develop Facebook into "a global leader on par with nations," and notes that Zuckerberg has stated, "'Companies over countries' [...] If you want to change the world, the best thing to do is start a company" (Losse 2013). According to Losse, Zuckerberg appreciates that companies have potentially more money and fewer structuring rules than countries, while countries remain a respected model of social organization to which citizens feel loyal. This latter connotation accounts for why Facebook often describes itself in national terms with phrasing like "Facebook nation" and user figures are announced in relation to countries' populations. In some ways, Facebook wants to be a company and a country, commanding the best powers of both. (Losse 2013)

The cultural work of *Lean In*, then, is to further blur the lines between corporations and countries, between corporate leadership and public power. The restructuring of the citizen self as worker and consumer is key for the corporate leader who wants to legitimate her political authority. Moreover, this restructuring fits nicely into U.S. mythologies of self-improvement, merit, and upward mobility through individual opportunity and is accepted as the "commonsense" solution to marginalization in contemporary culture; Sandberg's rhetoric stages an act of consumption (reading her book, joining a Lean In Circle, or Facebooking Lean In) as the *first step* to an improvement of the self for the good of others, legitimating her own stepping into the role of social authority. The attraction of Sandberg's text is that she convinces the reader to imagine that by empowering herself in the corporate world, she is changing the gendered structures of power in the world: women will now be put— more successfully—in the service of capitalism.

Her rhetorical strategy for managing hierarchy is structural. Sandberg provides statistics that show that most women don't have paid medical leave or that childcare is cost prohibitive for many women workers and then she continues with her argument so that while hierarchies are acknowledged, these do not shift the focus from techniques of self-improvement. Instead of engaging with women who need to discuss economic inequality, social policy, and racism, she parenthesizes their concerns and continues her monologue. Power, here, it should be noted, is the power to appropriate the labor of womanists such as Walker, to stifle their claims of resistance to Sandberg's social movement building. As with Facebook, Sandberg sets the terms of discussion, provides the site through which feminist discourse will be filtered, and lays out the networks through which women will talk with one another.[3]

---

[3] bell hooks makes a similar point about Sandberg's appropriation of feminism, calling it "faux feminism." There are, in fact, many feminist critiques of Sandberg, including Faludi's excellent essay discussed here.

Part of the allure of the empowerment fix is that it becomes a way not only of maximizing one's own opportunities, but also of being comfortable with validating or invalidating the choices of others. The gender essentialism of Sandberg goes so far as to make the claim that "We all want the same thing: to feel comfortable with our choices and to feel validated by those around us" (Sandberg 2013: 168). Being comfortable with our choices is clearly connected to the idea of external validation which suggests that others have the power also to invalidate our choices, to make us feel uncomfortable, or, as Sandberg herself noted when discussing the women who don't lean in, that other women can be "disappointed" in the choices "we" make. By making the need for external validation from other women the foundation for our choice making, Sandberg is able to rhetorically drive women to lean in.

Sandberg's postfeminist "we" suggests not the end to gendered policing but the invocation of the police in service of securing a sense of self. As with the reality television makeover expert who shows us that the makeover victim must "learn to make the 'right' choices herself" (Roberts 2007: 241), Sandberg refuses to resign herself to the idea that women can't learn to make the right ones. This is why she rejects affirmative action: affirmative action is bad for women because others will perceive the woman as a "token" and lacking in merit.[4] Again, it is the perception of others, in this case the ability of white males in power to validate one's merit, that is important. Thus, Sandberg is most concerned with making sure that women are able to demonstrate their worthiness.

Sandberg does spend a portion of the book admitting that external barriers exist in the workplace, but for a woman who claims to be restarting a revolution, she has little to offer as critique of the economic and social structure of work itself. While recognizing that she may be seen as asking women to assimilate to a system rather than challenging the barriers that are a part of its structure, she argues, "Both sides are right. So rather than engage in philosophical arguments over which comes first, let's agree to wage battles on both fronts. They are equally important. I am encouraging women to address the chicken, but I fully support those who are focusing on the egg" (Sandberg 2013: 9). On the surface such a pronouncement might seem fair. However, this rhetoric trivializes

---

[4]It is in an interview with Ken Auletta that Sandberg is most explicit about her rejection of affirmative action, although it is implied in many passages of the book.

the differences between these positions: first, by declaring both positions "right" (and therefore not necessarily in contradiction with one another or not one in danger of acting as a substitute for social change) and, second, by refusing to engage in "philosophical arguments" as if how we approach a problem does not matter to the end result. The liberal pluralism offered here ignores her own power, even as it trades on that power, since central to her movement is the idea that more women in power will make the world a better place for women. Moreover, she has the power to limit the possibilities for telling counternarratives as part of Lean In feminism, since the default structure of the Lean In website discourages alternative stories of feminism.

Lean In Circles: The Political Is Personal

Sandberg connects this personal empowerment to the architecture of a social movement by building feminism on the transactional nature of storytelling that is built into the architecture of Facebook's social networks. Her organization Lean In trades on lean-in stories as its primary means of engagement—both offline and online. Everyone is allowed a self to tell, but only if it fits the parameters of the interface. An example from a Lean In Circle diary illustrates the harmful nature of this transactional feminism.

Sandberg's Lean In Circles website focuses on the shaping of the self according to expert videos, corporate disciplines, and workplace volunteerism in achieving goals measured in raises and promotions or new "benefits." On the Lean In site, we see Sandberg's happy, smiling face, encouraging us to start a Lean In Circle, because "We are more creative, more confident, and accomplish more in groups." Lean In is committed to "shar[ing] Lean In Stories—short narratives of moments in life when we choose to 'lean in' or 'lean back' intended to inspire, teach and connect us." These stories are labeled to tell us what the message of the story is. Using a dropdown menu, users can choose from these topics, "Inspiration," "Overcoming Adversity," "Education," "Leadership," "Parenting," "Speaking Up," "Career Transitions," "Finding Balance," "Mentors and Role Models," and "Gender in the Workplace." But they must be stories that "inspire, teach and connect us." The interface limits the range of experiences, emotions, and actions that are available as forms of selfhood, perhaps, as Zuckerberg argues, to encourage more sharing. We can read the Circle Diaries of members to feel closer to the group. The diary, however, is not a narrative, but in the form of a short magazine interview, divided into categories such as "favorite Circle moment," "impact of the Circle," and "Circle Tips for Newbies." Sandberg trades on the conventional appeal of the diary as a personal mode of expression; but the diary is no longer an unstable writing of the self, receptive to the mundane and the dramatic, it is now a formulaic means for limiting that range of expression.

One diary is from the leader of a Lean In Circle for young girls who have been sexually abused, called "Change Your Shoes." According to the Diary, the Circle "aims to show that no matter what you have been through and no matter where you have come from, that you can 'change your shoes,' step out of all that holds you back, and lean in to all you want for your future." Kathy Andersen is the Circle Leader and we learn at the bottom of the page that she is CEO of Change Begins with One. From Andersen's website we learn that this Circle is part of her consulting work and that she is now President and CEO of Development Connect, a consulting service that helps facilitate global development, that she has a master's degree from the Harvard Kennedy School, and that she has written a book called *Change Your Shoes, Live Your Greatest Life!* Nowhere in her profile does it suggest that she has a degree applicable to working with teenagers who live on the streets or who are part of a rehabilitative juvenile program. But that is fine, because Sandberg is also working with them; Andersen tells us that they started their Circle with a video introduction from "Sheryl" and that the girls were touched by "what one of the richest and most powerful women in the world had to say. By the end of the video, there were tears. Isabelle sobbed from that deep place inside where all of our fears, sadness, and pain burn like a wildfire."

By the end of the session, one girl has this insight, "I'm trying to grow up. I'm trying to put all this bullshit aside. It's time for me to take care of me now and I know God's going to give me a good life and make me happy one day. Everybody has a purpose to be on this Earth, to do something with your life. It's up to you." The self that is narrated here is already shaped by the message of *Lean In*, but we cannot be sure who is writing this self and what the interface has omitted. Andersen encourages the personalization of their connection to Sandberg by calling her Sheryl and, at least in the diary entry, encourages the girls to think of her as someone who is speaking directly to their needs and desires. The connection made is not between the girls but with the powerful figures who provide a sense of care and empathy where there is none (it is a video produced for everyone). The lesson seems to be that we should listen to Sheryl because she is "rich and powerful" and direct our affect toward powerful representations of corporations rather than toward the other girls in the room.

It is no accident that Sandberg's book begins and ends with stories about Nobel Peace Prize winner Leymah Gbowee. Gbowee has written her own memoir about her struggles as a refugee, wife and mother, and her work to bring an end to Liberia's civil war. Gbowee's regional-based anti-violence work becomes an authorizing signature for the global significance of *Lean In*. If the book seems a lightweight contribution to career advice literature, then Sandberg's equation of her work with the work of Gbowee attempts to suppress the significant differences in their framings of the link between self and history. Whereas Gbowee led a protest movement against the corruption of her own government, Sandberg aligns herself with government leaders and corporations and has little involvement in women's social justice activism. That Sandberg remains silent on the most pressing issues of women's social justice movements in the U.S., including reproductive and sexual justice, interpersonal and state violence, racism, the living wage, poverty, and care leave, while attending such events as Davos and the EG8 summit should demonstrate the narrowness of her agenda. At the end of her book, Sandberg returns to Gbowee, reminding readers "All of this brings me back to Leymah Gbowee's insistence that we need more women in power. When leadership insists that these policies change, they will. Google put in pregnancy parking when I asked for it and it remains there long after I left. We must raise both the ceiling and the floor" (Sandberg 2013: 169). When Gbowee argues that we need more women in power, however, does she mean more women in power in corporations to act as experts? How does this affect change of the global power structures that Sandberg seems to gesture toward with her use of Gbowee as a frame for her own narrative?

Sandberg's feminism directs women and girls' energies toward the corporation as the structural site of empowerment. The Lean In website even has corporate "Partners." Sandberg has partnered with some questionable corporations that Lean In promotes on its website. The website allows a corporation to both provide a statement of its commitment to women and to link to its own corporate website and Facebook page. When Susan Faludi questioned Lean In executives (she was never able to speak with Sandberg) about the ethics of promoting corporations as Lean In partners, she received this response:

We reject this premise. There are over 200 companies who have joined as platform partners, and it seems early to judge their motivations. We are not setting up a watchdog organization or an audit function. Rather, we are providing high-quality educational materials and technology at scale that companies can use to improve their understanding of gender bias. We want to make these materials available to everyone—because every company can get better, and we want them to. (Faludi 2013)

Each company provides a statement as to how its corporation is leaning in. Gap Inc.'s statement, from Eva Sage-Gavin is, "We're proud to be leaning in because female leaders are a fundamental part of our company's DNA, starting with our co-founder Doris Fisher. Working across industries and borders to help women reach their fullest potential is one of our greatest strengths." While Gap Inc. and other corporations promote their women-friendly policies and the number of women members of their executive board, there is little discussion of these Fortune 500 companies abroad. Gap and Wal-Mart, for example, have long been named as sweatshop exploiters of women garment workers, many of whom have died due to unsafe working conditions. In the U.S., Wal-Mart's women workers filed an unprecedented class action lawsuit alleging gender discrimination. Lean In's partnership with corporations, as Faludi points out, provides a means for those companies such as Gap to launder their exploitation of women in the Global South, to whitewash their gender exploitative and discriminatory practices through an organization that promotes privileged women's equality in leadership and education.

Similarly, Lean In Circles become part of the public relations response to Sandberg's critics. For example, Sandberg was criticized for rejecting an invitation from Hilton hotel workers, predominantly women of color, trying to unionize on a property owned by Harvard, Sandberg's alma mater. The workers wanted Sandberg to visit and support the union as a Lean In Circle (Fig. 3).[5] According to *The Boston Globe*, Lean In responded by arguing that "it has partnered with several organizations that serve lower-income women, including Dress for Success, and supports Lean In circles of domestic workers in San Francisco, as well as rescued sex slaves in Miami." In other words, each Lean In Circle's group members become—not collective activists engaged in a movement—but beneficiaries of Sandberg's support.

[5] Thank you to Unite Here Local 26 and Emma Perdomo for the use of this image.

Fig. 3 Unite Here Local 26, a union of employees at the Hilton DoubleTree Suites hotel in Boston created leaflets to appeal for Sandberg's support. © UNITE HERE Local 26

Sandberg's indifferent response to the requests of the hotel workers is strikingly different from one reader's conflicted response on amazon.com to Lilly Ledbetter's *Grace and Grit*: "This book is a little unbelievable in that LIlly [*sic*] repeatedly subjects herself to punishment. Of course, that happens everyday to women who need financial security." The contradictory statement put forth by the reviewer demonstrates the ambivalence that many readers will experience while reading Ledbetter's story—the idea that she would subject herself to the hostility and discrimination she experiences seems, at first, unbelievable, but then, all too recognizable to many women workers.

Ledbetter's autobiography reads as a cautionary tale of leaning in, and a rebellion against the demand for self-improvement. While Sandberg's version of a feminist manifesto is a boon to corporate good "feeling," focusing on what women can do to improve their situations, Ledbetter's life story is a perfect example of "leaning in"; her husband, Charles, is even a good example of a partner who is partially transformed by his wife's ambitions. Her decision to return to work, and, then, to leave the reliability of her office manager job for the unknown and male-dominated workplace but increased challenge and economic rewards of Goodyear bears witness to her ambition and self-assurance.

However, Ledbetter writes of a very different experience of the connection between work and home, of representing the self in the workplace, from those experiences narrated in the Lean In diaries. She writes of the drive into work that she had to "leave behind worries about what was going on with the kids or Charles as I mused over the details that awaited me in the tire room. By the time I checked in at the gates of the plant, I'd have sealed off my emotions, ready for work" (Ledbetter 2012: 4). She arrives for work sometimes two hours early to prepare, fearful of making mistakes (Ledbetter 2012: 78) and tells readers, "I never socialized outside of work. It was always clear that I'd never be part of the boys' club—and that was just as well. It wasn't a club that I wanted to belong to. So I kept my boundaries clear" (Ledbetter 2012: 6). Ledbetter leans into her work while rejecting the sexism implicit in the fraternal order that has been established to evaluate her. All the while, her paycheck reflects Goodyear's indifference to her choices: "Those numbers said loud and clear that it didn't matter how hard I'd worked, how much I'd wanted to succeed and do the right thing: I'd been born the wrong sex, and that was that" (Ledbetter 2012: 7). Moreover, Lilly knows why she is in the room alone: "the handful of women managers along the way had come and gone, quitting or having nervous breakdowns and seeking professional help" (Ledbetter 2012: 149–150).

But her story also belies the memoir's trite title. Ledbetter did not suffer the daily humiliations of a hostile work environment and an unfulfilling home life with much grace at all really. She makes it clear that she was mostly stubborn, raised in a poor household by a mother who could not seem to love her, both of them unequipped for the rhetorics of therapeutic experts and psychological makeovers. Ledbetter lives all her life as a mostly ordinary woman, but it is how she narrates her transformation into a feminist historical subject that I find most interesting.

Except for an anonymous note filled with the pay figures of the more highly paid male managers and slipped into her locker, Ledbetter would not have become a public self worthy of our attention because of her experiences. The difference between Sheryl Sandberg's experience and Lilly Ledbetter's is that it is precisely through the anonymity of multiple identities of work and allegiance that Ledbetter has access to public articulation and that we have access to her contrasting story of leaning in. Autobiographical stories of working-class women have always raised significant questions about the relations between attention and value, and the individual nature of narratives that are about class. Ledbetter tells us that but for an anonymous note we would never know who she is. In other words, her life comes to our awareness not by the nature of the work she does or the lessons she learns, but is itself an instruction in the absence of popular and political attentiveness to the stories of women already leaning in.

Juxtaposed these two stories tell a story about how U.S. feminist histories are reframed and assimilated into dominant interpretive communities to accommodate the architecture of "choice" in U.S. culture. This accommodation ensures that the "we" written into the timeline of the present reflects the dominant structures already in place, pushing to the margins version of the past that challenge this architecture and excluding women's stories that do not fit into the dropdown menu of "Facebook feminism" (Faludi 2013). These cultural fictions act as a form of "active misremembering" that narrows and impoverishes the historical resources available to us for telling stories for a collective feminist future.

WORKS CITED

Auletta, Ken. "A Woman's Place." *New Yorker*, July 11, 2011. www.newyorker.com. Accessed on March 11, 2016.

Baxandall, Rosalyn. "Historical Life Stories." *Feminist Studies*, vol. 34, no. 3 (2008): 412–424.

Couser, G. Thomas. "Genre Matters: Form, Force, and Filiation." *Life Writing*, vol. 2, no. 2 (2005): 139–156.

Faludi, Susan. *Backlash: The Undeclared War against American Women*. New York: Crown Publishers, 1991.

Faludi, Susan. "Facebook Feminism, Like It or Not." *The Baffler*, n.p., 2013. Accessed on March 14, 2016.

Gillis, Stacy, Gillian Howe, and Rebecca Munford. *Third Wave Feminism: A Critical Exploration*. New York: Palgrave Macmillan, 2007.

Hawkesworth, Mary. "Feminists Versus Feminization." In Michaele L. Ferguson and Lori Jo Marso (eds.), *W Stands for Women: How the George W. Bush Presidency Shaped a New Politics of Gender*. Durham: Duke University Press, 2007, 163–190.

LEAN IN AND TELL ME A (TRUE) STORY   87

hooks, bell. "Dig Deep: Beyond Lean In." *The Feminist Wire*, October 28, 2013. Accessed on March 12, 2016.

Johnston, Katie. "Workers Trying to Unionize Appeal to Sheryl Sandberg." *Boston Globe*, May 24, 2014. bostonglobe.com. Accessed on January 20, 2016.

Kennedy, Tanya Ann. *Historicizing Post-discourses: Postfeminism and Postracialism in United States Culture*. Albany: State University of New York Press, 2017.

Kirkpatrick, David. *The Facebook Effect: The Inside Story of the Company That Is Connecting the World*. New York: Simon & Schuster, 2010.

Lean In. LeanIn.Org, n.d. Web. December 30, 2014. http://leanin.org/.

Ledbetter, Lilly M. and Lanier Scott Isom. *Grace and Grit: My Fight for Equal Pay and Fairness at Goodyear and Beyond*. New York: Crown Archetype, 2012.

Lejeune, Philippe. *On Autobiography*. Minneapolis: University of Minnesota Press, 1988.

Losse, Kate. "Feminism's Tipping Point: Who Wins from Leaning In?" *Dissent Magazine*, March 26, 2013. Accessed on March 14, 2016.

Marichal, José. *Facebook Democracy: The Architecture of Disclosure and the Threat to Public Life*. Farnham, UK: Ashgate, 2012.

McNeill, Laurie. "There is No "I" in Network: Social Networking Sites and Posthuman Auto/Biography." *Biography*, vol. 35, no. 1 (Winter 2012): 65–82.

Palmer, Daniel. "The Paradox of User Control." *Design Philosophy Papers*, vol. 1, no. 3 (2003): 127–135.

Parkins, Wendy. "Bad Girls, Bad Reputations: Feminist Ethics and Postfeminism." *Australian Feminist Studies*, vol. 14, no. 30 (1999): 377–385.

Roberts, Martin. "The Fashion Police: Governing the Self in *What Not to Wear*." In Yvonne Tasker and Diane Negra (eds.), *Interrogating Postfeminism: Gender and the Politics of Popular Culture*. Durham: Duke University Press, 2007, 227–248.

Rose, Nikolas. *Governing the Soul: The Shaping of the Private Self*. New York and London: Routledge, 1990.

Sandberg, Sheryl. *Lean In: Women, Work, and the Will to Lead*. New York: Knopf, 2013.

Smith, Sidonie and Julia Watson. *Reading Autobiography: A Guide for Interpreting Life Narratives*. Minneapolis: University of Minnesota Press, 2001.

Snitow, Ann. "Refugees from Utopia: Remembering, Forgetting, and the Making of *The Feminist Memoir Project*." In Yifat Gutman, Adam D. Brown, and Amy Sodaro (eds.), *Memory and the Future: Transnational Politics, Ethics, and Society*. New York: Palgrave Macmillan, 2010, 141–157.

Van Dijck, J. "'You Have One Identity': Performing the Self on Facebook and LinkedIn." *Media, Culture & Society*, vol. 35, no. 2 (2013): 199–215. Accessed on February 7, 2016.

Walker, Rebecca. "Becoming the Third Wave." *Ms.* 39 (January 1992): 39–41.

Zuckerberg, Mark. "Timeline Launch." *Facebook*, 2011. Accessed on January 20, 2015.

PART II

Black History in Auto/biographical Texts

The Many Lives of Ida B. Wells: Autobiography, Historical Biography, and Documentary

Delphine Letort

Biopics are a popular genre in Hollywood cinema, providing "valuable civic lessons" (Custen 1992: 16) by informing the audience about the history of the nation. Biopic scholar George F. Custen argues that "the Hollywood biographical film created and still creates public history by declaring, through production and distribution, which lives are acceptable subjects" (1992: 12). This statement calls into question the type of historical narrative shaped by Hollywood cinema; we should interrogate the choice of the characters that are expected to embody American history on screen. All too often, the focus on a single life tends to overshadow the grassroots movements that undergird the flow of history. Some historical periods have drawn significantly more attention than others: from *Gone with the Wind* (Victor Fleming, 1939) to *Lincoln* (Steven Spielberg, 2012), the Civil War turns into epic melodrama—lavish productions that stun their audiences with extravagance—whereas the Reconstruction

---

D. Letort (✉)
Le Mans University, Le Mans, France
e-mail: delphine.letort@univ-lemans.fr

© The Author(s) 2018
D. Letort and B. Lebdai (eds.), *Women Activists and Civil Rights Leaders in Auto/Biographical Literature and Films*,
https://doi.org/10.1007/978-3-319-77081-9_6

91

92 D. LETORT

period has yielded few films apart from the highly controversial *Birth of a Nation* (David W. Griffiths, 1915) that "made heroes of the Klansmen who had invented the horrors of lynching" (Stokes 2007: 191). Slave narratives were also adapted to screen (*12 Years a Slave*, Steve McQueen, 2013) and a few biopics retrace the Civil Rights movement through the commitment of its iconic figures (*Malcolm X*, Spike Lee, 1992; *The Rosa Parks Story*, Julie Dash, 2010), thus earning them a place in the pantheon of American history. Jonathan Lupo and Carolyn Anderson have recently noted an increasing diversity among the subjects tackled by biopics that now include the "lives of people of color and non-heterosexuals" (Lupo and Anderson 2008: 50) whereas Tom Brown and Belén Vidal have pointed out slave biopics that emphasize "the minutiae of the day-to-day lives of slaves and their manifold means of resistance" (Brown and Vidal 2014: 131), conflating with the 1990s' revisionist trends promoting histories that highlight slave agency in a system of oppression and domination.

African American documentarians support such progressive enterprises, taking part in the "struggle to be seen" which characterizes their dedication to the nonfiction genre. Phyllis R. Klotman and Janet K. Cutler contend that African American documentarians use filmmaking as a tool of investigation to retrieve historical episodes and figures from oblivion while also giving shape to cultural forms. While biopics constantly blur the boundaries between the public and the private realms, interweaving history and fiction, biographical documentaries claim the authenticity of sources (biographies, autobiographical accounts, historical narratives, documentaries, newspaper articles, etc.) to shed light on the political dimension of their subjects' lives. Director William Greaves dedicated his nonfiction filmmaking to such political purpose, advocating the power of film and television to produce social change:

> Films from a black perspective are films that are more in the order of weapons in the struggle for freedom, for equality, for liberation and self-expression, and for all those human rights, if you will. They tend to agitate in the tradition of Frederick Douglass. (Klotman and Cutler 1991)

Greaves considered television offered an empowering tool to African American filmmakers that aimed to challenge stereotypical representations of race. Part of his activist career was devoted to recovering the memory of African American political leaders whose historical legacy

THE MANY LIVES OF IDA B. WELLS   93

was all too often forgotten. From *Booker T. Washington: The Life and the Legacy* (1982) to *Ralph Bunche: An American Odyssey* (2001), his biographical films portray African American activists whose fight he pursues through documentary filmmaking.

This article aims to interrogate the memory discourse shaped by William Greaves' documentary *Ida B. Wells: A Passion for Justice* (1989) in relation to the female activist's autobiographical testimony *Crusade for Justice: The Autobiography of Ida B. Wells* (Wells 1970). Wells related her lifelong commitment to anti-lynching campaigns in an autobiography that historians and biographers have thoroughly exploited to reconstruct her persona. In much the same way did William Greaves, when selecting from her written words including from her trenchant and cutting editorials, retrace the woman's life story in a documentary that endeavors to grasp the personal and political motives of her consistent engagement with racial issues. Greaves further aimed to shed light on the ideological legacy of Wells' commitment to anti-lynching campaigns, calling attention to acts of individual resistance that were long left in the shade. Wells died before she finished the manuscript of her autobiography in 1931 and her daughter Alfreda Duster was not able to have it published before 1970, "at a time when black history and women's history were finally beginning to receive widespread attention" (Bay 2009: 11). Greaves strove to keep the memory of her work alive and a variety of books have since been devoted to recovering her singular voice.[1]

This article questions the adaptation process behind the biographical narrative fashioned by Greaves, capturing details that may reveal constraints he negotiated while working on television; the many biographies written since the late 1990s further testify to the difficult task of historians endeavoring to understand the woman's character in a context of coercion. The posthumous publication of primary sources, including *The Memphis Diary of Ida B. Wells* (1995), and of a list of secondary sources allows for a comparative approach that spotlights

---

[1]Among them: Linda O. McMurry, *To Keep the Waters Troubled* (New York: Oxford University Press, 1998); Wanda A. Hendricks, *Gender, Race, and Politics in the Midwest* (Bloomington: Indiana University Press, 1998); Paula J. Giddings, *Ida, A Sword Among Lions: Ida B. Wells and the Campaign Against Lynching* (New York: Amistad/HarperCollins, 2008); James W. Davidson, *'They Say': Ida B. Wells and the Reconstruction of Race* (New York: Oxford University Press, 2009); Patricia A. Schechter, *Ida B. Wells-Barnett and American Reform 1880–1930* (Chapel Hill: University of North Carolina Press, 2001).

different personality traits depending on the authors' perception of Wells' role in history as influenced by contemporary scholarship trends; some emphasize her identity as a "black feminist" and a "race woman" whereas others characterize her as a "pragmatist" and a "liberal progressive" (Curry 2012: 457). The memory of Wells seems to arouse conflicting interpretations, which she was also a victim of during her lifetime. Historical biographer Paula Giddings explains that "her place in history was hardly assured" when Wells began to write her autobiography in 1928 although she had led the first anti-lynching campaign, co-founded the National Association for the Advancement of Colored People (NAACP) and organized the Negro Fellowship League to support poor blacks in Chicago.[2] Both Wells' autobiographical work and the current biographical essays researching her life and career pinpoint the conflicting tensions that arise from gender and politics. Interestingly, such discussion is subdued in Greaves' film aimed at a mainstream audience that may be unaware of her pioneering work among the anti-lynching activists.

Gender and Politics

Ida B. Wells explains in the preface to her autobiography that her impulse to write her life story was prompted by a question: "A young woman recently asked me to tell her of my connection with the lynching agitation which was started in 1892" (Wells 1970: 23). Although Wells' activism drew international attention after she traveled to Great Britain in order to rally the support of former abolitionists to her cause (1893, 1894), her figure was soon overshadowed by the emergence of a new generation of male leaders—including W.E.B Du Bois and Booker T. Washington. Writing her autobiography in the late years of her life, Wells aimed to leave a testimony about the events she had witnessed, thereby

---

[2] Paula Giddings, "Missing in Action: Ida B. Wells, the NAACP, and the Historical Record," *Meridians: Feminism, Race, Transnationalism*, vol. 1, no. 2 (2001): 1–17. The article by Tommy J. Curry illustrates this controversy: "Ida B. Wells (1862–1931) has earned the coveted status of a canonical figure in the American Academy. The recent texts dedicated to her life by Paula Giddings and Mia Bay not only establish Wells-Barnett's significance as a black historical figure, but argue that our current study of black intellectual history is in fact incomplete without her presence. [...] However, the trajectory of the scholarship which serves as the foundation of Wells-Barnett's canonization has also had a narrowing effect on particular aspects of her thought" (Curry 2012: 457).

THE MANY LIVES OF IDA B. WELLS   95

taking responsibility for shaping an image of herself that had often been stained by her detractors. Her writing therefore extends the autobiographical tradition of African American literature; literary critic Joanne Braxton contends that "for the black woman in American autobiography, the literary act has been, more often than not, an attempt to regain that sense of place in the New World" (Braxton 1989: 2). Wells' writing was motivated by her desire to record an account of the black experience during the Reconstruction period, most of which was "buried in oblivion" at a time when "only the southern white man's misrepresentations are in the public libraries and college textbooks of the land."[3] Wells' autobiography articulates her desire to resist dominant history by relating collective history from her perspective as a woman whose public engagement relied on her activist journalism. Henry Louis Gates understands the autobiographical pact as an act of bearing witness among African American writers whose life writing intermingles with history: "The ultimate form of protest, certainly, was to register the existence of a 'black self' that had transcended the limitations and restrictions that racism had placed on the personal development of the black individual."[4]

Wells was confronted with race and gender barriers as a woman whose commitment to politics broke with the conventional definition of domesticity that prevailed in the late 1890s, confining a woman's place to the home—which accounts for "the absence of women from conventional historical accounts" (Steedman 1992: 42). Wells' testimony prompts us to question the reductive effects of the public/private divide by offering a narrative that challenges these boundaries. *Crusade for Justice: The Autobiography of Ida B. Wells* (Wells 1970) is no female autobiography *per se*, for Wells had little concern with the emotional and domestic details that make women "the visible heroines of the historical romance"

[3] She mentions "the gallant fight and marvellous bravery of the black men of the South fighting and dying to exercise and maintain their newborn rights as free men and citizens, with little protection from the government which gave them these rights and with no previous training in citizenship or politics" (Wells 1970: 24).

[4] "Of the various genres that comprise the African-American literary tradition, none has played a role as central as has black autobiography. [...] Through autobiography, these writers could, at once, shape a public 'self' in language, and protest the degradation of their ethnic group by the multiple forms of American racism. The ultimate form of protest, certainly, was to register the existence of a 'black self' that had transcended the limitations and restrictions that racism had placed on the personal development of the black individual" (Gates 1991: 3).

96   D. LETORT

according to historian Carolyn Steedman (1992: 42). Wells was a woman who demanded a public voice, using her editorials and her anti-lynching campaigns as a platform for voicing her radical thoughts about racial relations. Her autobiography is tinted with bitterness as she comments on the derogatory remarks that targeted her as a black woman—from white and colored men and women alike.[5] She resentfully writes about her lone fight after she brought the Chesapeake and Ohio Railroad before a court to protest her eviction from the white ladies' car at a time when race progressively subsumed gender in the Southern states: "None of my people had ever seemed to feel it was a race matter and that they should help me in the fight" (Wells 1970: 41).

Biographer Patricia Anne Schechter underscores Wells' strong character by underlining her persistent presence in public spheres: her life was threatened after overtly criticizing the motives used by a white mob for the lynching of Thomas Moss, Calvin McDowell, and Henry Stewart in the editorial of *Free Speech*. When an undercover law officer was shot after a scuffle broke out that opposed black residents fearing for their lives and a bunch of white men wishing to avenge a children's dispute, Moss and McDowell were arrested and jailed on suspicion of murder. The cruelty of the mob that broke into the prison and dragged them outside translated into gruesome journalistic accounts that Wells analyzed as eyewitness accounts; she spotted graphic details in the morning papers' columns that proved that either the journalists had attended the event themselves or knew those who were implicated (Wells 1970: 70). Wells' inflammatory editorials not only put her life in danger of deadly retaliation, but they also caused the Memphis office of *Free Speech* to be rampaged. Her autobiography demonstrates that her reflections on lynching are based on her own life experience: the lynching of Thomas Moss proved the turning point of her whole career, for it affected her understanding of lynching and prompted her to leave Memphis where her provocative editorials fueled hatred against her pen name Iola. She explains that the whole incident had provided the killers with "an excuse to get rid of Negroes who were acquiring wealth and property and thus

---

[5] Her autobiography refers to several cases of insult, including a menacing editorial published in the *Commercial Appeal* that targeted her (although her pen name preserved her anonymity): "The black wretch who had written that foul lie should be tied to a stake at the corner of Main and Madison Streets, a pair of tailor's shears used on him and he should be burned at a stake" (Wells 1970: 86).

keep the race terrorized and 'keep the nigger down'" (Wells 1970: 84). Writing allowed her to look back at the events that fueled her sharp pen whereas reading her autobiography offers the reader insight into the progress of her thinking; Wells wrote at length on the power struggle that undergirded the establishment of a segregationist system, acrimoniously noting the underlying economic motives for racial subjugation.

Wells pioneered investigative journalism when researching cases of lynching that led her to posit a link between the killing of African American males and the subjugation of "white Juliets" who nurtured a growing appreciation for "colored Romeos."[6] Her caustic remarks reveal a sarcastic sense of humor; she ironically uses biblical images in her anti-lynching pamphlet *Southern Horrors: Lynch Law in All Its Phases* (Wells 1892) calling for the defense of "Afro-Americans Sampsons [*sic*] who suffer themselves to be betrayed by white Delilahs," arguing that "white men lynch the offending Afro-American, not because he is a despoiler of virtue, but because he succumbs to the smile of white women."[7] Wells challengingly reverses responsibility for miscegenation by exposing the moral failings of white women, undermining patriarchal authority in an 1892 scathing editorial of *Free Speech*:

> Nobody in this section believes the old threadbare lie that Negro men assault white women. If southern white men are not careful they will overreach themselves and a conclusion will be reached which will be very damaging to the moral reputation of their women. (Wells 1970: 84)

Interestingly, her autobiography hints at the reflexive stance that pervades her writing as she quotes from previous texts to account for the logic of her thinking. Distance from the South permits her to develop an incisive pen as she is able to comprehend the power of stereotypes that she feels compelled to overturn when realizing their damaging effects:

---

[6]"Why is it that white women attract negro men now more than in the former days? There was a time when such a thing was unheard of. There is secret to this thing and we greatly suspect it is the growing appreciation of white Juliets for colored Romeos." See her article in the *Indianapolis News*, Tuesday, August 16, 1887. http://www.newspapers.com/clip/1221668/the_indianapolis_news/, accessed on November 30, 2017.

[7]Ida B. Wells, *Southern Horrors: Lynch Law in All Its Phases* (1892). http://www.digitalhistory.uh.edu/disp_textbook.cfm?smtid=3&psid=3614, accessed on November 22, 2017.

98   D. LETORT

> Like many another person who had read of lynching in the South, I had accepted the idea meant to be conveyed—that although lynching was irregular and contrary to law and order, unreasoning anger over the terrible crime of rape led to the lynching, that perhaps the brute deserved death anyhow and the mob was justified in taking his life. (Wells 1970: 84)

Her *Crusade for Justice* was never adapted to screen although it provides the dramatic climaxes that would make for a compelling biopic. Through recounting the history of lynching representations on screen, Ellen C. Scott demonstrates that its racial underpinning was a repressed subject in Classical Hollywood cinema: such films as *Fury* (Fritz Lang, 1936) may illustrate public concern with the breaking of public law by outraged mobs, but the brutality of lynching is aimed at a white man in the film thereby obscuring the racist dimension of the crime (Scott 2015). Striving to avoid censorship that would damage profitability in the Southern states, the Production Code Administration warned against the screen treatment of controversial racial subjects. The industry's ideological complicity with the Southern states' racist concerns favored the oblivion of reconstruction promises, permitting such figures as Ida B. Wells to be obscured from national memory.

It is noteworthy to mention that William Greaves' documentary *Ida B. Wells: A Passion for Justice* preceded the many scholarly works dedicated to Wells, pointing out the filmmaker's ground-breaking commitment to reviving the memory of the female activist whose name had attracted little research yet. Funding came in 1989 from the Public Broadcasting Service (PBS) for its *American Experience* series, a program whose didactic purpose the director had to keep in line with.

WILLIAM GREAVES' TELEVISION DOCUMENTARY

As a television program, *Ida B. Wells: A Passion for Justice* (1989) hardly conveys the African American director's ingenuity that made his *Symbiopsychotaxiplasm* (1968) a unique feature experiment influenced by the improvised, observational approach of Direct Cinema. Greaves strove to introduce originality in a program whose well-established format permitted few innovations. Film scholar Clyde Taylor contends that Greaves' choices may have been limited due to an ideological context that privileged some subjects over others:

THE MANY LIVES OF IDA B. WELLS   99

The Reaganite retrenchment in funding for public television drove all directors aiming for PBS toward "classic", high profile subjects. Specific public television venues set bland, big-picture agendas, entitling their series *Great Americans, Great Performances, American Experience*? [...] Black documentarians who might have pointed toward grassroots figures or themes now realized their chances for funding and exhibition would improve if they focused on indisputably great black Americans. (Taylor 1999: 125)

Significantly, Greaves also investigated Booker T. Washington's accommodating philosophy and Ralph Bunche's career as the first African American diplomat working for the United Nations.[8] While the figure of Ida B. Wells might have been more controversial, PBS host David McCullough introduced the woman as the "kind of heroic figure we should all have grown up with in school." Movie critic Linda O. McMurry argues that, while the film's treatment of some people and events may be misleading and simplistic, "the story is truly remarkable" and Greaves does "a remarkably good job of interweaving the stories of the person and the environment, using a rich array of photographs, interviews, and superbly effective readings from her memoirs and writings by Toni Morrison" (McMurry 1992: 1275). By contrast, Clyde Taylor regrets the all-too-conventional dimension of Greaves' biographical endeavor, which makes use of an invisible male narrator (Al Freeman) as an omniscient voiceover that seems to frame the woman's story and make it submit to the patriarchal order she consistently defied.[9] According to him the documentary downplays the outspoken character of the crusader:

Freeman's narration and Morrison's reading impose a distant respectability that becomes an anodyne to the feelings the real Ida B. Wells must have aroused. The elements of her story are exciting enough. But as rendered

---

[8] *Booker T. Washington: The Life and the Legacy* (1986) and *Ralph Bunche: An American Odyssey* (William Greaves, 2001).

[9] Melba Joyce Boyd wrote: "If there is one incongruity in the film, it is the narration. Since the man behind the voice, Al Freeman, Jr., is never shown in the film, the narration hovers over the film like an omniscient eye. Consequently, even though this is a film about a black woman from the past, the subliminal effect of the male voice, which gives the first and the last words on the subject, suggests that the larger intelligence and the broader view of history is male" (Boyd 1994: 134).

here, the feeling is one of polite deference. Wells becomes a laminated icon, a talisman to be caressed for good luck in contemporary times. Such memorializing biographies of great leaders condescend by suggesting that we have nothing to learn from them except as pious examples. (Taylor 1999: 137)

Dealing with a woman of the past whose autobiographical voice can only be interpreted, the documentary fails to convey the audacious style of a character that refused to tone down her accusations in a growing conservative climate.

Ida B. Wells: A Passion for Justice opens in 1965 with drawings that evoke the Reconstruction period through the figures of happy black men celebrating their newly acquired rights at the end of the Civil War: the right to marriage, to raise one's children, to own land. The director conjures the atmosphere of the past through the ringing bells and the singing voices that can be overheard; however, the still black-and-white images tend to undermine the narrator's statement about a "time of great optimism." The narrator borrows from Martin Luther King's familiar rhetoric when indicating that Wells, though born a slave, belonged to a generation that soon realized that "promises made were not to be kept" [00:49], thus acknowledging the legacy of her fight in a history of African American activism: "Wells would launch a campaign against oppression that reverberates through all America till this day" [00:54].

The film draws a portrait of Wells through an array of fragments that underline the director's reconstruction efforts, using archive images as historical proofs to a racist context which historian Paula Giddings evokes through calling Wells' father "a race man" who educated his daughter by reading from the press. Greaves introduces racist cartoons to signify the repressive state that put an end to reconstruction, underlining the legacy of slavery through the sound of clicking chains and iconic images of tortured bodies:

As Ida was growing up, the South was in convulsive change: devastated by war, suffering crop failure, deprived of slave labor, the economy was in crisis. The African American was the scapegoat. A massive propaganda campaign was unleashed in the press; the schools and the church reinforcing the belief that black Americans were genetically inferior, that freed from bondage, they had to be restrained. [4:42]

Toni Morrison may speak in the first person to embody the words inscribed in the book she holds in her hands; however, she fails to translate the opinionated character of the writer. Although some passages are seen in close-ups that aim to intensify the relationship between the reader and the text, *mise-en-scène* fails to convey the power of the written word. When Wells explains that she first encountered segregation on board the Southbound train, Morrison reads from the text with a soft voice that sounds a little at odds with the anecdote denoting the Jim Crow social order that was progressively being enforced:

> [The conductor] told me I would have to go into the other car. I refused, saying that the forward car was a smoke, and I was in the ladies' car I proposed to stay. He tried to drag me out of the seat, but the moment he caught hold of my arm I fastened my teeth in the back of his hand. (Wells 1970: 38)

Morrison's reading seems to contain the violence of Wells' response; when Paula Giddings further explains what happened afterward "They physically took her off that train" [11:30], no image helps understand the shocking power of the scene. Giddings describes the facts whereas Wells comments on the cruelty of the spectators' gaze in her autobiography:

> I had braced my feet against the seat in front and was holding back [...]. He went forward and got the baggage man and another man to help him and of course they succeeded in dragging me out. They were encouraged to do so by the attitude of the white ladies and gentlemen in the car; some of them even stood on the seats so that they would get a good view and continued applauding the conductor for his brave stand. (Wells 1970: 38)

The film's narrative tends to downplay the events that shaped Wells' character, selecting passages from her autobiography that highlight the woman's tenacity and will. Determined to win over the railway company whose employees disregarded her rights, Wells brought the case to court and was first allocated $500 compensation before the Tennessee State Supreme Court overturned the decision. Morrison quotes from her personal diary and thereby gives access to Wells' intimacy: "I have firmly believed that the law was on our side and would, when we appealed to it, give us justice. I feel shorn of that belief and utterly discouraged [...]" [12:38].

102   D. LETORT

The words are separated from the actions behind them, losing the power to express the narrator's subjective state of mind. After her life was threatened in Memphis, the narrator explains that "the power structure was angry with her" [21:00], which sounds like a euphemism considering the brutality of the events that led her into exile.

Film theorist François Niney argues that the omniscient voiceover used in nonfiction films competes with the documentarian's voice and finally wins over. While the filmmaker devises the narrative structure and organizes the elements of *mise-en-scène*, the disembodied voice of the omniscient narrator seems always to comment on those images "objectively" (Niney 2000: 112). The subjective dimension of the film is obscured by the repeated use of the voiceover, which dominates the characters' interviews and reduces the authenticity of the archive documents to visual illustrations. Niney contends that even the voiceover narration reframes the characters' *in situ* interviews while denying the director's construction of meaning. The television apparatus deprives Greaves of his authorial voice (Niney 2000: 113).

While the documentary eschews the cult of personality that more often than not undergirds the biopic, the portrayal of Wells tends to downplay the woman's sharp character and fierce sense of humor. Morrison's reading does not permit the feminist writer to verbally respond to the text she is reading, which might have yet furthered the viewer's understanding of Wells' legacy. The use of the third person narration by the voiceover and the interviewed historians fails to convey the virulence of the attacks she was confronted with after exploring various cases of lynching. She defiantly wrote about the "chivalrous white men" that accused "the black wretch who had written that foul lie should be tied to a stake at the corner of Main and Madison Streets, a pair of tailor's shears used on him and he should then be burned at a stake" (Niney 2000: 86). The violence of those words is lost in the edited interviews of people speaking about a context they never encountered. The documentary neutralizes the tension that pervades the first-person narration of the autobiography. Clyde Taylor argues that the narrative was adapted to satisfy a white audience:

> The limitation I speak of come mainly through this concern for white audience and its sensitivities […]. Fiction films have the advantages of emotion dramatized. (Taylor 1999: 139–140)

Reading through the autobiography suggests that Wells' provocative statements were toned down and the same concern for a white audience may account for the reason why her life was not made into a biopic. Even though a stamp was created to honor her memory, neither her face nor her name have achieved iconic status. The documentary produces an intellectual discourse on the activist; yet it does not translate the deep commitment of Wells to the fight she pursued away from the limelight by helping the poor of Chicago; nor does it convey the feelings that she provocatively inspired through her incisive pen. Little attention is paid to her protest against the World's Columbian Exposition which she challenged along with Frederick Douglass by handing out pamphlets that denounced the racist representations of the African tribes presented there and the absence of African Americans.[10]

Pointing out the differences between fiction and nonfiction, documentary theorist Bill Nichols evokes the reasons which may account for the shortcomings of such biographical endeavors as *A Passion for Justice*:

> Fiction attends to unconscious desires and latent meanings. It operates where the id lives. Documentary, on the other hand, attends to social issues of which we are consciously aware. It operates where the reality-attentive ego and superego live. Fiction harbors echoes of dreams and daydream, sharing structures of fantasy with them, whereas documentary mimics the canons of expository argument, the making of a case, the call to public rather than private response. (Nichols 1991: 4)

While striving to assume a historical objective posture, the film fails to translate the intimate passion for justice that drove Wells throughout her

---

[10] "In contrast with the few privileges granted to white upper class women, African American and native people did not gain the right to represent themselves; African American women and men made vain attempts to have at least one black woman integrate the *Board of Lady Managers*. During the exhibition, African American activists Ida B. Wells, Irvine Garland Penn, Ferdinand L. Barnett, and Frederick Douglass handed out ten thousand copies of their pamphlet entitled *The Reason Why the Colored American Is Not in the World's Columbian Exposition* (Rydell, 1999). They denounced the inherent racism of the Dahomeys' village exhibited in the Midway Plaisance, which used black Africans as the representatives of 'race in the White city.' The African American protestors were able to challenge their official exclusion thanks to regular demonstrations which pressured the committee into devoting one day to them on August 25." See http://www.cccg.umontreal.ca/pdf/Annick%20Druelle_fr.pdf, accessed on October 28, 2017, my translation.

104   D. LETORT

career. Although her autobiography tells the story of her development as a public figure without dwelling on the conflicts between the political and the domestic spheres, revealing little of her marriage and her raising a family, historian Patricia A. Schechter reintroduces the role of gender in her career. She argues that Wells played out her femininity as a speaker that comfortably expressed her emotions in public to draw sympathy to the cause: "By talking through tears, Wells carried out a demanding and highly political public performance while keeping femininity in display."[11] By contrast, Wilma Peebles-Wilkins and Francis E. Aracelis emphasize her unconventional femininity through an analysis of her work ethics:

> The personal presentation of Wells-Barnett did not fit the traditionally feminine mold. Using a logical, scientific, and fact-finding approach (deductive reasoning), she presented statistics about lynching to appeal to the American values of fairness and the rights to a trial by jury and to careful investigation. She was authoritative and objective and argued effectively without projecting the feminine stereotype. (Peebles-Wilkins and Aracelis Francis 1990: 99)

The documentary does not flesh out her character, drawing a composite portrait that first and foremost aims to educate viewers about her achievements. Historian Mia Bay nonetheless stresses that she overstepped the limitations placed on her sex as "a woman who took more pride in her intellect than her domestic accomplishments" (Bay 2009: 165). Worse, she broke the law when acquiring a gun in a state where African Americans were not allowed to do so. Wells' defiant activist style marginalized her among the black elite who gained prominence at the turn of the century—including Booker T. Washington and W.E.B. Du Bois.[12]

---

[11] Schechter pinpoints Wells' biased confession in her autobiography: she explains that she had "no knowledge of stage business" when delivering her speech in New York whereas Schechter recalls that "living in Memphis, she had performed public readings, organized and acted in a dramatic club, and even been scouted by a New York talent agent" (Schechter 2001: 20).

[12] Schechter argues that "there emerged at the elite level a gender division of labor, which assigned political and intellectual leadership to men while entrusting to women a parallel role of prayer, education, and fundraising in female networks" (Schechter 2001: 165).

CONCLUSION

Although William Greaves' didactic documentary helps bring recognition to the work achieved by Ida B. Wells, it also buries her into the past through digging into lifeless archives. Her life story remains a topic for historians to discuss whereas her figure is turned into a stamped image that the documentary cannot bring back to life. The typed pages from which Toni Morrison reads constrain her own response whereas the male voiceover seems to repress the woman's voice in the grand historical narrative. The restrictions faced by Greaves himself echo those that Wells dealt with during her lifetime, highlighting her frustration over the race and gender barrier that she found herself confronted by—both within American society and within the Niagara Movement. Her fierce activism and outspokenness were and are still at odds with the political correctness that prevails, making it difficult to adapt her life story on screen. The biographies produced in the wake of Greaves' documentary are more in tune with her impetuousness—as suggested by such titles as Linda O. McMurry's *To Keep the Waters Troubled* (1998) and Paula J. Giddings' *Ida, A Sword Among Lions: Ida B. Wells and the Campaign Against Lynching* (2008).

Biography scholars Hans Renders and Binne de Haan point out that the interpretations of autobiographies all too often serve commemorative activities—as illustrated by Greaves' documentary. The authors propose "a fruitful association between biography and microhistory" as an alternative, prompting filmmakers and biographers to use the individual experience as a window into the past. The adaptation of Wells' life writing into a documentary makes visible the "reading of a reading and the writing of a writing" as Joanny Moulin puts it, disappointingly defining the biographical turn as "an organisation of matter encrypting information" (Moulin 2015: 6). Understanding a life requires more than facts, which Greaves may have tried to intimate through the continuous noises heard on the soundtrack, alluding to an unrepresentable off-screen space.

WORKS CITED

Bay, Mia. *To Tell the Truth Freely, the Life of Ida B. Wells*. New York: Hill & Wang, 2009.

Boyd, Melba J. "Reviews." *NWSA Journal*, vol. 6, no. 1 (Spring 1994): 134.

Braxton, Joanne. *Black Women Writing Autobiography—A Tradition Within a Tradition*. Philadelphia: Temple University Press, 1989.

Brown, Tom and Belén Vidal (eds.). *The Biopic in Contemporary Film Culture*. New York and Abingdon: Routledge, 2014.

Curry, Tommy J. "The Fortune of Wells: Ida B. Wells-Barnett's Use of T. Thomas Fortune's Philosophy of Social Agitation as a Prolegomenon to Militant Civil Rights Activism." *Transactions of the Charles S. Peirce Society*, vol. 48, no. 4 (Fall 2012): 456–482.

Custen, Georges F. *Bio/Pics, How Hollywood Constructed Public History*. New Brunswick, NJ: Rutgers University Press, 1992.

Davidson, James W. *'They Say': Ida B. Wells and the Reconstruction of Race*. New York: Oxford University Press, 2009.

Druelle, Annick. Mouvements internationaux de femmes et solidarities des interest au XIXe siècle." http://www.cccg.umontreal.ca/pdf/Annick%20Druelle_fr.pdf. Accessed on November 30, 2017.

Gates, Henry Louis. *Bearing Witness*. New York: Pantheon Books, 1991.

Giddings, Paula. "Missing in Action: Ida B. Wells, the NAACP, and the Historical Record." *Meridians: Feminism, Race, Transnationalism*, vol. 1, no. 2 (2001): 1–17.

Giddings, P.J. *Ida, A Sword Among Lions: Ida B. Wells and the Campaign Against Lynching*. New York: Amistad/HarperCollins, 2008.

Hendricks, W.A. *Gender, Race, and Politics in the Midwest*. Bloomington: Indiana University Press, 1998.

Klotman, Phyllis and Janet Cutler. "Interview with William Greaves." September 12, 1991. Black Film Center/Archives Interview Collection.

———. *Struggles for Representation: African American Documentary Film and Video*. Bloomington: Indiana University Press, 1999.

Lupo, Jonathan and Carolyn Anderson. "Introduction to the Special Issue." *Journal of Popular Film and Television*, vol. 36, no. 2 (2008): 50–51.

McMurry, Linda O. "Movie Reviews." *The Journal of American History*, vol. 79, no. 3, *Discovering American: A Special Issue* (December 1992): 1275.

McMurry, Linda O. *To Keep the Waters Troubled*. New York: Oxford University Press, 1998.

Moulin, Joanny. "Introduction: Towards Biography Theory." *Cercles*, vol. 35 (2015): 1–11.

Nichols, Bill. *Representing Reality: Issues and Concepts in Documentary*. Bloomington: Indiana University Press, 1991.

Niney, François. *L'Epreuve du réél à l'écran, Essai du le principe du réel documentaire*. Bruxelles: De Boeck, 2000.

Peebles-Wilkins, Wilma and E. Aracelis Francis. "Two Outstanding Black Women in Social Welfare History: Mary Church Terrell and Ida B. Wells-Barnett." *Affilia*, vol. 5, no. 4 (Winter 1990): 87–100.

THE MANY LIVES OF IDA B. WELLS   107

Renders, Hans and Binne de Haans (eds.). *Theoretical Discussions of Biography: Approaches from History, Microhistory, and Life Writing* (1st edition: Edwin Mellen Press, 2013). Leyden: Brill Academic Publishing, 2014.

Schechter, Patricia A. *Ida B. Wells-Barnett and American Reform 1880–1930.* Chapel Hill, NC: University of North Carolina Press, 2001.

Scott, Ellen C. *Cinema Civil Rights, Regulation, Repression, and Race in the Classical Hollywood Era.* New Brunswick, NJ and London: Rutgers University Press, 2015.

Steedman, Carolyn. "*La théorie qui n'en est pas une,* or, Why Clio Doesn't Care." In Anne-Shapiro Louise (ed.), *History and Feminist Theory.* Middletown, CT: Wesleyan University, 1992, 33–50.

Stokes, Melvyn. *D.W. Griffith's the Birth of a Nation. A History of the "Most Controversial Picture of All Time."* New York: Oxford University Press, 2007.

Taylor, Clyde. "Paths of Enlightenment: Heroes, Rebels, and Thinkers." In Phyllis R. Klotman and Janet K. Cutler (eds.), *Struggles for Representation: African American Documentary Film and Video.* Bloomington: Indiana University Press, 1999, 122–150.

Wells, Ida B. *The Indianapolis News.* Tuesday, August 16, 1887. http://www.newspapers.com/clip/1221668/the_indianapolis_news/. Accessed on November 30, 2017.

———. *Southern Horrors: Lynch Law in All Its Phases* (1892). http://www.digitalhistory.uh.edu/disp_textbook.cfm?smtid=3&psid=3614. Accessed on December 1, 2017.

———. *Crusade for Justice: The Autobiography of Ida B. Wells,* ed. Alfreda M. Duster. Chicago: The University of Chicago Press, 1970.

Filmography

Booker T. Washington, the Life and the Legacy (William Greaves, 1986).
Ida B. Wells: A Passion for Justice (William Greaves, 1989).
Ralph Bunche: An American Odissey (William Greaves, 2001).

Malcolm X: From the Autobiography to Spike Lee's Film, Two Complementary Perspectives on the Man and the Militant Black Leader

Dominique Dubois

This paper proposes to analyze Spike Lee's 1992 film about the life and death of the black leader Malcolm X in the light of the latter's autobiography, jointly written by Malcolm X and Alex Haley.[1] While it is a known fact that Spike Lee, and Arnold Perl, who wrote the screenplay, took their cue from the autobiography, it is also clear that the scope of the film, its tone, and the narrative choices made account for the very different feelings readers and viewers experience. Indeed, analysis of the film's cinematographic narrative shows that despite being faithful to the events of Malcolm X's life, the director has naturally chosen to concentrate on

---

[1] Malcolm X, with the assistance of Alex Haley, *The Autobiography of Malcolm X* (London: Penguin, 2001). All further references are to this edition.

D. Dubois (✉)
Université d'Angers, Angers, France
e-mail: Dominique.Dubois@univ-angers.fr

© The Author(s) 2018
D. Letort and B. Lebdai (eds.), *Women Activists and Civil Rights Leaders in Auto/Biographical Literature and Films*,
https://doi.org/10.1007/978-3-319-77081-9_7

Fig. 1 Spike Lee focuses on Malcolm X's public figure and political message. © Warner Bros./Photofest

action rather than on the intellectual itinerary of Malcolm X's political vision, to the extent that some critics have rightly argued that Spike Lee's aim was to put forward his own political agenda.

The analysis will therefore focus on the artistic license taken by Spike Lee and try to account for these differences, departures, and omissions. Some of the differences between the film and the autobiography no doubt stem from the fact that whereas the autobiography stops in 1965 the film encompasses the events up to Malcolm X's assassination, hence allowing for a more historical perspective. However, the autobiography and the film also appear to have different agendas. The autobiography, with its autodiegetic narrator, brings to light the journey toward self-realization of a private individual, who turned out to become a public figure. The film on the contrary focuses on the public figure and on the political message Malcolm X was advocating. But it is certainly these differences in perspective that make both the autobiography and the film invaluable documents to understand one of the greatest American black leaders (Fig. 1).

The Writing of Malcolm X's Autobiography

Considering the time gap (27 years) between the writing of the autobiography and the making of the film, it is no doubt necessary to give a brief reminder of the circumstances in which the autobiography and later the film were produced. The book was written in collaboration with Alex Haley, who later was to write the acclaimed saga *Roots* (1976). The collaboration took the form of lengthy interviews between the two men over a period of two years from 1963 to 1965 and it can safely be said that the actual writer was Haley even if Malcolm X suggested corrections along the way. And yet, the mode chosen to recount the events of Malcolm X's life—a first-person narrative, the self-effacement of Haley behind the compelling voice of the militant leader—definitely makes the work an autobiography rather than a biography. Haley's 77-page-long Foreword, which relates the circumstances of how he was asked to write an account of Malcolm X's life, how the latter finally trusted him enough to accept, with the benediction of Elijah Muhammad, and fully collaborated on the project is proof enough that if Haley held the pen, Malcolm X was the controlling voice behind the text. Indeed, on reading the Foreword, one is struck by the difference in voices between the two texts. In the Foreword, it is clearly Haley speaking; in the autobiography, it is definitely Malcolm X recounting his journey toward self-realization as a private individual and a very public figure.

The fact that it took 27 years for a director to make a biopic based on the autobiography of Malcolm X also deserves an explanation. For one thing, even after such a timespan, there were still some people who questioned the validity of the project on the ground that it might rekindle racial strife in the country. But such dissenting voices were a minority. Several million copies of the autobiography had been sold by then, revealing to the American public a charismatic, complex but humane individual, far removed from the frightening militant who, in his own words, was called "the angriest Negro in America" [because he had urged the blacks to "use arms, if necessary, to defend themselves" when "the law fail[ed] to protect Negroes from whites' attacks" (Malcolm X and Haley 2001: 483). *The Autobiography of Malcolm X* had become extremely popular and, as Manning Marable notes in *Malcolm X: A Life of Reinvention*, by then "it had been adopted in the curricula in hundreds of colleges and thousands of high schools" (Marable 2011: 20)

112   D. DUBOIS

In a word, the times were ripe for the great black leader to be celebrated in a motion picture. Marvin Worth, a Hollywood producer who had convinced Malcolm X's widow to grant him the rights, had acquired the rights to *The Autobiography of Malcolm X* for Warner Brothers Pictures as early as 1967. He felt that Malcolm X's life experience, his extraordinary itinerary from street hustler to becoming Minister Malcolm X, deserved to be made into a film. But, for three decades Hollywood was not ready for the venture. Despite hiring James Baldwin to write the screenplay and his dedication in making the project a reality, Marvin Worth failed. During the following decades, several attempts were made to set the project on rail.[2] All in vain, until Worth finally thought he had the perfect combination, with director Norman Jewison, playwright Charles Fuller, and actor Denzel Washington, who had successfully worked on the film *A Soldier's Story* (Norman Jewison, 1984), based on the eponymous play by Charles Fuller.

When Spike Lee, who had by then established himself as a successful but controversial director, heard that a white director had been chosen to direct the film, he started campaigning to be given the project on the ground that such a film could only be made by a black director. In his *Spike Lee Director*, Dennis Abrams provides a clear summary of Spike Lee's motives and strategy:

> Instead of approaching Worth or Warner Brothers directly, he [Spike Lee] went straight to the media. "I have a big problem with Norman Jewison directing The Autobiography of Malcolm X," Spike Lee told the New York Times. "That disturbs me deeply. It's wrong with a capital W. Blacks have to control these films. Malcolm X is one of our most treasured heroes. To let a non-African-American do it is a travesty." (Abrams 2008: 76)

Spike Lee's media-staged campaign stirred up such a heated debate that Jewison, a white Canadian Jew, suggested that Spike Lee should have a go as he was convinced that Malcolm X deserved to have a biopic made. Using the screenplay drafted by James Baldwin in the 1970s, Spike Lee and Arnold Perl started to work.

[2] In addition to James Baldwin, novelists David Bradley and Calder Willingham as well as playwright David Mamet tried their hand at the script. Famous directors, such as Sydney Lumet, Stuart Rosenberg, and Bob Fosse contemplated making the film but they all finally renounced largely because of the constraints imposed by the family, the Nation of Islam (NOI), etc.

From the Text to the Film

When we compare the autobiography with the film, it is no overstatement to say that Spike Lee's adaptation is a "traditional translation, which maintains the overall traits of the book [...] but revamps particular details in those particular ways that the filmmakers see as necessary and fitting," to adopt Linda Costanzo Cahir's terminology (Cahir 2006: 4). Indeed, anyone familiar with the autobiography will have no difficulty identifying all the major episodes that appear in the book to the point that some critics have underlined the film's hagiographic fidelity to the original.

Spike Lee's choice "to take up the classical celebratory majoritarian form" (Bingham 2010: 23) for his adaptation of the autobiography can possibly be ascribed to the fact that after the way he had secured the direction of the film meant many people in the film industry, the followers of Malcolm X, and above all his relatives would watch the result closely and would be up in arms if Spike Lee diverged from the original work. In his book, Dennis Abrams mentions that Spike Lee received a letter from a group calling themselves The United Front to Preserve the Legacy of Malcolm X which expressed concern about Spike Lee's authority and knowledge to make a film on Malcolm X (Abrams 2008: 79).

From the structural point of view, there is a very conscious attempt on the part of the director to stick to the way the events are recounted in the autobiography.[3] Not only are the three phases of Malcolm X's life—his days as a hustler in Boston and Harlem, his imprisonment and conversion to Islam, and lastly his becoming a Minister of the NOI—clearly identified, but Spike Lee also resorts to the voiceover from the mature Malcolm X to make comments on his life very much like it appears in the autobiography.

Given Spike Lee's obvious commitment to rely on the narrative structure of the autobiography and to stick to the events narrated in it, one may wonder about the choice made by Spike Lee to start the action in the 1940s when Malcolm Little as he was known at the time had already joined his sister Ella in Boston. Indeed, the opening scene of the film zooms on an

---

[3] This no doubt accounts for the exceptional length of the film, 201 minutes.

114   D. DUBOIS

elevated train coming into Dudley Street Station followed by a crane shot of a street, presumably Roxbury Street. The scene is visually quite effective: the clever use of sepia lighting, the contemporary music, and above all the numerous extras appearing in the scene bespeak a big-budget film. The impression is reinforced by a close-up of the two main protagonists, Malcolm X and Shorty, featured bopping in the street in their colorful zoot suits.

Such an approach may be good entertainment but seems to constitute a serious breach from the autobiography. Indeed, it omits to mention the reasons why Malcolm X had moved from Michigan to Boston, a period that covers two chapters in the autobiography and relates his father's murder by white supremacists, the family's fall into poverty, and Malcolm being placed with a foster family. One reason why this might be regarded as a questionable choice lies in the fact that the family background and the adolescence of Malcolm X play a central role in who he becomes in Boston first and later in prison when he becomes attuned to the ideas of Elijah Muhammad. Particularly important is the fact that his father was a follower of Marcus Garvey, a proponent of the Black Nationalism and Pan-Africanism movements that were precursors to the Nation of Islam.

It is therefore no surprise that this precision is given to the reader as early as paragraph two in the autobiography. This is how Malcolm X describes his father:

> My father, the Reverend Earl Little, was a Baptist minister, a dedicated organizer for Marcus Aurelius Garvey's U.N.I.A. (Universal Negro Improvement Association). With the help of such disciples as my father, Garvey, from his headquarters in New York City's Harlem, was raising the banner of black-race purity and exhorting the Negro masses to return to their ancestral African homeland—a cause which had made Garvey the most controversial black man on earth. (Malcolm X and Haley 2001: 79)

A little later in the chapter, we learn that being his father's preferred child, Malcolm X sometimes accompanied him to those Garvey UNIA meetings. One may assume that such early formative education must have played an important role in Malcolm's later conversion to the NOI. So it is surprising that these events seem to have been omitted by Spike Lee. Another key episode in Malcolm's realization of the racial divide seems to have been left out. The episode is the one in which his eighth-grade teacher tells him he should forget about becoming a lawyer because "a lawyer—that's no realistic goal for a nigger" (Malcolm X and Haley 2001: 118). Instead, he advises him to become a carpenter! The irony here is that the teacher's name was Ostrowski whose forebears were Polish—a community that had also suffered ostracism.

In fact, as it turns out, the first two chapters are not omitted as such but they reappear in the form of flashbacks, with a voiceover commentary by Denzel Washington impersonating the mature Malcolm X of the later period of his life. In a word, such departures are departures in form rather than in content, permitting the film director to capitalize on the dramatic action brought about by the flashbacks. Thus, the first paragraph of the autobiography relating the visit of the Ku Klux Klan to Malcolm X's parents as he was still in his mother's womb is related in a flashback. Here again, there is an obvious dramatic intensity in the vision of the white horsemen riding to the house late at night and threatening Malcolm's mother in a scene that is paradoxically resonant of *The Birth of a Nation* (D.W. Griffith, 1915). Retrospectively, one can see some coherence in Spike Lee's narrative choice of recounting events of Malcolm X's youth through memories, as they constitute a counterpoint to his gradual slipping into a life of debauchery and of mimicking the white man. In this respect the various scenes in which Malcolm is shown to conk his hair is symbolic of that blind allegiance.

After this initial parting from the autobiography's narrative structure, there is no significant disruption in the chronology of events provided in the written text and for the most part, when one can perceive a difference, it is usually a difference in tempo and length of time or space devoted to a given sequence. Once again, it seems that the main reason stems from the difference in medium and the fact that action is more effective on screen.

Still, sometimes a difference in emphasis clearly creates a change in perception from reader to viewer. One example is the scene when Malcolm X pretends to play Russian roulette with his acolytes and thus establishes his authority on the little gang of burglars he has set up with Shorty and Sophia, his white girlfriend. In the film the whole sequence is six minutes long, describing the gang in a car, their arrival at Harvard Square, and the Russian roulette episode itself. In the book the whole episode is dealt with in less than twenty lines (Malcolm X and Haley 2001: 234–235). Spike Lee's propensity for dramatic action is reinforced by the fact that he adds an element by having Malcolm X dare Rudy, who had questioned his leadership, to play Russian roulette. The scene's dramatic intensity is reinforced by Malcolm X first removing the bullets from his gun and putting them one by one on the table before putting

116   D. DUBOIS

one back, flipping the gun and applying it to his head. The other shift in perspective is equally dramatically effective, showing Malcolm put the gun to Rudy's face and propose to flip the gun for him.

The prison sequences are also given more dramatic emphasis in the biopic. There seems to be a deliberate attempt on the part of Spike Lee to dramatize the dreadful treatment reserved to black inmates in American prisons. Whereas Malcolm X summarizes what he had to go through in a few sober paragraphs in the autobiography, the film definitely makes an issue of it. Both the scene in which Malcolm is beaten up and dragged to a solitary cell for refusing to state his number and the one in which we hear him howl in his cell like an animal are highly charged, the film director obviously playing on the viewer's feelings and emotions so as to make the indictment of the system more convincing. A similar example occurs later in the film after Malcolm X has started working as a minister for the Nation of Islam. The event in question is Father Johnson Hinton being beaten up by the police because he was too slow to obey an order to "move on." Despite suffering from a head wound, he is taken into police custody, and only after a standoff by Malcolm X and his fellow Muslim brothers do the police send him to hospital. On the way to the hospital, Malcolm X and his brothers are joined by a growing crowd of angry black people. They will only disperse after being assured that Hinton is out of danger. Once again, there is a real difference in treatment between the book and the film. In the autobiography, Malcolm X minimizes the drama and instead stresses the importance of the event which gave the NOI the notoriety it didn't yet have and all this in less than two pages:

> I mentioned, you will remember, how in a big city, a sizable organization can remain practically unknown, unless something happens that brings it to the general public's attention. Well, certainly no one in the Nation of Islam had any anticipation of the kind of thing that would happen in Harlem one night. [...] For New York City's millions of readers of the downtown papers, it was, at that time, another one of the periodic "Racial Unrest in Harlem" stories. It was not played up, because of what had happened. (Malcolm X and Haley 2001: 336)

The book also mentions the aftermath of the event, $70,000 in damages, the biggest sum ever granted in a lawsuit for police brutality at the time. By contrast, the film plays up the dramatic intensity of the six-minute-sequence by depicting the humiliation of the police officers who have to cave in and give way to Malcolm X's demands. Their helplessness is cleverly contrasted with the quiet but implacable determination of Malcolm X. Interestingly, Spike Lee has one police officer remark that "that's too much power for one man to have" referring to Malcolm X's successful display of quiet determination and control over the crowd of his followers. The same policeman will reappear in the scene of the assassination at the end, one way for the film director to suggest possible involvement of the authorities—be it the NYPD, the FBI, or the CIA—in the assassination.

This observation is a fit transition to the analysis of more problematic differences between the book and the film, which will show that despite his fidelity to the autobiography, Spike Lee was pursuing a more personal agenda.

Spike Lee's Agenda

Although his initial request for a budget of $33 million had been flatly rejected by Warner Bros., Spike Lee was finally granted $28 million by the Hollywood studio—twice the amount of the most expensive film that Spike Lee had directed at that date (*Jungle Fever*, 1991). The funds allocated implied that Warner Bros. had an entertaining epic in mind while agreeing to the 2-hour 30-minute film duration. The film eventually grossed some $48 million out of a budget of $33 million and was very positively reviewed when it first opened in New York on November 18, 1992. In the words of critic Robert Ebert, the film was "one of the great screen biographies" (cited in Abrams 2008: 83). Particularly praised were the superbly detailed period costumes by Ruth E. Carter and the elaborate use of lighting by Ernest Dickerson who used starkly different shades and tones to comment on each of the film's three different parts.

Critical researchers like Thomas Doherty acknowledged Spike Lee's achievement in conveying the atmosphere of the period convincingly:

> In both the Boston and Harlem passages of Malcolm's unregenerate life, Spike Lee the director luxuriates in the high life of a big budget prestige project from Hollywood—lavish production numbers, panoramic crowd scenes, and precision recreations of period detail in set design, props, and wardrobes. The showstopping sequence is an elaborately choreographed dance number in the Roseland Ballroom. Swinging and Lindy Hopping to a live Big Band, ecstatic dancers leap in line, all gyrating in perfect coordination, as in a vintage Hollywood musical. A tastefully chosen soundtrack of period music sets the mood and comments on the action—the original tunes by the original performers, the kind of material whose copyright

118   D. DUBOIS

permissions do not come cheap, among them Joe Turner, Billie Holiday, Jackie Wilson, and the whitebread Perry Como. (Doherty 2000: 40–41)

The film was the first epic about black people directed by an African American director and with a black man as its leading actor (Denzel Washington). Spike Lee's determination, his forking out two million of his own money in the project and his successful borrowing from black celebrities when the Completion Bond Company refused to allocate more budget to the film are clear indications that Spike Lee's reputation as a film director was at stake. Right from the beginning, Spike Lee had stated that "Malcolm X is my artistic vision, the film is my interpretation of the man. It is nobody else's" (Doherty 2000: 29). In his assessment of Spike Lee's film, Dennis Bingham acknowledges the director's personal vision and remarks that "*Malcolm X* is a reappropriation from white-centered cinema of a black story, and it is an appropriation of a Hollywood genre and production values in order to tell that black story" (Bingham 2010: 189).

That Spike Lee had a personal agenda in making the film can be seen in a number of significant shifts from the autobiography. One aspect of the autobiography which is given more prominence in the film than in the book is Malcolm X's relationship with women, from Sophia, his white girlfriend, Laura, the black girl he was dating at the time he met Sophia, to Sister Betty, whom he married following Elijah Muhammad's suggestion. Here again, it seems that Spike Lee was bowing to the rules of the epic, which would not have been complete without some sort of love story. But Spike Lee's treatment of the three women to have crossed Malcolm X's path calls for examination.

In the autobiography, Malcolm's relationship with the white woman he says he will call Sophia (Malcolm X and Haley 2001: 152) starts in Chapter 4 entitled "Laura." The reason why the chapter is named after the black girl who was his first date stems from Malcolm's feeling of guilt at having brought about the ruin of the young girl (2001: 153–154).[4]

---

[4] "Laura never again came to the drugstore as long as I continued to work there. The next time I saw her, she was a wreck of a woman, notorious around black Roxbury, in and out of jail. She had finished high school, but by then she was already going the wrong way. Defying her grandmother, she had started going out late and drinking liquor. This led to dope, and that to selling herself to men. Learning to hate the men who bought her, she also became a Lesbian. One of the shames I have carried for years is that I blame myself for all of this. To have treated her as I did for a white woman made the blow doubly heavy. The only excuse I can offer is that like so many of my black brothers today, I was just deaf, dumb, and blind."

The film does narrate the girl's downfall but in an indirect way that is more graphic than effective: as Malcolm walks past a group of prostitutes in Harlem, he takes no notice of Laura. And as Malcolm walks away without seeing her, she is shown to perform oral sex on a white man in a porch. This scene is of course to be paralleled with an earlier scene in which Malcolm rejects Laura's offer of sex as they are lying on a deserted beach, a scene which is reminiscent of the famous love scene in *From Here to Eternity* (Fred Zinnemann, 1954). Once again, whereas the autobiography is trying to explain, the film chooses to romanticize and dramatize, pandering to the audience's taste for the sensational.

The same technique applies to the other two relationships. The sequence in which Malcolm X and Sophia drive to a secluded place and kiss at length is quite spectacular as the camera zooms in on Sophia's convertible and on the couple. Interestingly, the fourth draft of the screenplay mentioned Sophia removing her jumper and showing her breasts to Malcolm. Although these lines were removed from the final version, Spike Lee makes another significant addition. The sequence takes place in a flat. Malcolm and Sophia make love after she prepares breakfast, which she brings to Malcolm who is still in bed. What follows is a scene of accepted humiliation on the part of the white woman, forced by Malcolm X to kiss his foot and feed him. The scene, a clear addition to the autobiography, is a symbolic reversal of the master–slave relationship. It is clearly in line with Spike Lee's interest in black masculinity and sexuality, a theme that is prominent in his other films.

Similar discrepancies can be observed in the treatment of the relationship between Malcolm X and Sister Betty. The autobiography presents the marriage as a marriage of reason—a reverend has to be married according to Elijah Muhammad who thinks Betty will make a perfect wife but the film clearly emphasizes the romance. Betty is also instrumental in having Malcolm X denounce Elijah Muhammad's infidelities, which is not how the episode is presented in the autobiography. Being made for a major Hollywood studio and aimed at a wide audience, the film tones down the sexual content while simplifying the ambiguous relationship Malcolm X had with women for the sake of foregrounding black sexuality.

Other differences reveal even more clearly a shift in perspective between the book and the film. The first such difference in perspective concerns the presentation of the film's credits sequence. The gradual burning of the American flag reveals an X that epitomizes Malcolm's

120   D. DUBOIS

name and provides a statement on the state of race relations in the U.S. at the time of the film's release. The sequence is made even more potent because, as the flag is burning, a voiceover delivers Malcolm X's famous inflammatory speech indicting the white man and rejecting any possibility of an American dream for the African American. But the sequence is anachronistic as it shows the footage of an amateur film shot during the infamous beating of Rodney King by the Los Angeles police on March 3, 1991. Spike Lee thereby stresses that the situation of African Americans had not yet changed some 25 years after Malcolm X's death.

Such an interpretation is reinforced by the eulogy sequence that ends the film. The sequence is seven minutes long and pays tribute to Malcolm X after his assassination so that the film does not end on such a grim message. The sequence opens with archive footage showing Martin Luther King's reaction to Malcolm X's murder and underlining the absurdity of resorting to violence to solve the racial issue. The rest of the sequence focusing on Malcolm X's funeral appears as a subtle but strong counterpoint to Martin Luther King's message of nonviolence.

Interestingly, the funeral is also mentioned in the Foreword to the autobiography, and Alex Haley quotes from Ossie Davis' moving speech made as Malcolm X's coffin was laid to earth, which also appears in the film. Yet, an analysis of the two extracts shows the difference in perspective. Contrary to Alex Haley, Spike Lee does not cut the part of the speech in which Malcolm X is presented as a brave, gallant champion of the black cause. Spike Lee goes beyond Ossie Davis' vibrant message by superimposing archive footage of the real Malcolm X, mixing them with footage of police brutality, demonstrations by black people, a shot of Angela Davis, and even the famous 1968 Olympics Black Power salute by gold and bronze American medalists who took part in the 200 meters. When the eulogy ends, Spike Lee makes another subtle connection between Malcolm X and a famous defender of the black cause, Nelson Mandela. First, we see a group of Soweto children running joyfully and carrying posters of Malcolm X, followed by a similar scene in Harlem, featuring adults also carrying Malcolm X posters. The next sequence takes place on May 19, Malcolm X's birthday, and shows fourth-grade schoolchildren shouting "I am Malcolm X." The film ends with a speech about the dignity of the black man made by Nelson Mandela to South African children. Spike Lee is making a political statement about contemporary America, a post–Civil Rights America that has not yet put aside its worst racial demons. George H.W. Bush had succeeded Ronald Reagan, another Conservative US President, in 1989 and sporadic racial riots were still erupting in American big cities following racial murders or episodes of police brutality. For Spike Lee, it is a powerful way of saying that Malcolm X's struggle is far from over some 25 years after his death. Spike Lee also establishes an affiliation between the two black leaders, giving Malcolm X's fight an even more universal character by using it as a vehicle for commenting on the racial situation in the 1990s.

In this respect, and by way of a conclusion, it is fair to acknowledge that Spike Lee has achieved the impossible in his biopic. On the one hand, he has managed to capture the essence of a very complex individual, who was continuously evolving and maturing intellectually, while displaying the political heritage of a black leader, whose influence has grown in scope over the years. On the other hand, he has succeeded in overcoming the numerous challenges facing him, challenges that stemmed from the controversial personality whose life he had chosen to depict, from the fact that he had to adapt a text that was neither a biography nor an autobiography and, last but not least, the fact that he was making a film for a major Hollywood studio. His greatest achievement is therefore to have managed to propose his own artistic vision of Malcolm X's life within such constraints while making one of the great biopics ever produced by Hollywood.

WORKS CITED

Abrams, Dennis. *Spike Lee Director: Black Americans of Achievement Legacy Edition*. New York: Chelsea House Publishers, 2008.

Bingham, Dennis. *Whose Lives Are They Anyway? The Biopic as Contemporary Film Genre*. Piscataway: Rutgers University Press, 2010.

Breitman, George (ed.). *Malcolm X Speaks: Selected Speeches and Statements*. London: Secker & Warburg, 1966.

Cahir Costanzo, Linda. *Film to Literature Theory and Practical Approaches*. Jefferson, NC: McFarland & Co., 2006.

Curtis IV, Edward E. *Black Muslim Religion in the Nation of Islam 1960–1975*. Chapel Hill: University of North Carolina Press, 2006.

Custen, George. *Bio/Pics: How Hollywood Constructed Public History*. Piscataway: Rutgers University Press, 1992.

Doherty, Thomas. "Malcolm X: In print, on Screen." *Biography*, vol. 23, no. 1, *The Biopic* (Winter 2000): 29–48.

Dyson, Michael Eric. *Making Malcolm: The Myth and Meaning of Malcolm X*. New York: Oxford University Press, 1996.

El-Beshti, Bashir. "The Semiotics of Salvation: Malcolm X and the Autobiographical Self." *Journal of Negro History*, vol. 82, no. 4 (Autumn 1997): 359–367.

Malcolm X. Dir. Spike Lee. Prod. Marvin Worth and Spike Lee. Screenplay Arnold Perl and Spike Lee. Warner Brothers, and 40 Acres and a Mule Filmworks, 1993.

Malcolm X, with the assistance of Alex Haley. *The Autobiography of Malcolm X.* London: Penguin, 2001.

Marable, Manning. *Malcolm X: A Life of Reinvention.* New York: Viking Press an Imprint of Penguin Group USA, 2011.

Nasson, Bill. "'A Whiteout': Malcolm X in South Africa." *The Journal of American History*, vol. 80, no. 3 (December 1993): 1199–1201.

Norman, Brian. "Reading a 'Closet Screenplay': Hollywood, James Baldwin's Malcolms and the Threat of Historical Irrelevance." *African American Review*, vol. 39, nos. 1/2 (Spring/Summer 2005): 103–118.

Painter, Nell Irvine. "Malcolm X Across the Genres." *The American Historical Review*, vol. 98, no. 2 (April 1993): 432–439.

Michelle Obama: The Voice and Embodiment of (African) American History

Pierre-Marie Loizeau

Almost four centuries separate the arrival of the first African captives on American soil (1619) and the historical moment when Barack Obama swore his oath of office (January 20, 2009), with his hand on the Bible that President Abraham Lincoln had used at his first inauguration (1861).[1] The symbol was powerful since it associated two men following an historic trail linked by a powerful destiny, one as the father of the Emancipation Proclamation and ardent supporter of the 13th Amendment to the Constitution (1865), the other as the first African American president. US forefathers had made freedom a right. Lincoln had made freedom a law. Now, Obama was making freedom a reality.

---

[1] This was the first time an incoming president used Lincoln's Bible, which is part of the collection at the Library of Congress. The 1280-page volume was published in 1853 by Oxford University Press.

P.-M. Loizeau (✉)
Université D'Angers, Angers, France

© The Author(s) 2018
D. Letort and B. Lebdai (eds.), *Women Activists and Civil Rights Leaders in Auto/Biographical Literature and Films*,
https://doi.org/10.1007/978-3-319-77081-9_8

But the new president was not the only one in the Obama family to make history. The description of the inauguration ceremony would not be accurate without a special mention for Michelle Robinson Obama as she proudly held the Bible for her husband, following a tradition initiated by Lady Bird Johnson in 1965. For the 44th president's wife too, the symbol was very strong as she became the First African American First Lady. Beyond the emotional charge, the challenge before her exceeded her own destiny.

First Lady Martha Washington once declared with sadness that she "lived a dull life" in the presidential home and added: "I am more like a state prisoner than anything else. There is certain boundaries set for me which I must not depart from [*sic*]" (Anthony 1991: 42). When she arrived in the White House, Michelle Obama envisioned a different future. Her goal was simply to prove that she could do as well as, and possibly better than, her predecessors: be as determined as Eleanor Roosevelt, as glamorous as Jackie Kennedy, as protective of her husband as Nancy Reagan, as candid as Laura Bush, or be a combination of them all. Or simply be herself... As the first African American woman to hold this position, she distinguished herself from the traditional, political wife. Playwright Esther Armah explains: "For First Lady Michelle Obama [...], there are more subtle pressures attached to her role, ones that surely did not exist in the FLOTUS job-description pack of previous presidential spouses" (Armah 2012: 166). Unlike other presidents' wives, she had to show that a descendant of slaves who grew up in the South Side of Chicago could find her place at the top of political power and deserve the prestigious title of First Lady of the United States.

It is precisely this woman's complex personality and unpredictable trajectory that have been investigated in two biographies: *Michelle: A Biography* (Liza Mundy 2008) and *Michelle Obama: An American Story* (David Colbert 2009). Digging into the life of an individual, be it a prominent woman, a cultural leader or icon, or an ordinary citizen, offers a way to explore social movements, intellectual history, philosophical concepts, religious beliefs, notions of education, ethnicity, race, class, during specific periods of history, etc. The biographical genre illustrates what Mikhail Bakhtine calls the "dialogic" relation where the "text" and "context" influence each other in a reciprocal interaction (Bakhtine 1982). As Lois W. Banner explains, "biographers are detectives and interpreters, attempting to illuminate the past and to interweave its threads in new and compelling patterns" (Banner 2009: 582).

OF RACE AND STEREOTYPES

In Michelle Obama's case, black history is omnipresent, tracing her roots back to slavery times, and the very fact that she entered the White House with husband and children in 2009 was in itself, to quote Joanne Griffith, a specialist of the African diaspora, "historically transformative" (Griffith 2012: 21).

OF RACE AND STEREOTYPES

The most popular contemporary books about prominent African American female figures portray politicians, community organizers, civil rights leaders, and cultural icons. They include novelists, poets, musicians, actresses, journalists, athletes, government members, whose accomplishments have inspired generations of Americans. The list is long but some stand out like *Wrapped in Rainbows: The Life of Zora Neale Hurston* (Valerie Boyd 2002), *Naked at the Feast: A Biography of Josephine Baker* (Lynn Hane 1981), or the recent *Maya Angelou: A Biography* (Alex Roberts 2017). Rather than focus on Michelle Obama's cultural achievements or political activism, the biographers Mundy and Colbert have written the story of an "ordinary" African American woman with an "extraordinary" destiny. It is the tension between these two perspectives that has produced an exceptional biographical character (Fig. 1).

In 2008, several biographies had already been written on Barack Obama; he himself had authored his memoir *Dreams from My Father* (Obama 1995) and his politically oriented bestselling essay *The Audacity of Hope* (Obama 2006). However, no such literature was available for those interested in the aspiring First Lady; the release of Mundy's *Michelle: A Biography* filled the void. The book is a revealing and intimate portrait of a woman whose life story is inspiring to many Americans. Mundy admits that she wrote it without the protagonist's cooperation. Obama's political team declined access to Mrs. Obama and discouraged close friends from talking. Yet Mundy has produced a carefully reported work, drawing upon interviews with over 100 people including former college mates, colleagues, ministers, historians, and political consultants as well as vastly documented material from the media and academic record. The second, and slightly frustrating, point is that the book was published one month before the final election of November 2008 and so does not include Obama's victory. Although some readers and political fans were probably a little

Fig. 1 Michelle Obama on *The Ellen DeGeneres Show*, an "ordinary" woman with an "extraordinary" destiny. © NBC/Photofest

disappointed that it stopped where it did and would have liked to see Michelle Obama in the White House and follow her adjustments to being First Lady, the book offers a sympathetic account of the trajectory of a strong, outspoken, and opinionated woman whose husband's sudden and spectacular political ascent catapulted her into the spotlight. "It was more than a political rise; it was a political levitation," Mundy writes. "A political teleportation. Obama had been beamed up. He had ascended. Overnight he had become a household name" (Mundy 2008: 151).

Besides (or because of) its exceptional character, the presence of a black couple in the 2008 campaign raised suspicion, whether feigned or not, among opponents and conservative circles. The two protagonists were alternately targeted through a well-oiled mechanism of supercilious attacks and racial slurs. Right from the beginning of Barack Obama's first presidential race, some media reported that Hillary Clinton was briefed by her chief strategist, Mark Penn, to subtly stress Obama's "lack of American roots" (Dowd 2008: 23). His family background was the

MICHELLE OBAMA: THE VOICE AND EMBODIMENT ... 127

subject of a vast debate across the nation, sometimes triggering nonsense conversations about the color of his skin, like: "Is he black enough?" (Miah 2007). The persistence in pursuing these fantasies might be indirectly rooted in pervasive racism within American society, the 2011 birther issue being just its disguised form.[2] As Professor Eric Hehman of the University of Delaware explains in the *Journal of Experimental Social Psychology*:

> The influence of racial prejudice in contemporary U.S. society is typically manifested in subtle, indirect forms of bias. Due to prevailing norms of equality, most Whites attempt to avoid appearing biased in their evaluations of Blacks, in part because of a genuine desire to live up to their egalitarian standards, but also because of concern regarding social censure. (Vergano 2011)

Concluding that all Americans are racists would be a misrepresentation of reality. Instead, it seems fair to claim that Obama's presidential candidacy, like none before, has prompted a reevaluation of blackness and impacted notions of identity. His complicated family background, with "brothers, sisters, nieces, nephews, uncles and cousins, of every race and every hue, scattered across three continents,"[3] provided what Armah defines as "an expansion in [our] conversation about black identity" (Armah 2012: 174). With a black father from Kenya, Obama was a diasporic black man as well as an American of African ancestry. With a white mother who was born in Kansas and raised in Hawaii, he was also rooted in the American heartland. He spent some time in Indonesia with his mother and stepfather, but lived the better part of his childhood with his white maternal Midwestern grandparents, "Gramps" and "Toot," as he affectionately calls them in his autobiography. To reinforce her husband's all-American virtues, Michelle Obama claimed: "He was raised in his grandmother's home, and his grandmother is from Kansas, eating tuna with pickles in it" (Mundy 2008: 8). Although he could be technically

---

[2] The "not black enough" charge foreshadowed more brutal ones like the 2011 rumors about President Obama being a practicing Muslim who was not born in America. The birther movement, with Republican presidential aspirant Donald Trump at its head, questioned Obama's birth certificate validity, hence his American citizenship, and consequently, under Article Two of the Constitution, his eligibility to be President of the United States.

[3] "Barack Obama Speech on Race," delivered on Tuesday, March 18, 2008. https://www.youtube.com/watch?v=P_9al4IQOhk, accessed on March 15, 2017.

categorized as a "biracial" man, he preferred to identify himself as a "black American" and "a black man with a funny name" (Obama 1995, viii). With this mixed parentage, he also represented a perfect example of the American multicultural identity.

His wife, on her side, had little trace of white blood among her ancestors. Michelle LaVaughn Robinson, born on January 17, 1964, is the daughter of Fraser C. Robinson III (1935–1991) and Marian Lois Shields (1937). Fraser used to be a janitor or "city operator" at Chicago's water filtration plant where he was expected to sweep the floors and flush basins. In 1964, he was also an avid "precinct captain" Democrat who dedicated himself to telling African Americans about the benefits of voting. Marian occupied a job as secretary at mail order retailer Spiegel Catalog and at a bank. During the 2008 campaign, she tended her two granddaughters Sasha and Malia while their parents were busy on the campaign trail. This was a prelude to January 2009, when she moved into the White House along with the First Family to help raise the two little girls. She was the first grandmother to reside in the mansion since Elivera M. Doud, the mother of Mamie Eisenhower, which prompted some media to dub her the "First Granny." By maintaining those family ties, the First Lady revealed her "mom and daughter-in-chief" values and her desire to keep a sense of connection between generations, a philosophy of life she inherited from her own parents. They had named her Michelle LaVaughn because LaVaughn was the first name of her paternal grandmother. "The Robinsons were a family who liked to name children after antecedents," claims Mundy, "a tradition that affirmed the importance of relationship and connection" (Mundy 2008: 2).

If Michelle Obama inspired much admiration and enthusiasm, she also tended to be a "polarizing" figure. According to a survey published by the Pew Report in June 2008, Republicans disliked her more than Democrats disliked Cindy McCain (Republican contender John McCain's wife) and Democrats liked her more than Republicans liked Mrs. McCain (Mundy 2008: 11). Mundy points out that the campaign generated both adoration and skepticism about Michelle and showed how controversial she had become. There were some who thought it would be even harder for America to accept a black First Lady than a black president. Like her husband, and because his electoral chances of success were increasingly good, she soon became the target of right-wing hardliners who attacked her on several fronts. They delved into her college years, particularly at Princeton University where she focused on sociology and earned a certificate in African American studies. Those were the early days of Affirmative Action, "a time of real acrimony, real resentment, and real entrenchment," notes Mundy, during which "the now-ascendant forces of 1960s liberalism and the changes brought on by the civil rights era were coming into collision with the nascent conservatism of the Reagan era" (Mundy 2008: 62–63). In her thesis entitled "Princeton-Educated Blacks and the Black Community," she lamented that in a university where African American students made up less than 10% of the student body (with only 94 blacks out of more than 1100 students in her freshmen class), white professors and classmates always saw her as "black first and a student second" (Mundy 2008: 67). Critics deplored her paper's "oversimplification" and called it "a work of racial separatism" (Mundy 2008: 11), a movement embodied by the Black Nationalist Stokely Carmichael, a prominent civil rights activist, whom she quoted in her thesis. She also shocked a lot of people during a campaign speech in Milwaukee, Wisconsin, on February 18, 2008, when she said: "For the first time in my adult life, I am proud of my country because it feels like hope is finally making a comeback," calling America a "mean nation" which was "guided by fear" (Mundy 2008: 11). Republicans denounced her lack of pride in her country, although she was a living example of the American Dream, "with her own great history of both opportunity and achievement" (Mundy 2008: 12) including two Ivy League degrees, well-paid jobs in her career, making an income of several hundred thousand dollars a year and living a life that most ordinary Americans could only dream of. Conservative media hurled their rage at "America's unhappiest millionaire," representing the stereotype of the angry black woman supporting the "Black Separatist" ideology. The April 21 cover of the *National Review* (2008) referred to her as the disgruntled, lecturing "Mrs. Grievance" and *Fox News* dubbed her "Obama's Baby Mama" (Mundy 2008: 12). This description was directly connected to stereotypical figures of African American women such as the "angry black harridan," the seductive and promiscuous Jezebel, and the antagonistic and emasculating Sapphire. The Jezebel stereotype in particular came into play with the way some media outlets described her body and the clothes she wore. More than once, she was portrayed as such in political cartoons. The conservative press continued to demonize her and denounced her diatribes as a perpetuation of the culture of grievance whereby alleged racism is the systematic source of complaint for every embarrassment African Americans face in their lives.[4]

Liza Mundy's book explores Mrs. Obama's life story within the context of African American history at large and carves out her place in history. She portrays Michelle Obama's frustration and disappointment as reflective of collective sentiment, turning her into a mouthpiece for a people's anger produced by a heritage of oppression, discrimination, and racism. Yet Mundy is also keen to underline that Michelle Obama still represented traditional American values, which one Obama supporter enthused about during the campaign: "Michelle's story is a lot more mainstream American than Cindy McCain inheriting a brewery" (Dowd 2008: 23). "The day she was born," Mundy explains, "Michelle Robinson embodied the unique combination of discrimination and opportunity, hardship and overcoming, of being acted upon and acting, that would define much of black history in America. Of *history* in America, period" (Mundy 2008: 5). In a campaign interview, Barack Obama simply defined his wife as "the most quintessentially American woman I know."[5]

Beyond the commonly emphatic electoral rhetoric, Mundy depicts Michelle Obama as a woman shaped and challenged by American history, and particularly by black American history. She is characterized as the product of the complex and painful African American experience. It is an image that she willingly endorsed when, still awestruck by her privileged position, she confessed in a speech at a London school for girls in April 2009: "Nothing in my life's path would have predicted that I'd be standing here as the first African-American first lady of the United States of America. There is nothing in my story that would land me here."[6] Unlike the Obamas, the Robinsons have a heritage of African slave trade, Jim Crow, Civil War, Reconstruction, the Great Migration, segregation.

---

[4] See "the Sapphire Caricature", Jim Crow Museum of Racist Memorabilia, Ferris State University. http://www.ferris.edu/jimcrow/sapphire/, accessed on May 16, 2017. The conservative media's stereotyped image of "Michelle Obama as Sapphire" is discussed on this page.

[5] Joanna Coles and Lucy Kaylin, "Barack in the Saddle," *Marie-Claire*, August 15, 2008. http://www.marieclaire.com/politics/news/a1968/barack-obama-interview-women/, accessed on March 15, 2017.

[6] Daniella Silva, "Michelle Obama: The Historic Legacy of the First Black First Lady," *NBC News*, January 6, 2017. http://www.nbcnews.com/storyline/president-obama-the-legacy/michelle-obama-historic-legacy-nation-s-first-black-first-lady-n703506, accessed on March 6, 2017.

and the fight for civil rights. During her last commencement speech as First Lady at the City College of New York in June 2016, she pointed out the irony of her situation: "I wake up in a house that was built by slaves."[7] Indeed, the majestic palace she called home had been erected, to a large degree, by the forced labor of men of African descent who had been deprived of liberty like her own ancestors. With this in mind, the first black woman in the White House felt invested with a historical responsibility. Her image had a profound impact on the psyche of many African American families because her own (his)story spoke to their hearts and minds. Mundy quotes one Chicago minister as saying: "People who have not traveled the same road that African-Americans have traveled could not understand it" (Mundy 2008: 189), thereby contributing to weaving her family story into collective history.

FROM FAMILY STORIES TO COLLECTIVE NARRATIVE

Like most biographical literature on Mrs. Obama, Mundy's biographical endeavor remains silent on her early ancestry. The other biography explored for this article, *Michelle Obama: An American Story* (Colbert 2009), does provide an account of her family origins. Colbert's narrative strategy goes chronological and, with it, interesting details of the Robinson pedigree begin to emerge. It goes back to Michelle's great-great-grandfather, Jim Robinson, who lived on an old rice plantation, "Friendfield", near Georgetown, South Carolina. Jim was probably born around 1850 and lived there as a slave until the Civil War and as a "free man" afterwards. "In the story of American slavery, Georgetown stands out," Colbert writes (2009: 26). With about 300 slaves on each plantation, the town's average percentage of black population was several times higher than the figure found on farms at the national level. The enslaved men and women provided the backbreaking work needed for growing rice in the marshes and flooded fields that were home to alligators, snakes, and mosquitoes spreading malaria and yellow fever. Many of the slaves originating from rice-producing African countries (Senegal, Gambia, Sierra Leone, etc.) were familiar with the crop and resistant to the area's hot and humid climate as well as the threat of infectious diseases. Michelle Obama is descended from Jim Robinson's third

[7] *Idem.*

132 P.-M. LOIZEAU

son, whose name was the same as her own father, Fraser Robinson, and who was born in 1884, about twenty years after South Carolina slaves had been freed. At the age of ten, he had his left arm amputated after a bad infection that was not treated properly. Colbert's biography points out that this attitude became a family characteristic since his grandson, Michelle's own father, demonstrated the same determination when he was struck by multiple sclerosis: "Never complain about it. Never give into it. Another family legacy" (Colbert 2009: 36). Indeed, he learned to read and write on his own and took on three jobs throughout his life: a lumber mill worker, shoemaker, and newspaper salesman. Understanding an individual's life requires all kinds of historical investigation, including oral history. Like many stories about slaves and their first-generation descendants, orality remains a precious tool for transmission and the preservation of memory. Dorothy Taylor, one old resident of Georgetown, recalls that Fraser Robinson took home spare copies of the papers he sold to make sure his children could read. He took education very seriously, as the best avenue to a more comfortable life: "It was the belief that education was our salvation," Taylor related (Colbert 2009: 36). By retracing Michelle Obama's childhood through the oral stories transmitted by relatives and friends, biographers aim to give insight into the community culture which the Robinsons typify. Their family path is used to extol collective values that legitimate Michelle Obama's new role as First Lady.

Fraser Robinson's home was large enough to accommodate his wife and nine children including Fraser Jr., Michelle's grandfather. At the age of eighteen, Fraser Jr. was working in the local lumber yard and harbored a great deal of hope and ambition about his future. But, the Great Depression soon struck America and he lost his job. Unemployment was tough enough to endure for millions of Americans, but it was also accompanied by a resurgence of racial tensions and extreme violence against African Americans, recalling the worst episodes of Reconstruction.[8]

---

[8] In the post–Civil War period, former Confederate states saw white supremacy groups like the Ku Klux Klan terrorize blacks and whites who supported Reconstruction. With the Compromise of 1877 and the election of Republican Rutherford B. Hayes, a deal was reached with Southern states to remove federal troops based in the South and put an end to Reconstruction, leaving the field free for local anti-black legislation. Jim Crow laws of racial segregation were passed, denying African Americans their right to vote, and excluding them from many all-white facilities. Racial violence was rife and bloody riots broke out in South Carolina in May 1919, initiating the violent "Red Summer" that spread across the country with white mobs intimidating, lynching, and murdering African Americans.

"The lack of work, Jim Crow, violence: Michelle's grandfather decided he'd had enough," Colbert writes (2009: 43). Like millions of other Southern blacks, he moved north to Chicago in 1930. Colbert also explains that six generations separate Michelle Obama from one little slave girl, Melvinia, born in 1844 in South Carolina, the earliest known ancestor in the Obama family tree. She was moved to Georgia and at the age of fifteen was impregnated by a white man who, to this day, remains unidentified. Was it her second owner Henry Shields, in his late forties, or one of his four sons, aged 19–24? Or a casual visitor? "No one should be surprised anymore at the number of rapes and the amount of sexual exploitation that took place under slavery; it was an everyday experience," says Jason A. Gillmer, a Texas Wesleyan University specialist of slavery (Swarns and Kanto 2009). Melvinia gave the name of Shields to her first child, Dolphus, like two of his three siblings in the following years. Does the name prove his paternity or did she follow the tradition of former slaves taking their master's surnames? The question remains unsolved. Dolphus was listed on the 1870 census as a "mulatto." He later married Alice Easley, Michelle Obama's great-great-grandmother, and settled in Birmingham, then a boomtown in Alabama, where he became a prosperous carpenter, owning his own home and able to read and write. After they divorced, Alice worked as a seamstress and a maid. They had had two sons, Robert Lee Shields and Willie Arthur Shields but not much is known about them, except that Robert Lee's wife, Annie Lawson, left Alabama and headed to Chicago in the early 1920s with her son Purnell Nathaniel Shields, Mrs. Obama's grandfather. Like his father, Purnell was a painter and in 1930 he was employed in a syrup-producing plant. He had eight children, including Marian Lois Shields, born in Chicago in 1937. Marian married Fraser Robinson with whom she had two children Craig and Michelle, the future First Lady of the U.S.

BIOGRAPHICAL FOCUS ON CHICAGO

Chicago stands at the crossroads of Mrs. Obama's paternal and maternal branches in their similar historical destiny. Their situation was not exceptional since this was the period defined in history books as the "Great Migration," an experience that artist Jacob Lawrence (1917–2000) captured in a famous series of sixty panels in which he painted evocative portraits of African Americans like Fraser Jr. and Annie Lawson, who made the historic journey from the rural South to the urban North, their new "Promised Land" (Grossman 1989: 98), usually traveling by train, boat, or bus. Liza Mundy calls the migration "a vast exodus," "a massive stream of human movement" that would transform northern and western cities like Chicago shaken by a black demographic explosion (Mundy 2008: 2–3):

> By the time [Fraser] arrived, the African community had already ballooned to more than five times the size it had been in 1910. It was growing at ten times the rate of the city's overall growth. About one of every five new residents was African American. A quarter of a million African Americans lived in Chicago. (Colbert 2009: 44)

The biographer gives particular attention to the historical events that took place in the "Windy City" during the twentieth century, from World War I to the racial tensions of the 1960s. Many of the new arrivals found jobs in the busy South Side where the factories, foundries, and slaughterhouses faced a shortage of industrial labor. This is where Fraser Jr. settled, in close proximity to the mills, stockyards, and meatpacking plants. Work was close at hand and despite the different wage scales for black men and white men, it paid better than in South Carolina. However, as Upton Sinclair (1906) had described in *The Jungle*, working conditions were horrendous and sometimes dangerous, the novel providing vivid descriptions of overwork, lack of adequate safety measures, and child labor common in many plants (Sinclair 1906).

While Chicago, particularly the South Side, was prone to discrimination, poverty, and criminality, African Americans also developed a rich urban culture, a seedbed of black culture in the U.S. and American culture in general and an inspiration far beyond borders. Mundy contends that Chicago nurtured the political ambitions of civil rights figures:

> The South Side would give the world the blues of Muddy Waters, the fiction of Richard Wright, the poetry of Gwendolyn Brooks, the presidential ambition of Jesse Jackson, distinctive contributions from people who were discriminated against, but who out of that experience created music and art and literature and politics, as well as a sense of solidarity and cohesion. (Mundy 2008: 9)

In 1954, with its decision in *Brown v. Board of Education of Topeka*, the Supreme Court ruled that public schools should be de-segregated, overturning the *Plessy v. Ferguson* case of 1896, whose doctrine of "separate but equal" had institutionalized the division of society according to racial criteria. *Brown* was a major victory and paved the way for the upcoming Civil Rights movement. A decade later, the same year that Michelle was born, 1964, President Lyndon B. Johnson signed the Civil Rights Act putting an end to discrimination in public accommodation and housing. With major advancements favoring racial integration in jobs, housing, and education, with new residential opportunities, the Robinsons moved to a more peaceful and former whites-only neighborhood. Within a few years, though, the flow of African Americans to these areas caused racial tensions again, many whites resisting with violence, intimidation, or legal maneuvers to curb the trend. Transformation of the social composition eventually led to a new form of migration, this time involving the white middle-class population moving away to the suburbs, a widespread phenomenon in many US cities known as the "white flight." Colbert reports that "as African families moved in, white families moved out" and relates the testimony of Craig, Michelle Obama's brother:

> A moving truck in front of a neighbor's house, a car packed with valuables, and the last white family in the neighborhood saying goodbye before leaving Chicago for the suburbs. (Colbert 2009: 60)

Like many other black families, the Robinsons were able to establish a broad and rooted family on Chicago's South Side. Mundy and Colbert both provide insight into Michelle Obama's experiences during her childhood and teenage years in her tight-knit neighborhood. Mundy underlines that her parents belonged to the working class, which instilled in her and her brother a strong work ethic, quoting Michelle Obama in a 2007 interview: "My father had M. S. [multiple sclerosis] and worked every day and rarely complained" (Mundy 2008: 26). What stands out most is the emphasis on community and family, with uncles coming around and people visiting each other. So much so that at the dawn of her romance with Barack Obama, family was a real epiphany for him. She gave him a very close, united, and happy family, a model in sharp contrast to the father-seeking experience he evoked in *Dreams from My Father*. Her family environment helped her grow up and mature into an accomplished woman who was also shaped by her successful professional career as a lawyer and her work for the University of Chicago, and who built herself a strong, self-assured family.

CONCLUSION

Unlike most other published life stories of black women, the biographies of Michelle Obama defy traditional categorization. They place her in a perspective of collective history and, because of her personal success as a role model, also contribute to turning her into an African American icon, a term which has since been used in the prolific presidential literature and biographical material about the First Lady (Chambers 2017; Coignard 2012). If as "wife-of," she resembles her predecessors, the public wife certifying "his" respectability, as "black wife-of," precisely of a black candidate/president, she has no precedent, a factor that adds considerably to her exceptionality. On March 18, 2008, at the National Constitution Center in Philadelphia, Pennsylvania, during the Democratic presidential primaries, Senator and future President Barack Obama delivered his powerful "race speech" for a "more perfect union" in which he declared: "I am married to a black American who carries within her the blood of slaves and slave-owners."[9] Obviously, Michelle Obama's prominence and family history have brought into sharp focus the disturbing and complex reality of the "peculiar institution," an indelible stain on the American historical narrative. Because the scars of slavery cannot be removed, they connect her to the essence of the African American experience. "A lot of times these stories get buried," she said, "because sometimes the pain of them makes it hard to want to remember. You've got to be able to acknowledge and understand the past and move on from it." But her message did not give into negative feelings and pessimism:

> It is a process of uncovering the shame, digging out the pride that is part of that story—so that other folks feel comfortable about embracing the beauty and the tangled nature of the history of this country. (Murray 2008)

Memory acts like a cathartic form of purification as it draws upon man's struggles of the past to help him build a brighter future. With the knowledge of history, imperfect though it may be, the oppressive silence imposed on African Americans by years of discrimination gives way to

---

[9] "Barack Obama Speech on Race," delivered on Tuesday, March 18, 2008. https://www.youtube.com/watch?v=P_9al4IQOhk, accessed on March 15, 2017.

a process of liberation and transformation. In this perspective, Michelle Obama echoes the words of Martin Luther King: "Silence is betrayal,"[10] and those of Malcolm X, another outstanding black figure: "History is a people's memory, and without a memory, man is demoted to the level of the lower animals."[11]

WORKS CITED

Anthony, Carl Sferrazza. *First Ladies: The Saga of the Presidents' Wives and Their Power 1789–1961*, vol. 1. New York: William Morrow, 1991.

Armah, Esther. "A Quiet Victory for Emotional Justice." In Joanne Griffith (ed.), *Redefining Black Power: Reflections on the State of Black America*. San Francisco, CA: City Lights Books, 2012, 165–186.

Bakhtine, Mikhail. *The Dialogic Imagination: Four Essays* (Reprint Edition). Austin: University of Texas Press, 1982.

Banner, Lois W. "Biography as History." *The American Historical Review*, vol. 114, no. 3 (June 2009): 582.

Chambers, Veronica. *The Meaning of Michelle: 16 Writers on the Iconic First Lady and How Her Journey Inspires Our Own*. New York: St. Martin's Press, 2017.

Coignard, Sophie. *Michelle Obama—L'icône Fragile*. Paris: Plon, 2012.

Colbert, David. *Michelle Obama: An American Story*. New York: Sandpiper/Houghton Mifflin Harcourt, 2009.

Dowd, Maureen. "Mincing Up Michelle." *The New York Times*, June 11, 2008, A23.

Griffith, Joanne (ed.). *Redefining Black Power: Reflections on the State of Black America*. San Francisco, CA: City Lights Books, 2012.

Grossman, James R. *Land of Hope, Chicago, Black Southerners, and the Great Migration*. Chicago: University of Chicago Press, 1989.

Kloppenberg, James T. *Reading Obama, Dreams, Hope and the American Political Tradition*. Princeton and Oxford: Princeton University Press, 2011.

Miah, Malik. "Race and Class: What Is 'Black Enough'?" *Solidarity*, May/June 2007. https://www.solidarity-us.org/node/524. Accessed on December 12, 2017.

---

[10] Martin Luther King's "Beyond Vietnam: A Time to Break Silence," speech delivered on April 4, 1967, at a meeting of Clergy and Laity Concerned at Riverside Church in New York City. http://www.informationclearinghouse.info/article2564.htm, accessed on December 12, 2017.

[11] Malcolm X's first public address on behalf of the Organization of Afro-American Unity (OAAU) at the Audubon Ballroom in Washington Heights on June 28, 1964. http://www.blackpast.org/1964-malcolm-x-s-speech-founding-rally-organization-afro-american-unity, accessed on December 12, 2017.

Mundy, Liza. *Michelle Obama: A Biography*. New York: Simon & Schuster, 2008.
Murray, Shailagh. "A Family Tree Rooted in American Soil." *The Washington Post*, October 2, 2008, C01.
Obama, Barack. *Dreams from My Father: A Story of Race and Inheritance*. Edinburgh: Canongate, 2007. First Published in New York: Times Books, 1995.
———. *The Audacity of Hope: Thoughts on Reclaiming the American Dream*. Edinburgh: Canongate, 2008. First Published in New York: Crown Publishers, 2006.
Palmer, Colin A. (ed.). *Encyclopedia of African-American Culture and History: The Black Experience in the Americas*. New York: Macmillan, 1960.
Sinclair, Upton. *The Jungle*. New York: Doubleday, 1906.
Swarns, Rachel L. and Jodi Kantor. "First Lady's Roots Reveal Slavery's Tangled Legacy." *The New York Times*, October 8, 2009, A1.
Swain, Susan (ed.). *First Ladies: Presidential Historians on the Lives of 45 Iconic American Women*. New York: Public Affairs, 2016.
Vergano, Dan. "Study: Racial Prejudice Plays Role in Obama Citizenship Views." *USA Today*, May 1, 2011. http://content.usatoday.com/communities/sciencefair/post/2011/04/social-scientists-look-at-racisms-role-in-birther-viewpoint/1#.WMu-ETs1-Uk. Accessed on December 12, 2017.
Wilkerson, Isabel. *The Warmth of Other Suns: The Epic Story of America's Great Migration*. New York: Random House, 2010.

Ghost Writing and Filming Biography in *Twelve/12 Years a Slave*

Sylvie Charron

Twelve Years a Slave (Solomon Northup, 1853) participated in an effort to end slavery in the U.S. in the mid–nineteenth century and rode on the coattails of Harriett Beecher Stowe's bestselling novel *Uncle Tom's Cabin* (1852). Both works were written as a rebellion against the Fugitive Slave Act of 1850,[1] which made penalties for harboring fugitive slaves even harsher than the first fugitive act of 1793, and engendered in a new breed of slave catchers who would capture freed slaves

---

[1] The Fugitive Slave Acts were a pair of federal laws that allowed for the capture and return of runaway slaves within the territory of the U.S. Enacted by Congress in 1793, the first Fugitive Slave Act authorized local governments to seize and return escaped slaves to their owners and imposed penalties on anyone who aided in their flight. Widespread resistance to the 1793 law later led to the passage of the Fugitive Slave Act of 1850, which added further provisions regarding runaways and levied even harsher punishments for interfering in their capture: "Persons who gave shelter, food, or assistance to an escaping slave were liable for a fine of $1000 and six months in prison" (Eakin 2013: 264).

S. Charron (✉)
University of Maine at Farmington, Farmington Hills, ME, USA
e-mail: scharron@maine.edu

© The Author(s) 2018
D. Letort and B. Lebdai (eds.), *Women Activists and Civil Rights Leaders in Auto/Biographical Literature and Films,*
https://doi.org/10.1007/978-3-319-77081-9_9

in the North to resell in the South. *Twelve Years a Slave* relates the story of a freeman, Solomon Northup, who lived with his family in Saratoga Springs in the State of New York before he was kidnapped and sold into slavery to work on a plantation in Louisiana. Northup was held captive for twelve years (1841–1853) until devoted friends from the North achieved his release.

Historian Kenneth M. Stamp argues that slave narratives should not be taken at face value:

> We never hear directly from the former slave; instead we read what a white author tells us in *his* words a former slave told him. I do not propose that we reject altogether this hearsay evidence—we cannot be as rigid as courts of law—only that we use it with extreme caution and with a clear understanding of what it is. (Stamp 1980: 41)

French literary scholar Claudine Raynaud also contends that slave narratives raise questions of authorship and she therefore prompts readers to interrogate the terms of the collaboration behind the publication of slave narratives: "What is the nature and extent of collaboration in autobiographical works (co-)signed by ex-slaves? Whose voice do we hear when we read the slave narrative?" (Raynaud 2005: 8).

Twelve Years a Slave is a case in point: Solomon Northup may have been interviewed indeed, but he never actually wrote the tale of his own abduction and slave experience. His oral report served as a primary source for David Wilson who edited the story for public reading. In the Preface to the 1853 published version of Solomon Northup's story, David Wilson presents himself as an unbiased editor committed to retrieving the truth:

> Many of the statements contained in the following pages are corroborated by abundant evidence—others rest entirely upon Solomon's assertion that he has adhered strictly to the truth. The editor, at least, who has had an opportunity of detecting any contradiction or discrepancy in his statements, is well satisfied. [...] Unbiased, as he conceives, by any prepossessions or prejudices, the only object of the editor has been to give a faithful history of Solomon Northup's life, as he received it from his lips. (Northup 1853: xv)

Wilson was a distinguished lawyer, journalist, and poet from upstate New York with strong abolitionist views. Sensing the importance of the Northup tragic tale, he had two clear goals in mind. One was literary: to publish the book as hastily as possible to benefit from Harriet Beecher Stowe's immensely popular novel *Uncle Tom's Cabin*. The second was activist in nature, as a search for justice. He hoped that as a result of the publication Northup's slave traders would be arrested and punished. This, unfortunately, did not happen because African Americans were not allowed to testify in court, which led to the traders' acquittal.

Although *Twelve Years a Slave* indeed became a bestseller at the time of publication, it quickly fell into oblivion after reprint in 1856. Its revival as an essential document came from a chance discovery by a twelve-year-old white girl on a plantation in Bayou Boeuf where Northup had been enslaved. Horrified by what she had read and obsessed with unearthing the truth about the account, Dr. Sue Eakin later became a historian who spent a lifetime researching Solomon Northup's case and slavery in the South. She republished the book for the first time in 1968, over a hundred years after the original publication, with a final annotated edition in 2013. In turn, this publication served as a source for British film director Steve McQueen, who adapted the story for the silver screen in 2013 to extraordinary acclaim. This essay aims to show that the various documents relating the narrative of Solomon bear the traces of their author's interpretive grid. While Solomon Northup's story can be recovered from the source materials, his voice is enmeshed with David Wilson's in the original book version and it becomes the object of Steve McQueen's film adaptation. Try as she might to research the historical truth, it seems that Dr. Sue Eakin's motivations are rooted in her own family story.

David Wilson's Authorship

Twelve Years a Slave claims to be the autobiographical account of Solomon Northup, narrated in his own voice and from his limited point of view, as this quote makes clear:

> I can speak of Slavery only so far as it came under *my own observation*— only so far as I have known and experienced it in *my own person*. My object is, to give a *candid and truthful statement of facts*: to repeat the story of my life, without exaggeration, leaving it for others to determine, whether even the pages of fiction present a picture of more cruel wrong or a severer bondage. (Northup 1853: 18)[2]

---

[2] Emphases are mine in every quote.

Northup's autobiography claims to convey the truth by reporting factual events—in contrast to Stowe's *Uncle Tom's Cabin* which resorts to fiction. However, Northup's life narrative can only be accessed through the filter of an educated white man's words. Although Wilson can be credited for sharing Northup's tragic tale with a large public through the book's publication, the author fails to convey a clear sense of Solomon's voice or personality. A close analysis of the text shows that Wilson's own prose permeates the narrative. An example, among many, is how he describes Northup's father:

> He endeavored to imbue our minds with *sentiments of morality*, and to teach us to place our trust and *confidence in Him* who regards the humblest as well as the highest of his creatures. How often since that time has the recollection of his *paternal* counsels occurred to me, while lying in a slave hut in the *distant* and *sickly* region of Louisiana, *smarting with* the *undeserved* wounds which an *inhuman* master had inflicted, and longing only for the grave which had covered him, to shield me also from the lash of the oppressor. (Northup 1853: 20)

The insistence on the morality and Christian faith of the father seems designed to reassure the reader about the protagonist's good character. The other issue is semantic and syntactic: Wilson often uses lengthy sentences, replete with adjectives as can be seen in the second sentence of the quote, which includes six adjectives in three lines, highlighting its literary character. While, according to the Introduction, Northup knew how to read, it is doubtful that he could express himself with such elegance. This, in turn, creates a literary distance between the narrator and the protagonist, preventing the reader from hearing Northup's voice. By contrast, Harriett Beecher Stowe gives life to her enslaved characters by using unusual syntax and orthography to represent their dialects and colloquialisms. The book is replete with examples of this kind, such as this one in Chapter 4, entitled: "An Evening in Uncle Tom's Cabin." It illustrates Aunt Chloe's speech patterns:

> Here you, Mose and Pete! Get out de way, you niggers! Get away, Polly, honey,—mammy'll give her baby some fin, by and by. Now, Mas'r George, you jest take off dem books, and set down now with my old man, and I'll

GHOST WRITING AND FILMING BIOGRAPHY IN *TWELVE/12 YEARS A SLAVE* 143

take up de sausages, and have de first griddle full of cakes on your plates in less dan no time. (Beecher 1852: 41)[3]

Wilson, on the other hand, uses almost no dialogues which might flesh out the characters in the story. Northup's personality remains somewhat hidden behind a compelling and horrifying life story. Readers may wonder who he was as a human being or how he expressed himself, which in turn makes his account less intimate and may partly explain why the book was not reprinted for so long.

In addition, the text is sprinkled with David Wilson's own racial comments on slavery. For example, it is hard to imagine that his references to "simple minded slaves" with "simple hearts" could have been made by Solomon. The description of the Christmas dinner where whites and blacks sit together is particularly telling in that regard:

> The omnipresent Cupid disdains not to hurl his arrows into the *simple hearts of slaves*. Unalloyed and exulting happiness lights up the *dark faces of them all*. The *ivory teeth*, contrasting with their *black complexions*, exhibit two long, *white streaks the whole extent of the table*. All round the bountiful table board *a multitude of eyes roll in ecstasy*. Giggling and laughter and the clattering of cutlery and crockery succeed. (Northup 1853: 215)

In this scene, the enslaved are caricatured as they would later be in such films as *Gone with the Wind* (Victor Fleming, 1939). The phrase "a multitude of eyes roll in ecstasy" seems to evoke these early Hollywood representations. It is also noteworthy that this scene of common merriment for plantation owners and slaves does not appear in Steve McQueen's film which focuses instead on the horrors of slavery without respite, bypassing instances of communality.

The description of Patsey at the end of Chapter 18 also reads as a racially charged digression by Wilson:

> She had been reared no better than *her master's beast*—looked upon merely as a valuable and *handsome animal*—and consequently possessed but a *limited amount of knowledge*. And yet a *faint light cast its rays upon her intellect*, so that it was not wholly dark. She had a *dim perception of God* and

---

[3] Interestingly, this dialogue reappears at the very beginning of Harriet Beecher Stowe's play, based on the book, entitled *The Christian Slave* (1855), p. 5.

of eternity, and *a still more dim perception* of a Savior who had died even for such as her. She entertained but *confused notions* of a future life—*not comprehending* the distinction between the corporal and spiritual existence. (Northup 1853: 259)

Wilson clearly interjects his own opinions when referring to Patsey as a beast or an animal with limited intelligence (insisting on her "dim perception," "confused notions," and "not comprehending").

At the other extreme, Wilson gushes about the goodness of Northup's white owner William Ford while excusing him from any wrong (blaming his surroundings instead), which Northup may not have been so eager to do:

It is *simple justice* to him when I say, in my opinion, there was never a more *kind, noble, candid, Christian man* than William Ford. The influences and associations that had always surrounded him, blinded him to the inherent wrong at the bottom of the system of Slavery. (Northup 1853: 90)

In addition, at the end of the book, Wilson adds an apology of Mistress McCoy, also visibly destined to white readers, which is not likely to have been penned by Northup:

I would have the reader understand that all slave-owners on Bayou Bœuf are not like Epps, or Tibeats, or Jim Burns. Occasionally can be found, rarely it may be, indeed, a good man like William Ford, or an *angel of kindness* like young Mistress McCoy. (Northup 1853: 286)

This metaphor of a white mistress as an angel betrays an idealization of the Southern Belle and places her as an omnipotent protector of helpless inferiors. This posits her as innately superior, able to decide on the fate of slaves who should be grateful for any kindness received, not as a right, but as a gift. This phrase, in essence, accepts the premise and status quo of racial inequality.

Steve McQueen's Adaptation

Steve McQueen's film *12 Years a Slave* presents the tale through a different lens since it engages the viewer through sound, images, and the presence of actors who give flesh to the characters. As a result, the viewer receives a markedly different representation of Solomon Northup. He

GHOST WRITING AND FILMING BIOGRAPHY IN *TWELVE/12 YEARS A SLAVE*   145

becomes fully alive and personalized. In addition, images and sound affect the viewer in ways that words could not. Multiple senses are used to construct the characters and their surroundings, and bring them to life.

The film director's personal identity also influences the filters he uses for retelling the story. Northup's biography is now told through the eyes of a descendant of slaves from the Caribbean. At the same time, Steve McQueen is somewhat of an outsider to the American experience and demonstrates European training and sensibility in his use of photography and *mise-en-scène*. Steve McQueen also has a distinct perception of oppression. In other cinematic productions such as *Hunger* (2008), he uses the body of his character as a site of resistance during a hunger strike in Ireland. Similarly, in *12 Years a Slave* the camera lingers on the lacerated flesh of Patsey and on Northup's own abused body but indomitable spirit. Steve McQueen relates to the slavery narrative and conveys the oppressed enslaved's point of view. He places Solomon Northup, the African American slave, at the center of the film and the camera often portrays the world through his gaze. Yet, the film offers its own rewriting, as we can see through a few examples.

The way Steve McQueen uses music is particularly interesting in affecting our view of slavery. One central musical theme (as in the original story) is the fiddle. Indeed, Solomon was captured because he was a known fiddle player who was tricked into going South, under the pretense that he would be hired as a musician. In the film the fiddle appears as a recurrent trope to illustrate Northup's emotions: not only does he show his homesickness by writing the names of his family members on the fiddle, but a frown on his face expresses his disgust at playing music at white dances. Most tragically, he breaks the fiddle when Patsey is beaten almost to death, as a metaphor for his own broken spirit.

Shana L. Redmond adds that "music brings terrible, frightening splendor" as the film exhibits Northup's violin playing as labor, providing a "method of sadistic pleasure and control by enslaving communities" and "a method of refusal and cultural formation of repute" (Redmond 2015: 152). A couple of musical examples are particularly evocative of this power in the film. The first conveys the horror of slavery when the white overseer sings a particularly sadistic song, "Run, Nigger, run" and forces the slaves to clap their hands at his jeers. The camera travels between the white man's vicious glee at the sight of the slave's suffering, and the silently suffering and angry face of helpless Northup,

Fig. 1 The fiddle appears as a recurrent trope to illustrate Northup's emotions. © Fox Searchlight Picture/Photofest

which renders the scene intolerable. The spectator is placed in the position of the enslaved men, victimized by the power of the overseer and unable to stop his chant. In another example the opposite effect is created when soulful singing celebrates African American culture while Northup appears victorious in showing his master how to transport logs, against the wishes of the overseer. This time, music serves to celebrate the victory of the soul against white oppression. In these two examples, powerful negative and positive emotions are created for the viewer through the musical score (Fig. 1).

The film also uses vivid visual contrasts to increase the poignancy of the experience. This contrast actually was already present in the book, most tellingly in one of its most tragic passages:

> The *painful cries* and shrieks of the *tortured* Patsey, mingling with the *loud and angry curses* of Epps, loaded the air. [...] The lash was *wet with blood*, which flowed down her sides and dropped upon the ground. At length she ceased struggling. Her head sank listlessly to the ground. [...] I thought she was *dying*! [...] It was the Sabbath of the Lord. The fields *smiled in the*

GHOST WRITING AND FILMING BIOGRAPHY IN *TWELVE/12 YEARS A SLAVE* 147

warm sunlight—the *birds chirped merrily* amidst the foliage of the trees—*peace and happiness* seemed to reign everywhere, save in the bosoms of Epps and his panting victim and the silent witnesses around him. (Northup 1853: 257)

The spectators' immersion into the bloody scene brings powerful emotion. We, as Northup himself, become helpless spectators of this arbitrary ferocity. The violence is rendered more shocking when contrasted with the magnificent scenery that Steve McQueen's camera focuses on, alternating with the horror. Frank B. Wilderson observes that "the preponderance of medium and/or wide angle shots compels the spectator to luxuriate in the density of lush vegetation, magnolia trees and thickly bearded willow, ample grass, and a multitude of shrubs and bushes that choke the veranda and line the road" (Wilderson 2015: 140). The serenity and beauty of nature dramatically contrasts with the depravity of man. Steve McQueen creates a similar contrast when Solomon is almost left to die by hanging surrounded by the calm magnificence and indifference of the landscape. Film scholar Rizvana Bradley leveled criticism at the film's "sadomasochistic gaze that is technically reinforced by the manipulation of the camera" (Bradley 2015: 163), noting that *12 Years a Slave* relies upon "tropes of mastery and domination, pain and trauma" (Bradley 2015: 163) that ambiguously make a "spectacle of sufferance" (Hartman 1997: 21).

The film may indeed appear as overly aesthetic in its representation of nature and characters. Most shots are carefully constructed and often resemble elaborate paintings. Scenes and interactions between characters are obviously staged throughout the film. One example that comes to mind is a scene towards the end when Northup and Bass discuss his fate and possible escape to freedom. The architecture of the scene resembles a classical painting where the slave on the left (Northup) is bending forward while the carpenter on the right (Bass) leans back in a most beautiful, almost languid pose. The clothes, throughout the film, are impeccably clean, as are the characters, which detracts from the realism of the story. In addition, Bass, who is played by the universally known movie star Brad Pitt, appears more like a Hollywood heartthrob than a rough-and-tumble Canadian carpenter and woodsman. As a consequence, he unfortunately seems like a convenient and unrealistic *deus ex machina*, whereas Northup was indeed saved through the efforts and courage of this humble man.

Archival Research by Sue Eakin

Dr. Sue Eakin points out through her research of court records that Solomon Northup was convicted of assault and battery three times, in February and May, 1834, and again in May, 1839 (Eakin 2013: 271, note 20). She also suggests that he may have had a drinking problem since he was arrested on several occasions for disorderly conduct. In other words, Solomon Northup may have been more complex and less heroic than either the book or the film portray him to be, even though this information does not detract from the horror of his kidnapping and certainly does not justify enslavement for ten long years, and possibly a lifetime. In reality, Northup's frailty as a human being creates a more nuanced, endearing, and realistic vision of history.

As an academic and descendant of white plantation owners who had owned slaves, Dr. Eakin may have been compelled to search for other information because the story touched her so personally. Throughout her career, she researched and collected official documents and court proceedings, including the court proceedings when Solomon Northup went on trial to regain his freedom (Eakin 2013: 198–217). She observed from the trial archives that Solomon had inadvertently ignored warnings from friends who tried to dissuade him from going South with white strangers. As a Southerner with a sense of guilt, Dr. Sue Eakin aims at alleviating the shame of her own people. Noting that Northup disappeared after the trial let him free, she appropriates his story as a moral lesson to modern readers and claims for an unfortunately universal tale. She writes:

> The Solomon Northup story reeks of tragedy and injustice, not just in the South at the time, but across the nation. In our pride as citizens in a nation dedicated to freedom, equality, and justice, we must be reminded that these are ideals toward which we continually struggle. [...] In the United States, prior to the Civil War, slavery was a national, not merely a Southern, institution. [...] Residuals of racism exist among our diverse people across the United States. Facts of History must temper our pride and instill a determination to bring democracy nearer to the ideal of the Founding Fathers. (Eakin 2013: 217)

We can only surmise that her ultimate motivation to unearth historical documents may have been related to her own search for redemption.

Conclusion

These few examples demonstrate that Solomon Northup's autobiography may not be literally accurate. The events of his life were interpreted at the onset by a writer whose literary style interfered with Northup's narrative voice. While Dr. Sue Eakin played a crucial role in establishing that Solomon Northup had indeed been a freeman from the North, captured and enslaved for twelve years, by searching for the historical truth through lifetime research into court documents and other artifacts, she also undermined the original hagiography by portraying a flawed man. Finally, filmmaker Steve McQueen can be credited for giving flesh and blood to the character and for disseminating through vivid photography and sound this horrific historical event to a vast international audience.

David Wilson and Steve McQueen have shaped the story of Solomon Northup through different artistic means, both wishing to give a face to the horror of slavery in order to combat it. Dr. Sue Eakin tried to demonstrate that Northup's story was never the simple autobiography of an individual: *Twelve Years a Slave* has become a form of parable and a tool to fight oppression.

Works Cited

Beecher Stowe, Harriet. *Uncle Tom's Cabin.* Boston: John P. Jewett, 1852.

Beecher Stowe, Harriet. *The Christian Slave.* Boston: Phillips, Sampson, 1855.

Bradley, Rizvana. "Reinventing Capacity: Black Femininity's Lyrical Surplus and the Cinematic Limits of *12 Years a Slave.*" *Black Camera*, vol. 7, no. 1 (2015): 162–178.

Eakin, Sue. *The Autobiography of Solomon Northup: Twelve Years a Slave.* The Woodlands, TX: Eakin Films & Publishing, 2013.

Hartman, Saidiya. *Scenes of Subjection, Terror, Slavery, Self-Making in Nineteenth-Century America.* New York and Oxford: Oxford University Press, 1997.

Northup, Solomon. *Twelve Years a Slave: Narrative of Solomon Northup, a Citizen of New York, Kidnapped in Washington City in 1841, and Rescued in 1853.* Auburn, AL: Derby & Miller, 1853.

Raynaud, Claudine. "Let Miss Jane Tell her Story." *Lectures critiques de The Autobiography of Miss Jane Pittman.* Tours: Presses Universitaires François Rabelais, 2005.

Redmond, Shana L. "Tip Toes and River Rolls: Overhearing Enslavement." *Black Camera*, vol. 7, no. 1 (2015): 150–161.

Stamp, Kenneth M. *The Imperiled Union: Essays on the Background of the Civil War*. Oxford and New York: Oxford University Press, 1980.

Wilderson, Frank B. "Social Death and Narrative Aporia in *12 Years a Slave*." *Black Camera*, vol. 7, no. 1 (2015): 134–149.

PART III

Biographical Films and History

Biographical Motion Pictures and the Resuscitation of "Real Lives"

Taïna Tuhkunen

Attempts to reconsider the past through exceptional, emblematic individuals capable of reincarnating entire eras is as old as the history of motion pictures. As Mark Moss notes in *Towards the Visualization of History: The Past as Image*, when discussing the influence of visual culture on the study of history: "Since the advent of film, one of the most common ways of dealing with historical subject matter on film has been to resuscitate the Great Man/Person version of history" (Moss 2009: 126). This line of argument is extended by the author of *Whose Lives Are They Anyway?: The Biopic as Contemporary Film Genre*, Dennis Bingham who claims that while the "great (white) man biopic" has perpetuated tropes of triumph and evolved from "warts-and-all"[1] depictions to more

---

[1] The expression "warts-and-all" is a popular summary of the English military and political leader Oliver Cromwell's (1599–1658) request to the court portrait painter Sir Peter Lely whom he asked to avoid all visual flattery when painting his portrait: "Mr. Lely, I desire you would use all your skill to paint my picture truly like me, and not flatter me at

---

T. Tuhkunen (✉)
Université d'Angers, Angers, France
e-mail: Taina.Tuhkunen@univ-angers.fr

© The Author(s) 2018
D. Letort and B. Lebdai (eds.), *Women Activists and Civil Rights Leaders in Auto/Biographical Literature and Films*,
https://doi.org/10.1007/978-3-319-77081-9_10

154   T. TUHKUNEN

post/modern portrayals of accomplishment, the "female biopic" remains hampered by myths of suffering and victimization. The exception to this gender and genre rule would be the few "feminist biopics"[2] which challenge these conventions, yet whose mere scarcity proves how difficult it is to reinvent the female biopic (Bingham 2010: 10–11).

In spite of its limits,[3] Bingham's dualistic perception of the biopic as a codified, subgendered genre highlights the way biographical films have been influenced by a number of biased patterns, when pursuing their distortive aesthetic modalities. Although strictly gender- and/or race-based approaches to biopics certainly call for more nuancing,[4] for, as Steven Neale notes in *Genre and Hollywood*, the biopic "is often hybrid and multi-generic" (Neale 2000: 54), film directors seeking to bring "exceptional individuals" to life on screen also keep negotiating, sometimes quite explicitly, with constitutive assumptions and distinctive modes of "life-telling" perpetuated by film industry.

Equally thought provocative are George F. Custen's theorizations in his landmark 1992 study *Bio/Pics: How Hollywood Constructed Public History* where the biographical film is defined as "one that depicts the life of a historical person, past or present" (Custen 1992: 5). According to Custen, biopic portrayals, famous for their longevity, are mediated through symbol systems which predate cinema. Interestingly, this first major biopic study which sees biography as the basis of the earliest forms

---

all; but remark all these roughnesses, pimples, warts and everything as you see me, otherwise I will not pay you a farthing for it." (Walpole 1763: Chap. 1).

[2] As examples of feminist biopics, Bingham mentions Jane Campion's *An Angel at My Table* (1990), *Center Stage* (Stanley Kwan, 1992), *Erin Brockovich* (Steven Soderbergh, 2000), *The Notorious Betty Page* (Mary Harron, 2006), and *Marie Antoinette* (Sofia Coppola, 2006).

[3] In *The Postfeminist Biopic: Narrating the Lives of Plath, Kahlo, Woolf and Austen*, Bronwyn Polaschek explores cinematic representations of three woman artists, and proposes a further conceptualization of the biopic genre by introducing a third category alongside Bingham's paradigmatic female biopic and the overtly feminist biopic: "the postfeminist biopic." What's more, Polaschek sees artist biopics as a particularly interesting subgenre as they highlight creative and visionary, yet misunderstood individuals (Polaschek 2013).

[4] According to Bingham, only a few "feminist biopics" have managed to reverse the conventional strategies of the classical form of the biopic genre, thus proving how difficult it is to reinvent the female biopic (Bingham 2010: 10–11).

BIOGRAPHICAL MOTION PICTURES AND THE RESUSCITATION ... 155

of literature associates the biopic genre with "one of the oldest human impulses": the attempt to "record for posterity something of the lives of one's fellows" (Custen 1992: 5). When dealing with biographical films, it is indeed important to keep in mind Custen's idea of a primeval need to call back from the past "tales of ancestors and other previous significant figures" (1992: 5) which not only seem to underlie the classic Hollywood representations of "remarkable people," but also the more innovative, recent efforts to "remember" and reconstruct private as well as public history through memorizations performed by biographical moving pictures.

Today critics tend to group together, albeit somewhat misleadingly, quite a miscellaneous assortment of films on in/famous individuals beneath the same umbrella term "biopic"—an abbreviation of the words "*bio*graphical" and (moving or motion) "*pic*ture"[5]—in reference to films based on the life (or lives[6]) of a real, rather than fictional person (or people). On the other hand, in the field of film studies a more comprehensive critical approach to biographical moving pictures in the form of an actual "biopic theory" is still quite a recent phenomenon. Long neglected by academia, as if the biopics' very popularity had discouraged critical explorations, more extensive scholarly interest is gradually developing, not only in the English-speaking world, but also in France. It remains, however, arguable whether a more comprehensive definition or generic identity is conceivable, namely when taking into account the intertwined roots of biographical films which intersect with such firmly established film genres as westerns, gangster movies, melodramas, and musicals. In the absence of a definite iconography and character types, shared spatial markers and/or time frames, the debate is bound to continue over the tropes and parameters of this movable group of films, as pointed out by Tom Brown and Belén Vidal who see the biopic, quite

[5] As a sign of the biopic's ongoing definitions, Cheshire uses a hyphen between the prefix "bio" and the abbreviation "pic," which endows both parts of the term with a seemingly equal autonomy. In the epigraph of her book, *Bio-Pics: A Life in Pictures*, Cheshire provides, by way of definition, the following explanation: "This book is dedicated to all my friends and family who have to hear me say 'It's Bio-Pics as in Biographical Pictures (films about real people), not Bi-opics, which sounds like some kind of a sight problem'" (Cheshire 2015: vii).

[6] As evidenced by Sacha Gervasi's recent film *Hitchcock* (2012), a biopic can be as much about a celebrity as about somebody left in the shadow of the star figure; in *Hitchcock*, the famous filmmaker's wife Alma Reville (Helen Mirren).

rightly, as a "troublesome genre" in *The Biopic in Contemporary Film Culture* (Brown and Vidal 2013: 1), a stimulating ensemble of critical essays on contemporary biographical film production not only in the Western world (France, Italy, Great Britain, the U.S., etc.), but also in countries like Russia, India, and South Korea, thus proving that the biopic is not simply a transhistorical but a transcultural film category.

The genre trouble at issue here is furthermore complicated by the normative expectations of the spectators, accustomed to the "comebacks of the Great" in the form of cinematic rebirths and engaging reconstructions which blend—more or less lightheartedly, scandalously, or ingeniously—fiction and fact, if necessary with fantasy, when elaborating filmic portrayals of nonfictional characters. Similarly to the adaptation of literary narratives to film, adapting life stories to the screen often proves quite as subjective or arbitrary in its treatment of historical facts, as well as in its wish to convey resolutions and morality lessons through screen-created "exceptional individuals." Further points of tension remain the escapism and voyeurism cinematographic interpretations of the "larger-than-life" are frequently blamed for, especially when deliberately distorting and commodifying facts for dramatic and entertainment purposes.

Within the more global and intrinsically unstable genre system theorized by Rick Altman in *Film/Genre*,[7] the biographical film—which, according to Altman, established itself firmly as a genre at the end of the 1930s—raises numerous typological, narratological, discursive, and aesthetic questions when traced back to its early manifestations, through the hagiographic studio era, before the advent of contemporary celebrity culture and its "tabloid famous" (Altman 1999: 216–217). As this article wishes to argue, while certain less idealizing or idolizing biopic accounts challenge more classic iconizations, relatively rare are the "reel stories" which discard all idol worship when re/telling "real-life stories."[8] For, even when shifting the focus from greatness to "everyday-ness," the biopic is easily overwhelmed by plots and images of achievement, to try and prove the exceptionality of the outstanding subject. Rather than

---

[7] Interestingly, Altman's chapter on "The biopic" begins by highlighting the word "game" when evoking the way film genres tend to be named either retrospectively (by critics) or prospectively (by producers) (Altman 1999: 38).

[8] For instance, *An Angel at My Table* (Jane Campion, 1990), *Superstar: The Karen Carpenter Story* (Todd Haynes, 1998), *I'm Not There* (Todd Haynes, 2007), and *Howl* (Rob Epstein and Jeffrey Friedman, 2010).

endorsing the idea of distinctively gendered, ethnic, professional,[9] or other potential subgenres,[10] the compilation of which could be regarded as a proof of the existence of an autonomous, clearly delineated, single genre, our (necessarily limited) study relies on the hypothesis that in spite of their easy recognizability and marketability, biographical moving pictures ultimately fail to constitute a system of their own, and hence do not stand out as a perfectly coherent, easy-to-label body of work.

With these postulates in mind, we shall approach the biopic as a hybrid, crossbred genre, both at the same time a deeply rooted and a wide-ranging critical category with spongy borders that enable the absorption and adaptation of selected biographical and historical facts, as well as interaction with more firmly established categories, such as the "history/historical film," "historical biography," "documentary," "docudrama," "costume drama," and "heritage film," not to mention larger drama and epic film genres biographical films also intersect with. Sharing Rick Altman's need to probe well beyond "the seemingly uncomplicated world of Hollywood classics" (Altman 1984: 6), we shall interrogate the biopics as a process by looking into the various resuscitations, revivals, and revelations practiced by these polygeneric films. For, in spite of the "nearly monochromatic view of history" (Altman 1984: 3), sustained by Hollywood for roughly three decades, today's biopics offer a far more polychromatic vision of "the famed" than one might expect.

From Hagiography to Latter-Day Biopic Saints

In *Jesus of Hollywood*, the biblical scholar Adele Reinhartz points out that since the beginning of commercial cinema, there have been well over a hundred celluloid incarnations of Jesus, before adding that people now tend to learn more about the life of this religious and historical figure

---

[9] This is the case, for instance, in Ellen Cheshire's *Bio-Pics: A Life in Pictures* which examines American and British biographical films since the 1990s through professional categories.

[10] Strikingly, the biopic often tends to be a life story of a lawbreaker; not necessarily of a gangster, but a politician, a singer, a musician, a writer, a painter, or another type of artist or innovator, such as the computer wizard Steve Jobs, who creates rules of his (more often than her) own. Since the idea of transgression and defiance so clearly impact the biopic typologies, one might wish to ask to what extent this characteristic might even constitute a prerequisite for any biopic *persona* who is, in one way or another, to challenge the rules and codes of society in order to acquire the label "larger-than-life."

158   T. TUHKUNEN

from cinema than from any other medium. More interestingly, according to Reinhartz, "Jesus movies" mirror the concerns and values of the eras of their making by reshaping the past in the image of the present. Among the other most frequently revived historical figures on film—Cleopatra, Napoleon, Queen Elizabeth I, Queen Victoria, Henry VIII, Jesse James, and Adolf Hitler—the Christian victim and savior figure of resurrection *per se* cannot, indeed, be ignored when dealing with the history of biopics and the historical consensus biographical portrayals often seem to echo.

The impact of this early canonical character, present through countless latter-day disguises, messianic messages, and more contemporary figures of pacific resistance, is nevertheless far from simple. For, as Dennis Bingham recalls, the foundations of the biopic lie not only in "the lives of saints," but in other popular forms, such as legends, melodramas, or national myths (Bingham 2010: 31). Hence the necessity to look into *and* beyond individual biopic *personae*, however overpowering they may appear, to try and seize their often intensely hybrid nature and capacity for renewal in films which, despite their explicit interest in "extraordinary individuals" in the field of politics, arts, sciences, sports, etc., reflect far wider signifying systems and modalities of character construction.

Throughout the cinematic processing of overdetermined, visionary individuals[11] and cult figures—in many a sense secular equivalents of religious icons—what is striking is the way "bio-telling" of prominent people, past and present, has connected singular life stories with larger, collective, grand narratives,[12] and more specifically with the Christian master narrative of love, suffering, and redemptive resurrection.[13]

---

[11] Custen insists on "the biopic credo of the person who has personal visions where others merely wear blinkers" (Custen 1992: 191).

[12] The concept of metanarratives or "master narratives" (*"grands récits"*/"big stories") was introduced by Jean-François Lyotard in his 1979 essay *The Postmodern Condition: A Report on Knowledge* where he defined postmodernism as a form of incredulity towards metanarratives. This incredulity or disbelief is particularly notable in some recent biopics, such as Todd Haynes' *I'm Not There*, where the biographical subject remains beyond the reach of the generic biopic structure, both as an absence and a movable, multiple presence.

[13] Despite this essay's focus on Bible-inspired, Christian redemption and salvation narratives, this is, of course, not the only metanarrative impacting biographical films. In these films where collective and individual stories constantly crisscross, other frequent metanarratives include Freudianism, Marxist utopianism, bourgeois capitalism, Enlightenment, democracy, as well as feminism, insofar as it is possible to consider feminism as a homogenizing, ideological script.

Exceeding the category of religious subjects toward other culturally and inter/nationally integrative forms—in various allegoric and ideological manifestations—the threefold theological plot has left its embedded imprints on a long series of "leader biopics" which repeatedly mingle the secular and the "real" with the sacred and the legendary.

One such recent example of "a secular descendent of the life of saints" (Brown and Vidal 2013: 4) merging the hagiographic with edification, is Steven Spielberg's *Lincoln* (2012): a biopic where the sacrificed savior of the Union who freed America from slavery is presented both at the same time as somebody "homely" (literally "home-like") and saintly ("God-like"), the former attribute requiring to be understood in its etymological sense as something "simple and plain," "belonging to home or household." After several previous filmic portrayals of the great American president,[14] the most recent cinematic retelling of Lincoln's final years keenly seeks to animate the fixed image of the hallowed leader, traditionally typecast in a style reminiscent of the imposing granite profile of the Mount Rushmore National Memorial.

During his attempt to turn Abraham Lincoln (Daniel Day-Lewis) into something else than another static symbol or mineral monument, Steven Spielberg seems to transcribe into cinematographic language the paradox encapsulated by the title of Gary Alan Doris's biography *Abraham Lincoln, An Uncommon, Common Man: A Narrative of His Life*. Resonating with John Ford's jovial recounting of Abe Lincoln's early life in *Young Mr. Lincoln* (1939), Steven Spielberg focuses on the "common man" by foregrounding the president's folksy sense of humor and direct, unpretentious contact with (the) people. Relying on specific vocal and point-of-view strategies, he reinforces the impression of proximity, and presents the pedestaled president as a simple "daddy" to Lincoln's 12-year-old son Thomas "Tad" (Gulliver McGrath), something quite unthinkable in the early filmic portrayals of U.S. presidents.

The film's oscillating mode between the public (politician) and the private (husband and father) reaches its climax when Tad discovers the (off-camera) assassination of his father during a poignant scene

---

[14]See, for instance, *Her Country's Call* (Lloyd Ingraham, 1917), *The Dramatic Life of Abraham Lincoln* (Phil Rosen, 1924), *Abraham Lincoln* (D.W. Griffith, 1930), *Young Mr. Lincoln* (John Ford, 1939), and *Abe Lincoln in Illinois* (John Cromwell, 1940).

toward the end of the film. The indirect showing and telling of the much-expected murder scene confirms Steven Spielberg's refusal to cash in on gratuitous violence. On the other hand, by breaking into a moving (and smiling) picture Lincoln's iconic profile image (reproduced on one-cent coins after a black-and-white photograph[15]), he literally enlivens the officially "coined expression" of the political leader. Yet at the end the biopic returns the "common man" into a sanctified man of exception, as Lincoln's dead body is exposed in a quasi-Christic light during the deathbed scene of the film. Steven Spielberg's portrayal thus joins John Ford's Lincoln (Henry Fonda) who, in the film shot seventy-four years earlier, disappears behind the horizon, walking uphill towards his tragic destiny in the midst of a symbolic thunderstorm that proleptically closes on the greatest father figure of the American Enlightenment.

Before pursuing, it should be pointed out that the word "leader" is used, within this article, in reference to politically and spiritually, but also scientifically, artistically, and athletically iconic subjects. Whatever the type of biopic re/construction of potentially empowering role models, these films remain sensitive to master narratives of salvation, closely connected with survival stories, also in the metaphorical sense of outliving the past, as with the portrayal of Lincoln's ongoing legacy as the incarnation of truly American values. It is the agency of the protagonist which provides the biopic with its main dramatic impetus, underlining the trajectory that leads to the final breakthrough into fame and the collective consciousness. For, whatever the social origin or historical background of the outlasting hero, he is to be perceived as an "agent" who, according to etymology, is apt to "drive," "lead," or "act."

While this basic ability to set into motion applies to most biographical films pivoting upon male leaders (Thomas Jefferson, Abraham Lincoln, Roosevelt, Hitler, JFK, Che Guevara, Lumumba, Malcolm X, Richard Nixon, Ronald Reagan, Mandela, and Gandhi, to name a few notable examples), biopics still tend to view female leadership through their hereditary, non-elective positions, staging women, more often than not, as agents of disorder, when they are not seen as troublemaking instigators. While it has taken biographical films time to view, in a

---

[15] Called "The Penny Profile," the photograph taken by Mathew Brady in 1864 has served as a model for the Lincoln cent from 1909 onward.

BIOGRAPHICAL MOTION PICTURES AND THE RESUSCITATION ... 161

more polychromatic light, the lives of female political leaders (Margaret Thatcher, Eva Perón, Winnie Mandela, and other similarly hardheaded "iron ladies"), they still prefer turning their camera lenses on the spouses of royal or presidential husbands (Grace of Monaco, Diana, Eleanor Roosevelt, Jacqueline Kennedy, etc.).

In the Preface to *Royal Portraits in Hollywood: Filming the Lives of Queens*, Elizabeth Ford and Deborah Mitchell note that "Queens are in vogue, sometimes literally," when evoking the media coverage received by "more recent high profile cinematic rebirths" (Ford and Mitchell 2009: 1) of enigmatic queens. Sofia Coppola's controversial, patently hybrid queen biopic, *Marie Antoinette* (2006), is certainly one of them. The deliberately anachronistic pop-rococo biopic of the last queen of France exposes diehard gender systems, and discards old patterns while interrogating the polarized logics that include the so-called "strong woman biopics" (De Tirado 2009: 145–160). Indeed, alongside old trends, new ones are piercing through the old canvas. Among other striking recent royal biopics, the iconic Tudor queen reincarnated by Cate Blanchett in *Elizabeth* (1998) and *Elizabeth: The Golden Age* (2007): two films made by Shekhar Kapur which prove that in present-day biopics "not only leading men gain depth and sophistication with maturity" (Ford and Mitchell 2009: 2).

At a time when any social, cultural, or professional category is apt to generate a revelatory rendering of a biopic subject—however shocking, vulgar, or intentionally unsaintly these latter-day revelations may be[16]—the discovery of the man or the woman behind the mask of the public *persona* remains, of course, a matter of basically limitless filming techniques. And, as in the creation of other forms of cinematic personhood the "how" is, understandably enough, as essential as the "what" or the "who", as the subject-protagonist is brought into being through signifying postures and gestures, meaningful dialogue and camera angles, suggestive sound and musical effects, color codes, etc. in the mediated reality of the film.

---

[16]As a number of critics have claimed, contemporary biopics often foreground the personal problems of the subject, focusing on his/her sexual relations, drinking and/or drug abuse, family violence, etc. This seems to apply, more particularly, to biopics that follow a clear "rise-and-fall" pattern, functioning as formulaic "warning tales" that offer the spectator instances of warts-and-all voyeurism.

Magic, Early Biopics, and the Larger-Than-Life Scientist on Screen

After the first biographical films released at the turn of the twentieth century (many of which were, remarkably enough, about famous women[17]), cinematographic portrayals of "the Great" gradually multiplied until their first heyday between the 1930s and 1960s[18]—a period that highlighted the role and status of male creators in the fields of arts, sciences, and politics. This was followed by the biopics' fall into temporary unpopularity during the counterculture era, more interested in promoting collective actions than in sanctifying or worshipping individual heroes. After the 1960s' iconoclastic Protest and Civil Rights movements the revered individual was back at center screen; at the beginning of the twenty-first century this was also the case in the shape of a computer age wizard whose inventions resonated with the scientific discoveries celebrated in the 1940s. These days, during the second coming of the biopic, it takes but a few mouse clicks to access increasingly long lists of biopic titles, usually arranged beneath various subgenres or typological subspecies of what is, nonetheless, popularly perceived as a genre of its own.

In order to improve our understanding of these paradoxes and of the tenacious attempts to classify biopic narratives, including today's overtly postmodernist revisions of historical characters, it may be of use to recall the appropriations of the life of another well-known historical *persona*, that of Joan of Arc, whose representations range from the art of poetry to patriotic emblems, political cartoons, and video games: an apt illustration of the endless practice of adaptation, central to the storytelling imagination, as Linda Hutcheon suggests in *A Theory of Adaptation* (2006) which, we might add, also informs us about the cultural *praxis* of adapting life stories onto movie screens.

If, as Hutcheon writes, part of the pleasure of adaptations comes from "repetition with variation" (Hutcheon 2006: 6) or "repetition without replication" (2006: 7), we are to cast a "double vision" (2006: 15) on the very word "adaptation," to consider it as a product *and* as a process. On the other hand, cinematographic adaptation of life stories remains period bound: while part of a continuum, it is rendered distinguishable

---

[17] *The Execution of Mary Queen of Scots* (Alfred Clark, 1895), *Cleopatra* (Méliès, 1899), *Joan of Arc* (1900).

[18] During this period over 300 biographical movies were made in Hollywood alone.

BIOGRAPHICAL MOTION PICTURES AND THE RESUSCITATION ...   163

by its differing aesthetic and ideological appropriations of the subject. This is evidenced by the first filmic portrayal of Joan of Arc in George Méliès's color-tinted *Joan of Arc* (1900)[19]: a film that dates back to the era of the "cinema of attractions" defined, by Tom Gunning, as "the earliest phase of cinema as dedicated to presenting discontinuous visual attractions, moments of spectacle rather than narrative." According to Gunning, this first era was followed from 1906 onward by a period "in which films increasingly did organize themselves around the tasks of narrative" (Gunning 2005: 124). Although the distinction between "attraction" and "narrative" was later on contested and nuanced,[20] Gunning's conceptualization proves useful when trying to understand the somewhat fixed, visual elements worked into biographical motion pictures, animated by narrative forces that drive spectacular instants into action and motion.

Since the first filmic resuscitation of the legendary fifteenth-century maiden warrior, Joan of Arc's transition from a peasant girl into a Roman Catholic saint has been reenacted in more than forty feature films, not to mention various TV spectacularizations on the fabled savior figure also known as the Maid of Orléans (*Pucelle de l'Orléans*). With his tableaux effects, George Méliès's early appropriation of Joan of Arc differs radically from Carl Dreyer's later icon-like close-ups and focalizations on Joan of Arc's heresy trial and execution in *The Passion of Joan of Arc* (1928). As Gilles Deleuze pointed out, when discussing the close-ups of Joan's face which Dreyer's film so heavily depends upon, the film becomes the "affective film" *par excellence* owing to its emotional handling of the main character. To what extent the "pure affects" discussed by Deleuze concern primarily "female biopics" is a question we shall have to leave aside for lack of space. It would, nevertheless, be interesting to see if what Deleuze calls "affection-image" (contrary to "action-image") is,

---

[19] Since Méliès, the life story of Joan of Arc (embodied by Jeanne Calvière) has been readapted by several famous filmmakers, among them Cecil B. DeMille (with Géraldine Farrar, 1916), Carl Dreyer (with Renée Falconetti, 1927), Marco de Gastyne (with Simone Genevoix, 1929), and Victor Fleming (with Ingrid Bergman, 1948), to name some of the most notable examples.

[20] Charles Musser offered the following corrective: "attractions and narrative are efficiently combined because the theatrical turns that Méliès favored are also an integral part of the narration." See Charles Musser's 1995 article "Pour une nouvelle approche du cinéma des premiers temps: le cinéma d'attractions et la narrativité" (cited in E. Ezra 2000: 4).

on a purely visual plane, less predominant among what Dennis Bingham calls the "great (white) man biopic."

It was hardly a coincidence that the first biographical film on the life of Joan of Arc followed Méliès's adaptation of *Cinderella* (*Cendrillon*, 1899), a fairy tale fantasy made a year before *Joan of Arc*. Georges Méliès (1861–1938),[21] the great cinemagician of early silent cinema, rarely bothered his brains with the sense of realism, and well before the typical "based-upon" and "inspired-by-a-true-story" captions which were to open more canonical, biography-based biopics, the French film director's protobiopic did not conceal its spectacular, deliberately show-oriented constructedness.[22]

Despite their differences, some of the key events in the lives of a fairy tale figure and the medieval religious icon resonate with one another. Not only do they anticipate the highly selective and conventionalized patterns of narrative, both maidens and victim figures seem quite as sensitive to fantasy. The closing scenes of the two films put an end to the ordeals of the fairy tale princess and of the martyred maiden in an equally uplifting, pre-Hollywood décor in which Cinderella completes her ascension to royalty, while Joan of Arc is hoisted to the heavenly spheres.

As Tom Gunning pointed out, the early cinema "differs from later narrative cinema through its fascination in the thrill of display rather than its construction of a story" (Gunning 2005: 100). Conversely, we could add, while *féerie* (fantasy) features complicate the inclusion of Méliès's protobiopic among the more classic biographical movies, its place within the cinema of "attractions" (rather than of "narration") serves as an interesting early example of the way biopics combine historical fact with fantasy—well before the more experimental biopics that challenge the above-mentioned "attraction"/"narration" opposition. And, as Méliès's pioneering film on Joan of Arc underlines, we should not confuse the biopic with simple recounting of facts. As Giles Hardie claims in "Big names, big flops: Why the biopics have failed in 2013" (Hardie 2013), an article where he calls the biopic "a very crowded non-genre," the

---

[21] George Méliès appears in Martin Scorsese's *Hugo Cabret* (2011), a "partial biopic" in the sense that Méliès is not actually the main character of the film (that focuses on the life of a fictitious young orphan), but which nevertheless reads as a glowing tribute to the early French filmmaker.

[22] During an interview, Méliès admitted that he had been drawn to the elements of fantasy and spectacle present in Joan of Arc's life story (Musser 2011).

truth frequently turns out to be a "huge handicap to storytelling," simply because "real life doesn't come in three act structures." In this text—published, let us underline, two years before the release of Danny Boyle's *Steve Jobs* (2015), a particularly "theatrical" biopic due to its three-part structure—Hardie challenges the very idea of biopics forming "a genre," even if the entire movie industry, together with the Academy of Motion Pictures and Sciences, insist on viewing it as an independent generic category.

The same question could be raised when looking into the biographical movies produced during the classic Hollywood studio era of the 1930s, 1940s, and 1950s, marked by a conspicuous move toward scientific know-how, without, nevertheless, breaking totally away from the genre's hagiographic leanings. What counted was the strong recommendation formulated by film producer and studio executive Richard D. Zanuck who insisted on the necessity to make "[a]ll cinematic lives [...] understandable in terms that viewers would find congruent with their own experiences" (cited in Custen 1992: 20), however alienating the biopic character's actual life might have been.

During the classical period, biographical films produced by the major Hollywood studios were not only male-driven, but marketed as historically accurate. Emblematic scientists were visionary male geniuses (Louis Pasteur, Graham Bell, Thomas Edison, etc.[23]), while Marie Curie, the Nobel-winning scientist who discovered radium, was the only woman in this all-male scientific bio(pic-)sphere. And, as underlined by Mervyn LeRoy's heavily fictionalized *Madame Curie* (1943), when tracing the path to public recognition of the "token woman," Maria Sklodowska (Greer Garson) needed to be presented as a *madame*, Pierre Curie becoming in a sense the scientific guarantor for his wife's work. This was hardly surprising for in these essentialist biopics women not only occupied secondary roles, but functioned as more or less standardized foils accentuating the male subjects' extraordinary sense of enterprise and initiative.

When compared with contemporary films on male scientists and inventors, such as the recent Oscar-winning *A Theory of Everything* (James Marsh, 2014) on the British physicist Stephen Hawking (Eddie Redmayne), Bell, Edison, and Pasteur convey the impression of honorable, yet fairly arid destinies, which seem to tell a coming-of-age story

---

[23] *The Story of Louis Pasteur* (William Dieterle, 1936); *Graham Bell* (Irving Cummings, 1939); *Edison, the Man* (Clarence Brown, 1940).

of their heroes destined to become men of erudition in a world where scientific understanding of things has supplanted the theological view of the world.

Curiously, these always somewhat saintly and God-like scientists are back, particularly since such popular biopics as *The Imitation Game* (Morten Tyldum, 2014) and the above-mentioned *A Theory of Everything* on a great physicist whose heroic battle against physical decline due to amyotrophic lateral sclerosis turns him into a secular saint of sorts. The hero of *The Imitation Game* is the English mathematician and logician, Alan Turing (Benedict Cumberbatch), the inventor of artificial intelligence and the founder of computer science who helped crack the famous Enigma Code during World War II. Regardless of this scientific triumph, which is thought to have been decisive for the Allied victory in the Atlantic, Turing's life ended tragically, almost in martyrdom. As recalled by Tyldum's film, Turing was eventually arrested on homosexual charges and forced to undergo an excruciating chemical castration as the only alternative to prison. While these contemporary scientist biopics keep focusing on scientists who are just as obsessive, it is their faculty to experience and embody suffering—in other words, their down-to-earth capacity to be human—that seems to distinguish them from the scientist heroes of the earlier decades.

CONCLUSION

Faced with the current upsurge of biopics, those who tend to regard these films as something merely "anecdotal, conventional, not artistic, and unrealistic" (Berger 2014: 6), or as a symptom of the "Facebook age" obsessed with celebrity and star systems, may view the phenomenon with increasingly dubious, if not fearful eyes. For, as the French film journal *CinémAction* observed in its 2011 edition devoted to biopics, by using the metaphor *déferlante* (literally "a breaking wave"; Fontanel 2011: 18) when evoking the plethora of biographical movies released during recent years, there are no signs of weakening of the biopic flow inundating our film screens.

Since roughly the mid-1990s, films based on the true lives of real-life persons or fact-based life stories have turned into an increasingly popular and lucrative phenomenon, enjoying exceptional popularity among filmmakers, moviegoers, and critics. At the American Oscars and the French Césars, biopics are regularly honored with awards and, despite their low repute, have aroused the interest of a number of film scholars, even in France, famous for its *auteur* films where the biopic is still often considered as a particularly "maligned and misunderstood genre" (Cheshire 2015: 3).

Although the hagiographic patterns beneath the coming into being of "extraordinary individuals" remain prominent, heroic, sacrificial deeds are no longer quite as systematically applied in contemporary biopics. Nor are they as methodically gendered, if we are to believe some of the most innovative postmodern biopics that focus on the lives of their subjects through deliberate fragments, or "slices of lives,"[24] defying the principles of coherence and resolution. Despite the fact that postmodern incredulity concerning redemptive metanarratives still remains a fairly rare phenomenon within the creation and production of biopics, some recent biopics illustrate their capacity to be both mythmaking and mythbreaking, inventive and self-reflective, moving beyond the bounds set by the formulaic biopics of the studio era.

One such eye-opening example is Todd Haynes's experimental biopic *I'm Not There* (2007) where no fewer than six characters, both men and a woman, embody different stages and dimensions of Bob Dylan's potential *personae*. *I'm Not There* literally moves around, including geographically across the States, to foreground the subject's different facets (as a musical trendsetter, protester, reluctant superstar, major poet, etc.), making it impossible to fix Dylan within a single plot or iconic image. The tone is set by two brief utterances: "All I can do is be me. Whoever that is." The biopic conventions thus disrupted—by words pronounced by Dylan during a 1965 interview—the biopic *persona* (whose "true"[25] name is never mentioned) is now posited as something intrinsically elusive and plural. This inevitably leads to further interrogations regarding authenticity and veracity—pursued, as we know, through twentieth-century debates about adaptation of literary stories, here extended to that of cinematographic life stories. A later quote in Haynes's film—"inspired by the music and many lives of bob dylan"—reinforces the distance from predictable plots, the lower-case letters of the artist's name underlining a refusal to erect yet another monolithic monument in the honor of a

---

[24] "Less than full-blown portraits, [biofilms] should be seen and understood as slices of lives, interventions into particular discourses, extended metaphors meant to suggest more than their limited timeframes can convey" (Rosenstone 2012: 122).

[25] Bob Dylan was born Robert Allen Zimmerman.

"great real-life person." Dismantling the standard formula according to which "Every biopic is supposed to have a basis in reality" (Bingham 2010: 8), the film on one of the most debated troubadours of the twentieth-century ends up generating movable and multiple biographical pictures which no longer prove to be "based on real events."

These ongoing biopic explorations also impact, in various degrees, more conventionally constructed biopics. One may think, for instance, of the dream sequences woven into Steven Spielberg's biopic which bear the mark of some of Lincoln's diary entrances, showing and saying something far more than the *déjà-vu* hagiographic "Father Abrahams." When the President is suddenly spotted on an allegorical boat, in the middle of a dark night, the Gothic imagery of the film intersects with Timur Bekmambetov's fantasy biopic, *Lincoln: Vampire Hunter* (2012), released the same year as Steven Spielberg's far more classic *Lincoln*.

A similar, yet aesthetically different portrayal *process*, more than a *construction*, is set up by Rob Epstein and Jeffrey Friedman's *Howl* (2010) where animated sequences partake in the ephemeral portrayal construction of a famous poet. Through the movie, Allen Ginsberg's catalyzing poetry is not only heard but "watched" in its animated form. While the countercultural masterpiece poem *Howl* is read out loud during poetry readings, and tackled in courtroom hearings and interviews, the spectator sees it literally transmute from typed, black lines into vibrant music and animated pictures during its eroticized, colorful journey onto the film screen. Based not merely on a life, but on progressively more heterogeneous storytelling means and techniques, these crossover hybrids prove the ability of contemporary biopics to draw on an impressive variety of sources: any texts the biographical subject may have written, received, or been influenced by; pictorial and graphical materials; other archives and dustbins of personal and private history; without, of course, forgetting more subtle incorporations of subtexts, intertexts, and/or grand narratives.

In the light of recent examples of biographical pictures, it thus seems possible to conclude, albeit temporarily, on the potential of revelations and resuscitations with which these films are endowed. Alongside more traditionally constructed biographical scenarios, more innovative handlings of characters and narratives will most probably keep impacting what can be seen, as suggested in our introduction, as a hybrid and crossbred genre; a critical claim that leaves more room for contradictions and irresolution than before. Without turning their backs on well-delineated, iconic portrayals, the unstable historical portrayal of some contemporary biopics confirm the need to find more original means to represent multiple selfhoods on screen.

Consequently, and as Dennis Bingham seems to suggest by his heavily highlighted use of the conditional form in the following passage from *Whose Lives Are They Anyway? The Biopic as Contemporary Film Genre*, rather than reflecting the historical characters found in old history books, the biopic yet to come may indeed look increasingly intensely into the very means and techniques of its own construction:

> A postmodern biopic would present the subject as a series of performances or roles, on which continuity, coherence, or meaning cannot be imposed. A postmodern biography would call attention to its own operations, as a series of clues and influences from its culture. A postmodern biography would problematize its own ability to re-create the life of its subject; it might also speak in a variety of styles and formats, again denying unity to the overall work. (Bingham 2010: 133)

Works Cited

Altman, Rick. "A Semantic/Syntactic Approach to Film Genre." *Cinema Journal*, vol. 23, no. 3 (1984): 6–18.

Altman, Rick. *Film/Genre*. London: British Film Institute Publishing, 1999.

Berger, Doris. *Projected Art History: Biopics, Celebrity Culture, and the Popularizing of American Art*. New York and London: Bloomsbury Academic, 2014.

Bingham, Dennis. *Whose Lives Are They Anyway? The Biopic as Contemporary Film Genre*. New Brunswick, NJ: Rutgers University Press, 2010.

Brown, Tom and Belén Vidal (eds.), *The Biopic in Contemporary Film Culture*. London: Routledge, 2013.

Cheshire, Ellen. *Bio-Pics: A Life in Pictures*. London and New York: Wallflower Press, 2015.

Custen, George F. *Bio/Pics: How Hollywood Constructed Public History*. New Brunswick, NJ: Rutgers University Press, 1992.

De Tirado, Heidi Denzel. "Les biopics des femmes fortes: réécriture biographiste, idéologique ou générique?" In Roswitha Böhm, Andrea Grewe, and Margarete Zimmermann (eds.), *Siècle classique et cinéma contemporain* (Biblio 17, vol. 179), 2009, 145–160.

Doris, Gary Alan. *Abraham Lincoln—An Uncommon, Common Man: A Narrative of His Life*. Indianapolis: Dog Ear Publishing, 2014.

Elsaesser, Thomas (ed.), *Early Cinema: Space, Frame, Narrative*. London: British Film Institute, 1990.

Ezra, E. *Georges Méliès: The Birth of the Auteur*. Manchester and New York: Manchester University Press, 2000.

Fontanel, Rémi. "Biopic: de la réalité à la fiction." *CinémAction*, no. 139. Condé-sur-Noireau: Editions Corlet, 2011.

Ford, Elizabeth A. and Deborah C. Mitchell. *Royal Portraits in Hollywood: Filming the Lives of Queens*. Lexington: University Press of Kentucky, 2009.

Gunning, Tom. "Cinema of Attractions." In Richard Abel (ed.), *Encyclopedia of Early Cinema*. London and New York: Routledge, 2005.

Hardie, Giles. "Big Names, Big Flops: Why the Biopics Have Failed in 2013." *Sydney Morning Herald*. http://www.smh.com.au/entertainment/movies/blogs/get-flickd/big-names-big-flops-why-the-biopics-have-failed-in-2013-20131025-2w58m.html, October 25, 2013. Accessed on November 2, 2017.

Hutcheon, Linda. *A Theory of Adaptation*. New York and London: Routledge, 2006.

Méliès, Georges. "Le premier 'Jeanne d'Arc' de 1897." *Revue de l'Association Française de Recherche sur l'Histoire du Cinéma*, Varia 64 (2011). http://1895.revues.org/4397. Accessed on November 2, 2017.

Moss, Mark. *Towards the Visualization of History: The Past as Image*. Lanham, MD: Lexington Books, 2009 [2008].

Neale, Stephen. *Genre and Hollywood*. London and New York: Routledge, 2000.

Polaschek, Bronwyn. *The Postfeminist Biopic: Narrating the Lives of Plath, Kahlo, Woolf and Austen*. New York: Palgrave Macmillan, 2013.

Reinhartz, Adele. *Jesus of Hollywood*. New York: Oxford University Press, 2007.

———.*Cinema*. London and New York: Routledge, 2005.

Rodowick, David Norman. *Gilles Deleuze's Time Machine*. Durham and London: Duke University Press, 1997.

Rosenstone, Robert A. *History on Film/Film History*. London and New York: Routledge, 2012 [2006].

Walpole, Horace. *Anecdotes of Painting in England*, 1763.

"Negro Girl (meager)": Black Women's In/Visibility in Contemporary Films About Slavery

Lisa Botshon and Melinda Plastas

In 2013 two major English-language films were released that confront viewers with moral questions about the value placed on black lives under British and US slavery and, by extension, the legacies of those systems of racism levied against black people today. Our particular interest rests in the filmic positioning of historical black women figures within slave systems, including resistance to slavery. Echoing the insistence of the contemporary hashtag #BlackLivesMatter, we ask in what ways do black women's lives matter in the histories conveyed in these films? #BlackLivesMatter is, notably, a gender-neutral term, but, despite its creation by black queer women, it has mainly been deployed in the mainstream media to mark the violence that targets straight black

---

L. Botshon (✉)
University of Maine at Augusta, Augusta, ME, USA
e-mail: botshon@maine.edu

M. Plastas
Bates College, Lewiston, ME, USA
e-mail: mplastas@bates.edu

© The Author(s) 2018   171
D. Letort and B. Lebdai (eds.), *Women Activists and Civil Rights Leaders in Auto/Biographical Literature and Films*,
https://doi.org/10.1007/978-3-319-77081-9_11

men. We know, however, that black women are also very vulnerable to violence in the contemporary U.S. In her piece "A Herstory of the #BlackLivesMatter Movement," Alicia Garza, one of the hashtag's creators, insists that it applies to a much broader set of truths. Among other assertions, Garza notes that the hashtag "is an acknowledgment that black women continue to bear the burden of a relentless assault on our children and our families and that assault is an act of state violence," and "the fact that black girls are used as negotiating chips during times of conflict and war is state violence." Yet these girls and women are often invisible or portrayed in very problematic ways in the larger discussions about violence against black people. Given the long history of the silencing of black women's voices, we consider how the development of a black feminist perspective can alter the way we tell our stories (Crenshaw and Ritchie 2015).

Directed by black British directors, both 2013 films endeavor to tell the story of a specific historical figure for which slavery features prominently. *12 Years a Slave*, based on Solomon Northup's 1853 eponymous autobiography and directed by Steve McQueen, depicts Northup's horrifying journey from living as a free man of color in Saratoga, New York, to his illegal capture in Washington, DC, his ensuing enslavement in Louisiana, and his eventual return to freedom. Despite the fact that this narrative focuses on a black man's experience, both the original work as well as Steve McQueen's filmic version perceive black women as intrinsic to Northup's story. In *Belle*, director Amma Asante and writer Misan Sagay relate the story of Dido Elizabeth Belle, a British woman born in 1763 of a union between Sir John Lindsay, a British Royal Navy officer, and an enslaved woman about whom little is known. Belle, as Amma Asante calls her, was raised in luxurious circumstances by her great uncle William Murray, Earl of Mansfield, and the Lord Chief Justice of England. To construct their narrative, Amma Asante and Sagay consulted an array of documents, including court records, visitors' letters, and an oil portrait of Belle and her white half-cousin, Elizabeth Murray, in part because Belle left no written account of her life. As is the case for films based on historical figures or events, these two films have been scrutinized for the "truthfulness" of the depictions of the events in the lives of their lead characters. And, while *12 Years a Slave* has garnered a higher profile and has engendered more controversy about its portrayal of slavery in the media, both films are notable for the ways in which they grapple with the problem of the (invisible) black woman in American and British history.

The Function of Black Women in *12 Years a Slave*

12 Years a Slave is a film of many firsts. It is the first film of its kind to be based on a slave narrative, but it is also the "first major studio-backed slavery film helmed by a black director," and it won numerous prestigious awards, including three Oscars (Gay 2014: 228).[1] Steve McQueen understands this film as part of a process of black empowerment, asserting that for black people the fact of slavery's history is a given: "That's your start in the world... What I would like to do is to embrace that past—to make it yours, to own it, to take it, to master it" (cited in Romney 2014). Furthermore, he contends, "I think people actually want to reflect on that horrendous recent past in order to go forward" (George 2013). Steve McQueen's project is thus quite significant in both the subject on which he focuses and the way he represents that focus. What is less clear, however, is how black women might own and move forward with the history that he chooses to tell.

Steve McQueen's attention to Northup's text and the location in which his story took place is noteworthy. He has said that 80% of the film's dialogue has been taken straight from the book (Romney 2014), which would be difficult to dispute, and his decision to film on location in Louisiana results in a verdant and authentic-looking setting against which the major events of the narrative unfold. But it is worth pointing out that Northup's narrative, like many slave narratives, was a mediated text upon its original publication, "edited" by or perhaps co-written with a white man from New York, David Wilson, and containing multiple authenticating documents by various white authors.[2] Moreover, this book would not even be in print today—and thus adapted for film—if, in the mid-twentieth century, a white Southern woman, Sue Eakin, hadn't helped resurrect it through a great deal of historical research and annotation. As Sylvie Charron has suggested elsewhere in this book, each mediation, including Steve McQueen's, adds a new prism to the narrative.

---

[1] Steve McQueen's film is not, moreover, the first filmic adaptation of Northup's narrative. Gordon Parks created a made-for-TV version in 1984.

[2] In his Preface, Wilson writes that "the only object of the editor has been to give a faithful history of Solomon Northup's life, as he received it from his lips," which suggests that Northup did not pen this narrative himself, although we know that he was literate. In their book *Solomon Northup: The Complete Story of the Author of Twelve Years a Slave*, David Fiske et al. consider the authorship issue and conclude, "Even if not the actual person who put pen to paper, Northup was very involved in its content" (Fiske et al. 2013: 113).

This is not meant to cast aspersions on the film, but it is important to stress the director's volition in telling his own truth about Northup's story.[3]

According to critic Brenda Stevenson, one of the aspects of Northup's autobiography that appealed to director Steve McQueen was the narrative's very conscientious depiction of slave women. While the work of course focuses on Northup's own story, how as a free-born, native New Yorker he was kidnapped, transported across many state lines, and held as a slave in territory that was foreign to him, there are also numerous sections concerning other slaves. Particularly noteworthy in the original narrative are his representations of slave women as strong, capable workers who are the equal of men in traditionally masculine arenas such as logging, team driving, and field work. In a portrayal of lumbering in the bayou, for example, he describes "four black girls" who come to help him and another man cut trees. Northup asserts, "They were excellent choppers, the largest oak or sycamore standing but a brief season before their heavy and well-directed blows." Indeed, he contends, "There are lumberwomen as well as lumbermen in the forests of the South. In fact, in the region of the Bayou Boeuf they perform their share of all the labor required on the plantation. They plough, drag, drive team, clear wild lands, work on the highway, and so forth" (Northup 2014: 108). While one might imagine that such skills might be perceived with disapproval in antebellum US culture, as these are far from the desired domestic qualities often ascribed to the middle-class and upper-class white woman, Northup's narrative invites unadulterated admiration.

Moreover, Northup's depictions of the specific women he befriends, including Eliza, a Washington DC mother who believes that she and her children are about to be emancipated when, instead, they are quite literally sold down the river, and Patsey, a remarkable woman who excels at many pursuits, including riding, rail splitting, and cotton picking,

---

[3] In a piece about the film adaptation for the online journal *The Root*, Skip Gates writes, "Some will ask, Is everything in the film version of *12 Years a Slave* accurate? My response is yes *and* no, for the truth is Solomon Northup himself changed some of the facts, including his birth and marriage dates, the spellings of certain names and, in an early play version, he even made the character of Samuel Bass more of a 'Yankee' than a Canadian. This points to a deeper truth about African-American culture, and one I have written about throughout my career: that signifying or black signification, by its very nature, is an act of repetition and revision, of invocation and improvisation, and so to me, the far more relevant question to ask of any representation of *12 Years a Slave* is not whether it is strictly factual but whether it is true. To this I say yes, without question...."

"NEGRO GIRL (MEAGER)": BLACK WOMEN'S IN/VISIBILITY ...   175

are tender and sensitive. Eliza is brutally separated from her children, who are sold to different masters, and Northup shows us through the course of his narrative how she is eventually depleted of her will to live as a result. Of Patsey he tells us, "She had a genial and pleasant temper, and was faithful and obedient. Naturally, she was a joyous creature, a laughing, light-hearted girl, rejoicing in the mere sense of existence" (Northup 2014: 134). The reader also discovers that Patsey "wept oftener, and suffered more, than any of her companions" because of the excessive cruelty directed at her by their "licentious master and... jealous mistress" (Northup 2014: 134).

As Stevenson reminds us, in the nineteenth century:

Published descriptions of the plight of enslaved women... made for an important abolitionist device intended to gain sympathy for their cause. True stories of the inability of enslaved women to maintain the gendered conventions of the day—domesticity, sexual purity, and maternal sacrifice—because of their status as physical and sexual laborers who could not be legally married or have parental control over their children, abound in published accounts from the late antebellum era. (Stevenson 2013)

Arguably, Northup's inclusion of female characters assisted with his abolitionist agenda. However, these characters were also sufficiently varied as to provide a broad representation of enslaved women, even as he focused on his own story.

True to Northup's narrative, Steve McQueen populates his film with multiple representations of black women, including the characters of Eliza and Patsey, not to mention Northup's wife, Anne. Unlike Northup, however, Steve McQueen trains his lens almost exclusively on women who are raped or turned into concubines, providing the viewer with a narrow understanding of the black female slave experience. Similarly, Steve McQueen creates female characters for his film that fit this limited characterization, such as Mistress Shaw, the black wife of a neighboring white plantation owner who has been elevated from slave status to that of plantation mistress. Also notable is Steve McQueen's addition of a scene in which Northup witnesses a white sailor about to rape a slave woman. When another male slave attempts to intervene, he is stabbed to death. This scene does not exist in Northup's original text, and, moreover, as Stephanie Li contends, "the scene is historically suspect." Steve McQueen makes other, comparable alterations to Northup's narrative by omitting slave women characters who demonstrate great feats of resistance, including the character of Celeste, who, according to Northup's original narrative, successfully hid in a swamp for the better part of a summer in order to heal from a lingering sickness and to avoid being "whipped to death" by her overseer (Northup 2014: 177). Importantly, the strong lumberwomen that Northup so admires are utterly absent from the story that Steve McQueen recounts.

Because Solomon Northup has a unique experience as a free man who is kidnapped and tricked into slavery and then freed by his Northern white friends twelve years later, his narrative can hardly be perceived as a "standard" slave experience in the nineteenth-century U.S. Steve McQueen clearly wants to tell Northup's story as a singular, yet important chapter in the history of American slavery, not to mention national understandings of freedom more broadly, but he also gestures toward a larger slave history, a history that acknowledges that most enslaved black people were not liberated by well-connected friends; nor were they able to successfully escape their bondage. Steve McQueen does this primarily through the character of Patsey, whom the viewer sees demonically pursued by her sexually obsessed white male owner, Epps, tormented by her jealous white mistress, and ultimately left behind to suffer her situation interminably after Northup is restored to his previous circumstances as a free man. It is Patsey whom the viewer sees being raped, Patsey who is mercilessly flayed, Patsey who is erratically struck, and Patsey whose condition the viewer understands will not change until her death or emancipation in 1865, whichever comes first. Notably, the historical record continues to remain silent on Patsey's life beyond Northup's narrative.[4]

There was no small measure of controversy about Patsey in the blogosphere upon the release of the film, as her situation is so traumatic and unending, and because it is her body that bears the brunt of the film's violence while the narrative revolves around Solomon. And, indeed, as Janell Hobson argues, "the focal point for much of Patsey's suffering... is on her body, from scarred back to disfigured eye (at the hands of her mistress). Patsey's body is the object of our horror and pity, but her internal reflections remain hidden" (Hobson 2013). Commenting on the scene in which Patsey is brutally whipped, first by Northup at Epps'

---

[4]In a lengthy piece for *Vanity Fair*, Katie Calautti chronicles her nearly two-month search through archives, town records, and the like for any evidence of Patsey after the Civil War to no avail.

insistence, and then by Epps himself, Roxane Gay asserts, "The scene is visceral, as it should be, but it also feels gratuitous because the scene is not designed to amplify Patsey's plight. The scene is designed to amplify Solomon's plight, as if he is the more tragic figure in this situation" (Gay 2014: 230). She adds, "What I resent in *12 Years a Slave* is how the suffering of women is used to further a man's narrative" (2014: 231). Stephanie Li contends that the narrative "highlights the inability of black men to protect enslaved women from rape, physical abuse, and the hardships of work all slaves endured. While Northup is explicit in his written narrative about his despair in seeing women like Eliza and Patsey beaten, Steve McQueen repeatedly dramatizes male impotence" (Li 2014: 258).[5]

In other words, then, while Patsey's physical and psychological degradations at the hands of the Eppses are essential to the viewer's understanding of Solomon Northup's emasculation as a formerly free man who now toils at the brutal will of another, Patsey's voice is conspicuously absent from Steve McQueen's dramatization. The viewer of the film does not quite comprehend how exceptional Patsey is perceived to be by the textual narrative. As the daughter of a "Guinea" woman "brought over to Cuba in a slave ship," she is the only one of Epps' slaves with a close ancestral tie to Africa, and in the original narrative she carries an "air of loftiness in her movement, that neither labor, nor weariness, nor punishment could destroy" (Northup 2014: 133). Moreover, Northup assesses Patsey as a person who, in other circumstances, "would have been chief among ten thousand of her people" (Northup 2014: 133). In contrast, Steve McQueen's film depicts Patsey with lesser degrees of volition; in scenes that depart from the original text, she makes corn husk dolls during the little free time she is afforded; she seeks solace and soap from a neighboring plantation; and, most notably, she begs Northup to take her life as her existence on the Epps' farm is unbearable. However, these moments neglect to provide an equivalent sense of Patsey's extraordinary character. Neither do they add up to what bell hooks bids black women to do, which is to "see our history as a counter memory, using it as a way to know the present and invent the future." In fact, hooks herself has

---

[5]The use of Patsey to further Northup's story is also noted by scholar Vincent Woodard, who makes a parallel argument about the textual version of *12 Years a Slave*: he contends that the presence of Patsey and her transformation from "a joyous creature" to a constantly abused, depressed woman serves a "utilitarian purpose in relationship to Northup's assaulted masculinity" (Woodard 2014: 258).

condemned the film for "negat[ing] the black female voice." She asserts, "What I want for us all the time is a pushing of the imagination... I'm tired of the naked, raped, beaten black woman body. I want to see an image of black femaleness that alters our universe in some way" (hooks 2013). While, as Steve McQueen's numerous accolades attest, many aspects of *12 Years a Slave* are laudable, including his willingness to grapple with the violent history of Black people in the U.S., the director's erasure of the black woman's voice from these annals remains troubling.

BELLE: A BLACK WOMAN ENTERS THE DRAWING ROOM

Arguably, director Amma Asante is more successful at creating a fresh representation of a black woman character in her eighteenth-century biopic *Belle*. This work offers an interesting counterpoint to *12 Years a Slave* in its approach to larger questions about slavery, memory, law, commerce, spectatorship, and the black female body. The differences between the two films may be attributable to the (feminist) intentions of *Belle*'s filmmakers and the choices they made in relationship to the paucity of the source material available. However, the general lack of biographical and autobiographical material about Dido Elizabeth Belle also allows for a film that is less a study of the title character and more a meditation on how slavery and people of color are depicted and remembered. Further, the centrality of the infamous *Zong* slave ship to the film and Dido's racialized and gendered coming of age, especially when read alongside the rich postcolonial literature about the *Zong*, entreats us to embrace *Belle* as an opportunity to engage in the ongoing "hauntological rethinking of justice" (Baucom 2005: 63). For in the film Dido Elizabeth Belle signifies the potential embodiment of the irretrievable—from the enslaved mother she barely knew to the innumerable enslaved Africans jettisoned into the Atlantic. Finally, this film takes risks by utilizing a genre in which black women are almost never cast as the protagonist—the period costume drama.

The creation of the film began with screenwriter Misan Sagay's chance viewing of the 1779 portrait of Belle and her white half-cousin Elizabeth Murray at the Scone Palace in Scotland in 2004. The portrait intrigued Sagay for it seemed to mark a break in the convention of portraying women of color as subservient or "pets" to their white counterparts (BBC Woman's Hour Radio). Recognizing that the portrait might be "an entry into a much bigger story," Sagay spent the next six years researching and writing the script for what would eventually become the movie. Aware of the film industry's predilection for telling ostensibly black stories through the narration of a white savior, Sagay determined to forestall the "Wilberforcing" of her script (Scripts and Scribes 5). As she states: "I didn't want anyone to save 'free' Belle. She had to free herself" (Scripts and Scribes 3). Film director Amma Asante, whose Tumblr hashtag pronounces #tochangethegame, shared Sagay's interest in making a film disruptive of the raced/gendered politics and white redemption narratives endemic to the mainstream movie industry. And, like Sagay, viewing the 1779 portrait of Belle and her cousin figured significantly in her divining of Belle's interiority and fashioning of the film's aesthetics. For although the eighteenth-century portrait predictably positioned Belle, who is referred to as Dido in the film, behind her cousin, Dido's forward-focused and uncustomarily direct gaze set the course for the film. For Amma Asante Dido's pictorial gaze declared: "I am here. I'm relevant. I'm a lady. I'm brown. I'm made up of many things. I'm happy with who I am" (Kellaway 2014). Out of the silences of the archives and under the skillful fashioning of Sagay and Amma Asante, Dido Elizabeth Belle emerges as an eighteenth-century black protofeminist and as the heroine of the *Zong* slave case.

By birthright both a slave and an aristocrat, Dido must negotiate the complexity of late eighteenth-century British society and empire. These complexities are foregrounded in the opening scene of the film when Dido's father retrieves the six-year-old Dido from a London slum telling her, "I am here to take you to a good life, a life that you were born to."[6] Lord Lindsay, who must return to the navy, takes Dido to Kenwood Manor where she will be raised by his aunt and his uncle, the Earl of Mansfield. He instructs his aunt and uncle that although "she is black... she is my blood." When Lord Lindsay dies soon after Dido arrives at Kenwood, Dido's substantial inheritance amplifies the intricacy of her situation. Because of her race Dido is forbidden to dine with the Mansfields during the evening meal, while her paternal class lineage prohibits her from dining with Mable, the black maid. In this historical costume drama, the web of gender, race, wealth, and aristocratic law are made apparent when it comes to questions of marriage and love. Dido's patrilineal wealth elevates her suitability for marriage above that of her

---

[6] Quotations are from the 2013 film *Belle* unless otherwise noted.

white cousin, who possesses a meager dowry in comparison. Although monied, Dido must contend with the surveillance of her body and accompanying racially disparaging remarks by the white British elite— "she is intriguing," "she is a beast," "she is repulsive"—and mistreatment from suitors and their family members. In one dramatic scene the mother of a suitor gazes at Dido who is sitting silently and demands, "Does she have a tongue?" to which Dido forcefully replies: "I have a tongue!" In this moment, despite her racially marginalized position among British aristocracy, *Belle*'s filmmakers insist on providing her with a voice. And this voice allows her to both advocate for herself and all others affected by British slavery. Throughout the film Dido questions the conventions of the day, from marriage protocol, to the racial social rules within Kenwood Manor, to the legality of the trade in enslaved people.

Belle approaches the impact of slavery on the black body and psyche quite differently than *12 Years a Slave*. Two dissimilarities are readily notable: the lack of onscreen moments of physical violence in *Belle* and how *Belle*'s filmmakers instruct the audience in the visual politics of race and gender, something completely missing from *12 Years a Slave*. Because Sagay and Amma Asante elect to interrogate issues of slavery, race, and gender through the lens of a historical costume drama, they are able to point to moments of violence in ways that not only refrain from depictions of assaults against the black female body, but that remind the viewer of aspects of loss that are generally absent from our storytelling. As a domestic narrative focused on the legitimacy of kinship, *Belle* cannily displaces the violence of slavery to the drawing room. Unlike Steve McQueen's film, where Patsey's back story is never imagined, even as Northup reveals some of it in his text, in *Belle* the viewer is invited to imagine what it might be like for a "Negro girl (meager)" to lose her mother, to be simultaneously cherished by and segregated from her extended family, to negotiate marriage from a position of concomitant privilege and marginality, all of which is inflected by the specter of slavery (Fig. 1).

From the outset the filmmakers frame *Belle* as a multilayered and multidirectional reflection on the power of the gaze. The film self-consciously and actively engages the audience in a dialogue about the white gaze: how it may have affected Dido's self-consciousness, how it influenced and narrated the racial projects of the British Empire and how it shapes the cinema we consume today. The centrality of the gaze to the

Fig. 1 *Belle* (Gugu Mbatha-Raw) appears on equal footing with her half-cousin (Sarah Gadon). © Fox Searchlight Pictures/Photofest

film and the multivalence of the gaze itself emerge early when we watch a very young Dido walking along one of the lush hallways of Kenwood Manor that is lined with sculptures and paintings. Along her way Dido stops and studies a painting that depicts as happy and carefree a very young enslaved boy, similar in age to her, who is accompanying his master. Here Dido confronts the dialectics of human value and art and the dire consequences of the white imagination for black existence; in this moment she realizes that the painting reassures whites of the benevolence of slavery and the acquiescence of the enslaved. As such it, and the plenitude of similar paintings of the era, helped shape the conditions in which black lives become objects that could be purchased, owned, exchanged, ignored, or eternally removed. As Dido states, "Just like in life we are no better in paintings." As film viewers, we travel with Dido as her racial consciousness sharpens and she pieces together the interdependence of systems of racial signification, commodification, and value. Ultimately, Dido comes to recognize that the art that fills Kenwood Manor is directly implicated in the creation and maintenance of British slavery.

As we argue above, in the film version of *12 Years a Slave*, Steve McQueen produces a problematically reductive depiction of the impact of slavery on black women. The violent sexual mistreatment of the black female body, as presented by Steve McQueen, serves as a trope for black women's lives during slavery. As such, the complexities of the black female experience are erased, thus hindering our understanding of the multifaceted dynamics of slavery, including black women's vulnerabilities and resistances to slavery. Despite the significance of Steve McQueen's contributions to the representation of black American history, his film's portrayal of black women—and the multiple endorsements of that film—ultimately contribute to a circulation of problematic images of black women. *Belle*, on the other hand, while a much less celebrated film, provides us with a multidimensional experience of the black female presence on screen and in proximity to slavery. Dido, played by Gugu Mbatha-Raw, commands this historical costume drama with her serene and yet powerful poise and elegant beauty. Director Amma Asante explains that she selected Mbatha-Raw because she wanted someone who possessed an "innate grace" and "yet you look at her and say: she makes sense and doesn't." The issue of making sense references again the filmmaker's engagement with canonical visual portrayals of black women. The film breaks with the historical costume genre, one in which black women have never appeared except as servants and slaves, by portraying Dido as beautiful, desirable, and in charge of her own life. As Amma Asante explains, she wanted to "make a movie that had something to say and was lush and beautiful" (Rickey 2014). *Belle*, as a costume drama about slavery featuring a black female heroine, works to remind the viewer of the centrality of domestic spaces to the maintenance of the political, cultural, and social economies of slavery and race as it also, through Dido, contests ideas about race, beauty, and belonging.

NEGRO GIRL (MEAGER). I'M RELEVANT

Amma Asante's film highlights how violence against black bodies is ever-present and yet rarely at the center of the white Western gaze. Through the costume drama, *Belle* brings attention to the scores of now nameless victims of a particularly brutal incident during the eighteenth-century slave trade. In 1782 the *Zong*, a British slave ship transporting 442 enslaved Africans to Jamaica, became the center of a British legal battle over slavery and commerce when news broke that the ship's owner sought insurance reimbursement for the enslaved Africans who died during the Atlantic voyage. Over a period of three days, the ship's captain, Luke Collingwood, commanded the crew to kill 162 of the Africans by throwing them overboard alive. Some reports indicate that on the first evening of killings, "Fifty-four women and children were pushed through cabin windows" (Bryne 191). Reasoning that he could not fetch a good price for those who had become ill since leaving the West Coast of Africa, Collingwood decided it would be most expedient to "jettison" the ill and then make an insurance claim for the lost "cargo." White British abolitionist Granville Sharpe learned of the *Zong* in March of 1783 from fellow abolitionist Olaudah Equiano. Equiano, a former slave and a London abolitionist, notified Sharpe about the details of the atrocity and conveyed to him that a jury had just ruled in favor of the insurance claim made by the ship's owner, James Gregson. Sharpe helped fund the successful appeal of the decision and, along with Equiano and other abolitionists, made the *Zong* into what is now a canonical example of what Paul Gilroy, Ian Baucom, Gayatri Spivak, Marx, and others explore as the web of modernity, human value, and capital flow. The appeal of the *Zong* ruling occurred in 1783 and was adjudicated in both real life and in the filmic narrative by Belle's uncle, Lord Mansfield.

The actual role of Elizabeth Dido Belle in the appeal of the first *Zong* decision and Lord Mansfield's early antislavery decision, the Somerset Case, is much debated. According to some readings of the slim historical records, including that of Henry Louis Gates, it is possible that Belle functioned as a legal secretary of sorts for her uncle (Gates 2014). Others, including screenwriter Sagay and director Amma Asante, transform the silences of the written records into an opportunity to breathe black life into the white sanctum of legal history and history. Belle can be read as both a filmic ghost, a specter of black lives lost, and an agentive black superwoman who delivers a modicum of justice.[7] As divined and delivered by Sagay and Amma Asante, *Belle* coheres with the contemporary work of postcolonial writers, many of them black feminists, who have been exploring the meaning and place of the *Zong* in our rememberings and forgettings of the past and ongoing atrocities of the Black Atlantic.

---

[7] Many have written about the relevance of ghosts in depictions of the transatlantic slave trade. See, for instance, Guyanese novelist Fred D'Aguiar's 1997 *Feeding the Ghosts* and Ghanaian writer Ama Ata Aidoo's 1970 play *Anowa*.

For example, M. NourbeSe Philip's (2008) book-length poem sequence *Zong!* "is populated entirely by words and anagrammatic rear-rangements of letters from the 500-word legal decision" which were at the heart of Lord Mansfield's decision to hold a new trial (Fehskens 2012: 408). Philip, a Caribbean Canadian lawyer and poet, haunted by the high regard and finality bestowed upon the legal text, dismantles and restrings the letters and words that comprise it in hopes that, through her act of rearrangement, traces of the black lives lost might surface. Philip's work shares with other scholars an interest in "untelling" (Fehskens 2012: 409) the courtroom-heavy abolitionist-focused narrative of the *Zong* case and, in endeavoring to reimagine the story from what Saidiya Hartman calls the "locus of impossible speech," the speech of all the black lives lost to slavery (cited in Fehskens 2012: 409). Or as Lindon Barrett contends, the historical dehumanization of black lives requires that we "pursue novel or original access to meaning, voice, value and authority" (Philip 2008: 207).

Through her creation of *Belle*, Amma Asante continues the contem-porary quest for an "untelling" in order to create a new narrative of the slave trade and its meaning for black possibility. Dido marks and embodies the black absences in the *Zong* legal proceedings and decision. The legal decision in the *Zong* case may have announced that the slave trade was reprehensible, and the killing of enslaved people for money wrong, but it told us little about the enslaved Africans who were killed. They were now to be considered something other than (human) cargo, but what? And who were they? What were their names, their loves, and their desires? In preparing to write her two hundred and twenty-page poem *Zong!* Philip reviewed the ship's logs in hopes of finding names registered for the Africans on board. No names were listed, only columns enumerating the numbers of men, women and children. One entry, *Negro Girl (meager)*, as troublesome as it was, offered Philip a glimmer of embodiment, and a hint to the humanity of the jettisoned lives (Saunders 2008: 7).

The most consequential enactment of black female subjectivity occurs when Dido is depicted stealthily stealing a document from her uncle's office that will prove pivotal to the positive outcome of the appeal. At this moment the filmmakers render Dido as ultimately responsible for the resurrection of the lives of the 162 murdered Africans. As such, it is Dido's actions that render it possible to officially and publicly mourn and honor all lives lost to the slave trade. Significantly, one of the lives Dido brings forward from ghostly existence is that of her mother. Although her mother did not die on the *Zong*, details about her life are lost to

Dido. As Dido explains early in the film: "I knew little of my mother, other than the color she has given me." These words spoken by Dido serve as the powerful marker of the impact of slavery on the black female body. By birthright and law, Dido, like her mother and those on board the *Zong*, was a slave. Her own legal freedom, in fact, was not secured until Lord Mansfield's death, when his will revealed, "I confirm to Dido Elizabeth Belle her freedom."

The filmic Dido is assigned an unprecedented degree of autonomy for her class, gender, and race in both her quest for legal justice for the victims of the *Zong* and when she is depicted falling in love with aspiring abolitionist John Davinier who is white, but below her in class; the son of a clergyman, Davinier yearns to be a lawyer. Belle first meets Davinier and learns about the *Zong* when Davinier visits Kenwood Manor to engage Mansfield about the case. Belle, who assists her great-uncle with his work, witnesses the conversation. Earnestly, Davinier explains to Belle that he "wants to make the laws and change this world." Belle's witnessing represents more than her first knowledge of the *Zong* case; this scene exposes Belle's gendered and raced position. Unable to be one who "makes the laws" through the vagaries of race and gender norms, Belle actively watches over the proceedings between the patriarchs, establishing herself as the collective consciousness of those unnamed black lives lost at sea: *Negro Girl (meager). I'm Relevant.* Upon learning from Davinier during a conversation in one of the grand hallways at Kenwood Manor that the *Zong* was a "human cargo ship," Dido determines to assist in the case. From this point on, she becomes confrontational with her great-uncle, one of the most powerful men in Britain and the judge who will ultimately determine the outcome of the *Zong* case.

In order to find the ship owners guilty of insurance fraud, the prosecution needed to secure evidence that the captain lied about the health of the enslaved "cargo" and the captain's inability to obtain provisions necessary to keep the slaves alive. Lord Mansfield initially insists to the abolitionists that no such evidence exists. Yet Dido finds ship records in Lord Mansfield's study that indicate fraud on the part of the captain and his business partners. Belle steals the documents, delivers them to Davinier and his male abolitionist friends, who render them visible—and thus actionable—to Mansfield. In Amma Asante's telling, it is Dido's securing of the incriminating materials that changes the course of history. Killing black people in order to make an insurance claim could no longer be justified in British jurisprudence. Amma Asante's Lord Mansfield rules, "It is not legal, nor is it right."

CONCLUSION

Although neither Amma Asante nor historians know, for sure, what Dido's influence was on the case and Lord Mansfield's ruling, in the film Belle is cast as an actor as well as a witness. The viewer observes Dido arrive on the upper balcony of the courtroom just in time to watch the announcement of the decision. The balcony is full of men, mostly white, though some black. Positioning Belle, *Negro Girl (meager)*. *I'm Relevant*, in the balcony but on its periphery suggests the history of black female witnessing—a witnessing not bound by jurisprudence and regal courtrooms, but by humanity in the face of suffering, perseverance in the face of erasure. Dido's gaze instructs the film's viewers about how to see the past. While the gendered historicity of slavery offers at best a liminal black female standpoint, *Belle* foregrounds the black female presence. Moreover, it follows Hartman's invocation to "do the impossible" and "reclaim" the mother lost to slavery (Hartman 2007: 162). As such Amma Asante's bold, beautiful, and self-assured Dido haunts the world that forgets the lives lost in the Atlantic. Here, then, is an image of a black woman who matters in every sense of that word, and who is given the filmic time and space to assert her relevance to *Belle*'s viewers. Amma Asante successfully transforms Dido's gaze from the original eighteenth-century painting into a contemporary portrait that is assertive and canny. As such, *Belle* disrupts the dominant filmic slave narrative as it foregrounds the interiority of slavery's violence and consequences. Viewers conditioned to expect depictions of physical brutality are now directed to consider the various registers of harm precipitated by slavery including the role on intimates, like Dido's Mansfield family, in justifying and prolonging the "peculiar institution."

12 Years a Slave and *Belle* both contend with the ongoing and impossible quest to reconcile the histories and legacies of slavery and engage forthrightly, as Hartman and others do, with critical questions about memory, forgetting, and loss.[8] As such, the films offer us venues for contending with today's echoes of slavery, including the 1800-plus lives, 93% of whom were black, lost in 2005 during Hurricane Katrina in Louisiana; the ongoing tragedies as thousands of Africans attempting to reach Europe are either lost at sea or detained; and the entrenched structural racism in the U.S. that violently restricts and assaults the lives of people of

[8] See, for instance David Scott, "Introduction: On the Archaeologies of Black Memory." *Anthurium: A Caribbean Studies Journal*, vol. 6, no. 1 (2008), Article 2.

color. While the impact of slavery on the lives of black women has received increasing attention from scholars, artists, novelists, and filmmakers, the task continues. The efforts produce uneven results, as the two films we have discussed here reveal. In an interview soon after the release of *Belle*, director Amma Asante contended, "I would not want audiences to come to see *Belle* and think they were going to see a *12 Years a Slave Mark 2*." Amma Asante's need to assert that *Belle* is not a derivative slave film, and neither are black women's experiences derivative experiences of slavery, signals the irony of the current moment in which we live. And, indeed, Amma Asante is able to forward a vision of an historical black woman figure who is able to make her way in the world with vision and purpose. In this way, Amma Asante contributes to the call of the queer feminist founders of the #BlackLivesMatter movement to bring the marginalized into the center of the movement, history, and our consciousness.

WORKS CITED

Aidoo, Ama Ata. *The Dilemma of a Ghost and Anowa*. London: Pearson, 1995.

Baucom, Ian. *Specters of the Atlantic: Finance Capital, Slavery, and the Philosophy of History*. Durham, NC: Duke University Press, 2005.

Calautti, Katie. "'What Will Become of Me?' Finding the Real Patsey of *12 Years a Slave*." *Vanity Fair*, March 2, 2014. Accessed on June 18, 2015.

Charron, Sylvie. "Ghost Writing and Filming Oral History in *12 Years a Slave*." In Delphine Letort and Benaouda Lebdai (eds.), *Civil Rights Auto/Biographical Film and Literature*. Basingstoke: Palgrave Macmillan, 2018.

Cliff, Michelle. *Free Enterprise: The Making of Mary Ellen Pleasant*, 1994.

Crenshaw, Kimberle and Andrea J. Ritchie. *Say Her Name: Resisting Police Brutality Against Black Women*. New York: African American Policy Forum, July 2015.

D'Aguiar, Fred. *Feeding the Ghosts*. Long Grove, IL: Waveland Press, 1997.

Fehskens, Erin M. "Accounts Unpaid, Accounts Untold, M. NourbeSe Philip's *Zong*! and the Catalogue." *Callaloo*, vol. 35, no. 2 (Spring 2012): 407–424.

Fiske, David et al. *Solomon Northup: The Complete Story of the Author of Twelve Years a Slave*. Santa Barbara, CA: Praeger, 2013.

Garza, Alicia. "A Herstory of the #BlackLivesMatter Movement." *The Feminist Wire*, October 7, 2014. Accessed on January 14, 2015.

Gates, Henry Louis. "*12 Years a Slave*: Trek from Slave to Screen." *The Root*, March 3, 2014. Accessed on June 17, 2016.

Gates, Henry Louis. "The Political Romance of 'Belle'." *Ms.*, June 4, 2014.

Gates, Henry Louis. "Who Was the Real Dido Elizabeth Belle?" *The Root*, August 26, 2014.

Gay, Roxane. *Bad Feminist: Essays*. New York: Harper Perennial, 2014.

George, Nelson. "An Essentially American Narrative: A Discussion of Steve McQueen's Film *12 Years a Slave*." *New York Times*, October 11, 2013. Accessed on February 8, 2016.

Hartman, Saidiya. *Lose Your Mother: A Journey Along the Atlantic Slave Route*. New York: Farrar, Straus & Giroux, 2007.

Hobson, Janell. "Imagining Patsey's Rescue by Harriet Tubman (Or, Marie Laveau's Vengeance)." *The Feminist Wire*, November 8, 2013. Accessed on January 14, 2016.

hooks, bell. "The Oppositional Gaze: Black Female Spectators." In Amelia Jones (ed.), *The Feminism and Visual Culture Reader*. New York: Routledge, 2002.

hooks, bell. Interview. "Watch this Amazing Conversation Between bell hooks and Melissa Harris-Perry." *Bitch Magazine*, November 8, 2013. Accessed on February 8, 2016.

Kellaway, Kate. "Amma Asante: 'I'm Bi-cultural, I Walk the Division that Belle Walked Every Day." *The Guardian*, May 18, 2014.

Li, Stephanie. "*12 Years a Slave* as a Neo-Slave Narrative." *American Literary History*, vol. 26, no. 2 (2014): 326–331 (*Project MUSE*, Web, accessed on January 9, 2015).

Northup, Solomon. *12 Years a Slave [1853]*. Los Angeles: Graymalkin Media, 2014.

Philip, M. NourbeSe. *Zong!* Middletown, CT: Wesleyan University Press, 2008.

Rickey, Carrie. "A Portrait and the History It Holds: 'Belle' and Slavery's End in Britain." *New York Times*, April 25, 2014.

Romney, Jonathan. "A History of Violence." *Sight & Sound*, vol. 24, no. 2 (2014): 28–32 (Art Full Text (H.W. Wilson), Web, January 9, 2015).

Saunders, Patricia. "Defending the Dead, Confronting the Archives: A Conversation with M. NourbeSe Philip." *Small Axe*, 63–79, June 26, 2008.

Scott, David. "Introduction: On the Archaeologies of Black Memory." *Anthurium: A Caribbean Studies Journal*, vol. 6, no. 1 (2008), Article 2.

Stevenson, Brenda. "The Surprisingly Central Role of Slave Women in *12 Years a Slave*." *History News Network*, October 18, 2013. Accessed on February 8, 2016.

Walvin, James. *The Zong: A Massacre, the Law and the End of Slavery*. New Haven: Yale University Press, 2011.

Williams, Andreá N. "Sex, Marriage, and *12 Years a* (Single) *Slave*." *American Literary History*, vol. 26, no. 2 (2014): 347–353 (*Project MUSE*, Web, accessed on January 9, 2016).

Woodard, Vincent. *The Delectable Negro: Human Consumption and Homoeroticism within U.S. Slave Culture*. New York: New York University Press, 2014.

Queering the Biopic? *Milk* (2008) and the Biographic Real

Isabelle Van Peteghem-Tréard

According to Dennis Bingham, the emergence of highly self-reflexive biopics, such as *Man on the Moon* (1999) and *I'm Not There* (2007), provides evidence of the genre's "evolution from classicism to parody to contestation and critique" or "deconstruction" (Bingham 2010: 18). Bingham applies this term to describe films which attempt to provide alternative approaches in the representation of biographical subjects portrayed on screen. This marks a departure from the classical generic form which is typically defined by its "official" biographical depiction of a "real person whose real name is used" (Custen 1992: 5). The function of the biopic, as Bingham asserts, is not historical precision: it is a form of entertainment that demonstrates how or why that star persona is significant and how this may help us, as film audiences, learn about our own society and culture.

In a *Newsweek* article, published in February 2010 under the banner headline "The Death of the Biopic," the commentator announced the following: "Like popcorn and Milk Duds, the biopic has long been a Hollywood staple and often a big moneymaker [...] but in the

---

I. Van Peteghem-Tréard (✉)
CinéSup, Nantes, France

© The Author(s) 2018   189
D. Letort and B. Lebdai (eds.), *Women Activists and Civil Rights Leaders in Auto/Biographical Literature and Films*,
https://doi.org/10.1007/978-3-319-77081-9_12

190   I. van PETEGHEM-TRÉARD

last five years it has begun to feel as dusty and outdated as the set of Encyclopedia Britannicas in your parents' attic" (Setoodeh 2010). According to the article the biopic is considered too staid and outmoded to appeal to modern audiences. Such opinion is typical of negative critical accusations leveled toward the biopic, leading some to claim that "it may be the most maligned of all film genres" (Bingham 2010: 11). Indeed, one might regard the iconic status of historic personalities as a problematic hindrance to any creator's originality if it entails more hagiography than creativity. In assessing how the biopic functions as an "official" portrayal of a "real" person, it is clear a potent tension exists between the dual impulses of realist depiction and creative conjecture.

Gus Van Sant's celebratory portrait of pioneering gay activist Harvey Milk, played by Sean Penn, shows him earning his place in history by being elected in 1977 to the San Francisco Board of Supervisors, the first openly gay man to hold public office in the U.S. As a biographical movie, *Milk* raises several questions that are typical of the biopic genre itself, the issue of truthfulness, respect, representation, legacy, bias, which are also central to other films such as *The Iron Lady* (Phyllida Lloyd, 2011), *Lincoln* (Steven Spielberg, 2012), *J. Edgar* (Clint Eastwood, 2011), to quote but a few recent ones. But it also fueled controversy as to the treatment of queer identity politics which was analyzed as far too mainstream by some critics.

Art transforms reality into reality effects, which implies staging and appropriation, and a sublimation of reality. Gus Van Sant's cinema is more real than realistic, from the Lacanian notion of the *Real*[1] as what remains inexpressible in the symbolic but returns to haunt the subject. His films are suffused with a return of the repressed which is

---

[1] The Lacanian concepts of real, imaginary, and symbolic are the structures of the psyche that control our desires and constitute the three orders of the intersubjective world, as theorized by Lacan. The concept of the imaginary indicates both the capacity to form images and the alienating effect of identification with them, as in the mirror stage. The symbolic is primarily the order of culture and language; this is the order into which the subject is inserted or inscribed thanks to the Oedipus complex and submission to the name of the father. It is the social world of linguistic communication, intersubjective relations, knowledge of ideological conventions, and the acceptance of the law (also called the "Big Other"). The real is not synonymous with external or empirical reality, but refers to that which lies outside the symbolic and that which returns to haunt the subject in disorders like psychosis (Lacan 1986: 71).

displayed through circularity, repetitions, long sequences. Van Sant, the experimental director of *Gerry* (2002), *Elephant* (2003), *Paranoid Park* (2007), and *Last Days* (2005), resorts to *cinéma-vérité* techniques but also abandons the documentary mandate to impose his own filmic obsessions and aesthetic idiosyncrasies in *Milk*. But Van Sant is not only an emblem for independent cinema, he also directed Hollywood block-busters such as *Finding Forrester* (2000) or *Good Will Hunting* (1997). His elasticity and adaptability are therefore clearly established as both an *auteur* and a mainstream artist. Of course, the difference here stems from his choice of subject matter since this is the first time the filmmaker chose to focus on a real political figure and icon, Harvey Milk.

Harvey Milk was born on Long Island, New York, in 1930, the son of Eastern European Jews. The Korean War veteran held jobs on Wall Street and in 1964 worked for the presidential campaign of right-wing Republican Barry Goldwater. Swept up by the counterculture of the 1960s and 1970s, Milk openly acknowledged his sexual orientation and eventually fell in with a bohemian milieu in San Francisco. He became an advocate of gay rights, and finally ran for public office before he was assassinated by Dan White in November 1978, along with the city's mayor, George Moscone. Van Sant's film essentially recounts Milk's six-year career in San Francisco politics.

Thus, this article engages with Gus Van Sant's aesthetic choices in an effort not only to appropriate the history of a murdered politician and tackle the political issue of homophobia and the evolution of San Francisco in the 1970s, but also to bring his own personal touch to the biopic. The mixed feelings of some gay critics about the movie come indeed from the tension between exploring a popular genre and repre-senting queer identity in a transgressive creation both in form and con-tent. Focusing on *Milk*'s compliance with the generic frame of the biopic, this essay will also explore the political and poetical Real of the movie *Milk* and the difficult process of sublimation of history and legacy (Fig. 1).

THE BIOPIC: FIDELITY AS A FRAME

The first challenge posed by the biopic is the constraint of historical accuracy. It implies a relation of truthfulness to a period and also some research on the original subject so as to imbue the movie with reality effects. Being underpinned by reenactment, biopics often stage and value similarities with the original personality and subject matter.

Fig. 1 Gus Van Sant's celebratory portrait of pioneering gay activist Harvey Milk (Sean Penn) shows him earning his place in history. © Focus Features/Photofest Photographer: Phil Bray

QUEERING THE BIOPIC? *MILK* (2008) AND THE BIOGRAPHIC REAL   193

Here is how Gus Van Sant presented his relation to the historical material and the difficulties stemming from the charisma and stature of Harvey Milk:

> This is the first time that I have really made something that is a historical document. But it really is something else. When Henry Fonda plays young Lincoln, you are not supposed to be thinking that he is actually Lincoln. It is a pantomime or a political passion play. As a creator you want to be able to play with it and not be overburdened by the historical accuracy. But at the same time, you want to stay true to Milk. In some cases, it was easier since we had actual footage, so what we shot was what was exactly what happened. (Bowen 2008)

Indeed, Gus Van Sant had to do some research on biographical elements and also decide upon which aspects to focus. He was also well aware of the existence of prior works. Before the movie *Milk*, there was *The Life and Times of Harvey Milk: The Mayor of Castro Street*, written by Randy Shilts and published in 1982. The journalist interviewed many people who knew Milk from school, work, as friends or enemies. Shilts even offered a complete "transcript" of Milk's "death tape," which named possible successors and ruled others out. The book also created a controversy because several gay historical figures, among whom Cleve Jones, who is depicted in the biography, disagreed with some statements.

In the Academy Award-winning documentary *The Times of Harvey Milk* (Robert Epstein 1984), Epstein explained that he wanted to create a *vérité*-styled film and that he determined the three core ingredients to his film would be news footage, archival footage, and original interviews. Van Sant's movie thus exploited some of the resources and elements present in Epstein's version while integrating his own relation to temporality. Even if the director has an *auteurist* approach to filmmaking, the biopic relies on conventions that cannot be eschewed considering that the genre relies on a process of recognition which will allow the historical subject to be identifiable by the public. Van Sant was also faced with this difficulty in his desire both to exploit previous material while leading his own research and shed new light upon Milk's story:

> We were striving for as true-to-life a re-creation of the story as possible in the sets, the costumes, the performances and the dialogue. Since these people have very detailed, sometimes painful but also beautiful memories

of what really happened, that helped us re-create so much more. There was this whole other layer of meaning and truth and beauty in making *Milk* that you don't usually get on projects. It was extraordinary. (Nicoletta 2008/2009)

The first element often displayed by biopics in order to achieve accuracy is resemblance. Indeed, a major component of what makes *Milk* such a compelling film is the acting. On a purely technical level the combination of skilled casting and makeup created a group of actors who all bore an uncanny resemblance to the actual people that they played in the film. It got Sean Penn the Oscar for Best Actor. Always a chameleon actor keen on method acting, Penn was usually more used to male chauvinistic parts than to gay impersonation. With *Milk*, Penn himself vanished, as he became Harvey Milk, down to every last minute mannerism and quirk in his speech. Just as well handled as the impersonation itself was the handling of the character arc, in which Milk made a gradual but compelling transformation from an insecure and casual "hippie" to a charismatic, heavily burdened leader and champion of civil rights.

The film uses costume and hair design aspects of *mise-en-scène* to perfectly capture and convey the environment of the 1970s. From the abundance of tight jeans to a variety of long or Afro hairstyles, one can really feel immersed in the atmosphere of Castro. Clothes do not function only symbolically for the narrative but also diegetically to symbolize the period correctly. The director resorted to fashion's ability to generate discourses on all aspects of society—gender, sexuality, class, politics. Stella Bruzzi explains that "costume films that, conversely, choose to look at clothes, create an alternative discourse and one that usually counters or complicates the ostensible strategy of the overriding narrative" (Bruzzi 1997: 36). Film costume is not just subordinate to narrative, it may create its own alternative discourse. The use of clothes in the movie seems to authenticate historical representation and background and entail a myriad images about the period which is anchored through these reality effects. Yet, the narrative conveys a wider and more universal meaning that cannot be limited to America in the 1970s. Costume, *mise-en-scène*, actors' bodies, film technology and techniques are all marked by the contemporary period in which the film is made (in this case 2008), while attempting to appear as though marked by the past time period in which it is set, the 1970s here. Through historical denotation, costume creates enough distance from contemporary events and issues that these same events and issues may then be reflected back to the spectator from the safety of an "historical" viewpoint. In other words, clothing does not only revive the past, it also signifies the artist's own relation to the past and to the present. Also impressive is the make-up, as a prosthetic nose, teeth, and hairline are given to Sean Penn, making him bear an almost frighteningly striking resemblance to the actual figure he is playing. Here again, as with *The Iron Lady*, resemblance can be seen as performance and draws the attention of many critics. It might appear paradoxical to cast a famous actor in a biopic and then to transform his looks, his voice, his gait, his manners, but this is a deliberate strategy to enhance both the director and the actor's skills. Sean Penn and Harvey Milk merge in the eye of Pygmalion/Van Sant's camera to form a composite character.

Explicit attention to detail was given to everything from the apartments to the cars, faithfully recreating a time period so similar and yet so different from our own. Production designer Bill Groom declared:

> We were working already from thousands of photographs and hours of film and video, but everybody from back then helped us interpret those materials. There were a lot of 'aha!' moments along the way when someone stepped in and put the pieces together. People who have been in the Castro for a very long time just started coming forward with not only photographs, but objects from Harvey's camera store. (Nicoletta 2008/2009)

Biopics often build narratives of nostalgia, here for a time of sexual liberation and enthusiasm. They are also organized as stories of loss charting an imaginary historical trajectory from stability to instability, charting the process of decay, the fall from a utopian ideal. The camera style when filming Castro can appear to be pictorialist, insisting on art photography, aesthetic refinement, and set-piece images. The effect is to transform the narrative space of Harvey Milk's political itinerary into heritage space of America in the 1970s; the gaze is therefore organized along props and settings (clothes, shops, candles).

The discourse of authenticity means that references should be historically accurate, that the image of the past should not be anachronistic. A common device used to display an effect of authenticity is often provided by the projection of archive footage. This is a typical technique, even in experimental movies on historic personalities, to insert Super 8 films or extracts from documentaries. Oliver Stone's opening sequence to *JFK* (1991) is a good example of nostalgic montage and oscillation between real images and recreated ones. *Milk* opens with footage of the 1969 Stonewall riots in New York City, a violent protest by the LGBT community against police brutality. Other images of men being beaten by police and crammed into paddy wagons—or hiding their faces from the camera to protect their identities—speak to a time when being gay was illegal or semi-legal in many places and, in general, there was widespread harassment and victimization of the gay community.

Working from a screenplay by documentarian Dustin Lance Black, Van Sant makes clever use of ample historical footage of both the Castro neighborhood (which is at times blended in so seamlessly with the modern-day recreations that it is impossible to tell the difference) and news footage of many of Milk's political enemies, most notably Anita Bryant, whose conservative Christian movement pushed to get Proposition 6 passed in California after first finding success in Florida. California Proposition 6 was on the November 7, 1978 statewide ballot in California as an initiated state statute, where it was defeated. Known as The Briggs Initiative, Proposition 6 would have banned gays and lesbians from working in California's public schools. Dan White was the only member of the Board of Supervisors who refused to vote for the San Francisco gay civil rights bill, which would prevent gays from being fired from their jobs if they came out—a cause especially close to Milk's heart. Nevertheless, the bill went through in the spring of 1978. White resigned from the board; then, some days later, he asked to be reinstated. Moscone refused White's request; several days after that final rejection White showed up at City Hall and killed Moscone, then Milk, before turning himself in at a local police station.

The other obvious characteristic of biopics is dramatic irony because the public can never be truly surprised at the outcome. Apart from the public's knowledge of historical facts regarding Harvey Milk's life and death, the beginning of the film is ominous and imbued with tragedy as *Milk* begins with Penn dictating his last will and testament into a tape recorder.

However, what might matter more in Van Sant's film is not the expected murder of Milk. Crafty editing and *mise-en-scène* choices actually transform historical realism into political and poetical Real. Even if the film ends with a sequence that shows the real-life figures that the film's characters were based upon—from Cleve Jones (who would go on to create the Names Project AIDS Memorial Quilt) to Danny Nicoletta (a photographer who documented much of the era's struggles), Van Sant has also transformed Milk's tragic fate into an aesthetic discourse upon the ephemeral and vacillating quality of human essence.

THE POLITICAL AND POETICAL REAL IN *MILK*: QUEERING THE BIOPIC?

Isn't this what biopics are for? Hagiography; and a retelling of the saint's story for those who don't know it? [...] The very visual closeness Van Sant has achieved—the characters do look amazingly like their counterparts— highlights this effect, since likeness is to identity as fiction is to history. The film reminds us where we were and asks where we are. This is perhaps an answer to the second question about biopics. If we are wondering 'why now' perhaps we need to wonder a little more. (Wood 2008)

Directing the movie *Milk* was challenging for Van Sant because of its representation of a murdered gay politician and the queer implications of the movie were therefore highly political, even if the openly gay director had never intended his movie as LGBT. The New Queer Cinema movement that emerged in the 1990s sought to appropriate the term "queer" and fight against stereotyping that had dominated cinema's representation of gay characters. Gus Van Sant cemented his position in this movement with his 1991 film *My Own Private Idaho*. B. Ruby Rich, a prominent queer theorist, noted that "[w]hat was so striking about the 1990's when I came up with this term 'Queer Cinema' [...] was a meeting of political engagement and aesthetic invention" (Rose 2004). In this respect, and in comparison with *My Own Private Idaho*, *Milk* is much less avant garde. Although the frank depiction of gay sexual relations in *Milk* seemingly places it in the New Queer Cinema canon, the film is at a formal level extremely conventional: there is little "aesthetic invention," compared with *Elephant* or *Last Days*. Therefore, it seems that, although *Milk* is a movie about a gay politician's fight, the representation of LGBT desire, while blatant, appears far more conventional than in Van Sant's previous movies. There are many scenes of partying and kissing but, paradoxically enough, the biographical and therefore quite didactic dimension appears to prevail over innovative perspective on the gay community. Indeed, as a biopic, it is a movie about an exceptional man and it operates more as a tribute than as an original work.

In *Mapping Contemporary Cinema*, Hannah Mary Farr argues that *Milk* aims to keep a largely heterosexual mainstream audience engaged by avoiding the political issues of the day (Farr 2011). However, the film is one of the first high-profile biopics about an openly gay activist, depicting gay life in San Francisco in the 1970s as promiscuous and unruly, thereby securing support from gay viewers. The treatment of sexual discrimination was highly sensitive, particularly as the release of the movie coincided with the controversy surrounding Proposition 8. While Milk defeated Proposition 6, which would have meant the mandatory firing of LGBT teachers in schools, the film failed to counter Proposition 8, which reversed the California Supreme Court ruling that legalized same-sex marriage. Indeed, the passing of Proposition 8 has been described as the biggest political setback to the American Gay Rights movement in years. *Milk* premiered on the 30th anniversary of Milk's death, three weeks after the passing of Proposition 8, thereby missing the opportunity to feed the debate (Proposition 8 was ruled unconstitutional in 2010 and repealed in 2013).

Although the film may not have changed the vote, its late release actually highlights the producers' desire to distance themselves from gay rights' activism in order not to alienate the wider audience. When interviewed, Van Sant explained that they refused to align the film with the political issues of the moment and aimed to lengthen the life of the film beyond the contemporary moment, yet he conceded that if Milk had been in charge he would have done it differently (Bowen 2008). So one may wonder whether Van Sant truly managed to imprint this movie with originality and creativity, as such critics as Hilton Als seem to suggest:

> The screenwriter, Dustin Lance Black—Mormon-raised and a former writer and producer on the Mormon-themed, critically lauded television series *Big Love*—pretty much follows the standard biopic formula: subject grapples with self, finds self, becomes a public self, weathers controversy, triumphs personally and/or professionally, and then dies. Black's attempts to dress up this schema in the gay trappings afforded by his subject do nothing to meaningfully pervert the form—or *Milk*'s emotional tidiness. (Als 2009)

Director Gus Van Sant has depicted the doomed lives of young people in various films, capturing the way they speak and relate to the world around them. His characters are frequently young men who are somewhat lost and removed from mainstream society, with death being a reoccurring theme—including in *Elephant* and *Paranoid Park*. Helped by his director of photography Harris Savides, famous for exploring the different possibilities of the long take, Van Sant captures Harvey Milk's alienation and solitude by isolating him in the frame and in the space of a disaffected environment; he thus shifts from realism to psychoanalytical Real. Using different types of stock footage (formats including 16-mm film, 35-mm film, and video), Van Sant accentuates gaps and heterogeneity in the representation to endow the film with some distinctive style and not remain purely documentary.

In his article "Milk and Political History" (2009), Harry Benshoff explains that the film also features some Van Sant signature auteur touches: slow-motion shots of falling chads that recall the fizzing bubbles washing over the images of *Drugstore Cowboy* (1989), along with multiple split-screen images of a telephone tree that suggest both the magazine cover pin-ups of *My Own Private Idaho* (1991) and Van Sant's Warhol-inspired urge for serial reproduction. Most obviously, the floating Steadicam shots that follow Dan White through the corridors of City Hall the morning of his murderous rampage bring to mind their similar use in *Elephant*. He concludes that Van Sant's intermingling of the real and the fictionalized remains at the core of *Milk*'s queer style. Some *mise-en-scène* choices actually bring some originality to the movie and display Van Sant's recurring obsessions, particularly in his characteristic relation to temporality. Van Sant exploits the theme of alienation by resorting to intimate penetrating close-ups and observational traveling long takes of the Town Hall and of Castro that isolate the protagonist from his environment (both human and natural). His aesthetic of slowness uncompresses time, distends it, renewing the ability of the shot to represent a sense of the phenomenological real. Herein lies the marked tension between fast and slow: whereas speed perpetually risks gratuitous haste, fragmentation, and distraction, reduction intensifies the spectator's gaze, awareness, and response to the protagonist's journey into public recognition.

Some sequences disrupt linearity; for example, by skipping back eight years to the eve of Milk's 40th birthday when he is still in the closet and working on Wall Street. This *in media res* beginning (doubled in the case of *Milk*) gives the opportunity of "beginning the story at the moment just before the subject begins to make his/her mark on the world" (Bingham 2010: 5). This is particularly relevant as the encounter with Scott Smith (which happens at the beginning of the movie) was the turning point in Milk's life. Documentary footage is used in the closing sequence where, after Milk's death, the streets of San Francisco are filled with people attending a candlelit vigil. The size of the gathering is striking as the camera zooms out to show the seemingly never-ending crowds. This closing shot expresses the devastating effect of the murders on the community and serves to highlight the tragedy of the story, made no less poignant by the fact that the viewer knows Milk's fate from the outset.

Another specificity of Van Sant's cinema is his portrayal of characters haunted by traumatic events and disconnected from their surroundings. The intimate *malaise* of his male characters is not voiced through dialogues but *extimated* as the *real* is not expressed through language but through Freudian slips, fantasies, repetitions. The term "extimacy" is an English translation of the French neologism (extimité) coined by the psychoanalyst Jacques Lacan. The notion of "extimacy" is used to designate "this central place, this intimate exteriority, this extimacy, which is the Thing" (Lacan 1992: 171). Lacan identifies extimacy with the Thing after enigmatically describing this Thing as the "excluded interior" (Lacan 1992: 125), the "subject's inside" that becomes "the first outside," the first exteriority around which the subject orients his way (Lacan 1992: 65). In cinema, the access to intimacy is made possible thanks to various techniques which enable the directors not only to externalize fleeting and evanescent moments in the psyche of the protagonists (i.e., on the diegetic level), but also to promote their own aesthetics of intimacy as a characteristic mark of their cinematic writing.

The ambiguous relationship between Harvey Milk and Dan White (Josh Brolin) is *extimated* on the screen in a very subtle way. White might stand for the man Milk could have become had he married and remained closeted. The real Dan White committed suicide after a five-year prison sentence. Thirty-one years old and a new father, White, a former fireman, cannot make ends meet. In their relatively brief scenes together, the more politically savvy and charming Milk tries to connect with White, to build some intimate connection, to get him to talk about his sense of failure. Brolin and Penn bring a homoerotic element to their scenes reminiscent of the shower scene in *Elephant*. They let their words drift as they pause, or go markedly silent as the other talks. Penn mutes his voice in his private scenes with Brolin, like a particularly caring coach. Brolin's impersonation of White builds uncanny echoes with his part as Bush in *W.* by Oliver Stone, released the same year. Brolin brings a very intimate touch to these two men who are shown not as ideologists but as wounded men, spurred by frustration and resentment. One of the most intimate shots in *Milk* portrays Dan White on the day of the double murder, lying in his underwear on his couch, his beautiful body exposed, his vulnerability enhanced by a fetal position. This shot clearly brings forth other vulnerable male bodies in Van Sant's films and it reinforces the ambiguity of the character, torn between his desire and his moral background. It epitomizes the director's paradoxical aesthetics of softness present in *Elephant, Gerry, Paranoid Park*: characters who are about to commit terrifying deeds appear as fundamentally split. Their appearance evokes a form of innocence, of purity which is contradicted by their ruthlessness.

His representation seems to insist on a cinematic de-realization or de-materialization, as the new condition in which the image prevails over the object present so the virtual prevails over the real, as analyzed by Paul Virilio (1989: 73). His fuzzy shots magnify the feeling of retinal persistence as their projected images form a clutter of fantasies persisting for a short time after the photogram has moved on, favoring the illusion of continuous movement. In a manner reminiscent of Tarkovsky's insistence that the "dominant, all-powerful factor of the film is rhythm, expressing the course of time within the frame" (Tarkovsky 1987: 13), Van Sant's art is, therefore, immediately identifiable because of a common thread (some critics would call mannerism) that runs through his creations. Slow motion and a peculiar softness characterize his movies and this is particularly obvious in *Milk*. The director revisits the melodramatic format by promoting a heightened stylized vision. The artist paradoxically uses softness as a form of distancing from the chaos of society, from the terrible void and dislocation of the protagonist's intimate world.

To abolish, temporarily, the violence of the real, Van Sant resorts to filters, veils, and gauze; eerie soundtracks contribute to the synesthesia of softness and slowness extimated on the screen. Another concept central to this analysis is the notion of sublimation as transformation, metamorphosis, conversion of grief into art, but also as an oneiric filmic apparatus to render "extimate" the fundamental vacillation of the subject. According to Lacan, when the cherished love object is adulated and elevated in sublimation (as is the case in troubadour and surrealist poetry), this serves, albeit temporarily, to complete the subject's existence, to relocate what Lacan terms the ego's "prehistoric Other" (Lacan 1975: 87)—commonly perceived as the subject's "other half"—without which the individual labors with a certain sense of existential vacuity. Lacan terms this unspecified sense of psychic lack *das Ding* (German for "the thing"). The exact formula for sublimation given by Lacan is the raising of the object "to the dignity of the Thing" (Lacan 1975: 138) implying an undue exaltation of and overinvestment in the Other. In other words, from identifying a desirable "something" in the external world, the subject mythologizes and refashions it into the signifier of its complementary Other with the implications of dreamlike romance, false hopes, and emotional self-deception this entails.

Music and particularly the repetition of Puccini's *Tosca*—one of Milk's favorite operas—serves as a sublimating device and a background for important events in his life and dramatizes his political and personal struggles. The music of *Tosca* underscores one scene in particular, in which Milk laments to Scott that he is **40** and has done nothing with his life. This scene, which occurs at the beginning and is repeated near the end, functions as both a visual and musical refrain that emphasizes Milk's meteoric rise and tragic fall. *Tosca* will thus be used as intradiegetic and extradiegetic music, linking Harvey Milk's intimacy with his public fate. The shooting scene is a striking example of sublimation and de-realization. The horror of the scene is transferred to an opera stage. Harvey Milk the politician is united with the tragic heroine of *Tosca*. After White blows a couple of holes in Milk's hand and chest, the victim starts to fall in very slow motion. As he lands, the camera backtracks and we see what he does in an eyeline match: a banner announcing the San Francisco Opera's production of *Tosca*. The spectator remembers that Milk was a fan of the opera about tragically thwarted love. Milk falls to the ground, his hands flailing in slow motion—reminding us of previous scenes showing him conducting along to his opera records and gesticulating while he talked. Politics and art merge in this pivotal scene, the historical and the Lacanian real blend to frame Van Sant's cinematic obsession, death as kaleidoscopic spectacle.

CONCLUSION

One of Van Sant's directorial techniques—borrowed from director Terrence Malick, and which the director first experimented with on *Milk*—is to direct the actors to perform the scene silently, without dialogue, with the actors moving through their lines internally, expressing their emotions with their eyes and faces. "The true language of art is speechless," claimed Adorno (1984: 164). Indeed, silence places an emphasis on gesture, dramatic action, and expression through visual meaning that is reminiscent of melodrama. In that respect *Milk* pays a tribute to Hollywood melodrama because it insists on the protagonists' inner dilemmas and the dissemination of the symbolic order, that of language, to magnify the *jouissance* of the Real, of the Kantian sublime—a pure thingness that underlies experience and surpasses our ability to describe or name it.

Most critics reviewed *Milk* favorably. Yet, some deplored the overwhelming weight the hagiographic mode, often inherent to the biopic, laid on Van Sant's artistic fluidity. For example, Hilton Als claimed that his aesthetic was "constricted by the fixed nature of biography." Mark Simpson in *The Guardian* accused Van Sant of stuffing the hero back into the closet by foregrounding a mainstream and reassuring representation of Harvey Milk. But *Milk* is also dedicated to an artist who "must find a new scene," as Scott tells Harvey Milk at the beginning of the movie and historic Harvey Milk is endowed with a new stature in Van Sant's movie. The public figure of the politician somehow vanishes behind the romantic *persona* whose death is transcended and magnified. Catabasis is indeed staged but in slow motion and in silence, as his physical collapse is filmed in slow and choreographed steps. *Milk* is imbued with softness and intimacy, which form a thread in Van Sant's cinematography and constitute his *real* touch, between queer cinema and oneiric melodrama. The paradox of *Milk* comes from the obvious militancy combined with the creator's desire to resist any essentialist definition. Van Sant's movie cannot be reduced to a political discourse, but it does reach a more universal and poetical goal by voicing the intimate, the unsaid. It is possible to analyze *Milk* as a queer biopic inasmuch as it displays a subversion of traditional genre and not only offers an explicit representation of LGBT desire on screen. As with *Last Days*, Van Sant's biopic can remind the public and critics of Magritte's *Treachery of Images. This is not a queer biopic.* Is it not, *really?*

Works Cited

Adorno, Theodor. *Aesthetic Theory*, trans. C. Lenhardt. London: Routledge & Kegan Paul, 1984.

Als, Hilton. "Revolutionary Road." *The New York Times*, N.p., March 12, 2009. http://www.nybooks.com/articles/archives/2009/mar/12/revolutionary-road/. Accessed on June 18, 2017.

Anderson, C. and J. Lupo. "Hollywood Lives: The State of the Biopic at the Turn of the Century." In S. Neale (ed.), *Genre and Contemporary Hollywood*. London: British Film Institute, 2002, 99–104.

Anderson, C. and J. Lupo. "Off-Hollywood Lives: Irony and Its Discontents in the Contemporary Biopic." *Journal of Popular Film and Television*, vol. 36, no. 2 (2008): 102–111.

Benshoff, Harry M. "*Milk* and Gay Political History." *Jump Cut: A Review of Contemporary Media*, vol. 51 (2009). http://www.ejumpcut.org/archive/jc51.2009/Milk/index.html. Accessed on June 19, 2017.

Bingham, Denis. *Whose Lives Are They Anyway? The Biopic as Contemporary Film Genre*. New Brunswick, NJ: Rutgers University Press, 2010.

Bowen, Peter. "Mighty Real: Gus Van Sant on *Milk*." *Filminfocus.com*, November 12, 2008. http://www.focusfeatures.com/article/mighty_real_gus_van_sant_on_milk?film=milk. Accessed on June 17, 2017.

Bruzzi, Stella. *Undressing Cinema: Clothing and Identity in the Movies*. London: Routledge, 1997.

Custen, George Frederick. *Bio/Pics: How Hollywood Constructed Public History*. New Jersey: Rutgers University Press, 1992.

Farr, Hannah Mary. *Mapping Contemporary Cinema*. Queen Mary: University of London, 2011. http://www.mcc.sllf.qmul.ac.uk/?p=1396. Accessed on June 18, 2017.

Lacan, Jacques. *Le Séminaire XX—Encore*. Paris: Seuil, 1975.

Lacan, Jacques. *Le Séminaire. Livre VII. L'éthique de la psychanalyse*. Paris: Seuil, 1986.

Lacan, Jacques. *(1959–1960) The Seminar of Jacques Lacan—Book 7, Ethics of Psychoanalysis*, trans. and ed. J.-A. Miller. London: Routledge, 1992.

Lacan, Jacques. *Séminaire XVI—D'un Autre à l'autre*. Paris: Seuil, 2006.

Miller, J.-A. "Dossier Suture: Suture (Elements of the Logic of the Signifier)." *Screen*, vol. 18, no. 4 (1977): 24–34.

Miller, Jacques-Alain. "Extimité." In Mark Bracher, M.W. Alcorn, R.J. Corthell, and F. Massardier-Kenney (eds.), *Lacanian Theory of Discourse: Subject, Structure, and Society*. New York: New York University Press, 1994, 74–87.

Nicoletta, Danny. "Milk." *Set Decor*, Winter, 2008/2009. http://dannynicoletta.com/pdfs/nicoletta_setdecor_milk.pdf, accessed on June 10, 2017.

Rose, Jennie. "The Last Refuge of Democracy: A Talk with B. Ruby Rich." *GreenCine.com*, May 7, 2004. http://www.greencine.com/article?action=view&articleID=119. Accessed on June 12, 2017.

Setoodeh, Ramin. "The Death of the Biopic." *Newsweek*, N.p., February 2, 2010. http://www.newsweek.com/death-biopic-75249. Accessed on June 10, 2017.

Simpson, Mark. "There's Just One Problem with Milk: It Castrates Its Hero." *The Guardian*, N.p., January 28, 2008. http://www.theguardian.com/film/filmblog/2009/jan/28/milk-gus-van-sant-sean-penn. Accessed on June 15, 2017.

Tarkovsky, Andrei. *Sculpting in Time*. Austin: University of Texas Press, 1987.

Virilio, Paul. *War and Cinema: The Logistics of Perception*. London and New York: Verso, 1989.

Wood, Michael. "At the Movies." *London Review of Books,* June 2008. http://www.lrb.co.uk/v31/n01/michael-wood/at-the-movies. Accessed on June 15, 2017.

In Search of Purcell's Legacy: Tony Palmer's *England, My England* (1995)

Nicole Cloarec

Subtitled "The Story of Henry Purcell," Tony Palmer's film *England, My England* was first broadcast in December 1995, which marked the three-hundredth anniversary of Henry Purcell's death. In the same year, music critic and former Controller of the BBC Proms Sir Nicholas Roger Kenyon quoted Vaughan Williams who stated in 1951: "We all pay lip service to Henry Purcell, but what do we really know of him?" only to add "More than forty years on, are we much the wiser?"[1] Although Purcell has been called "Our Musical Shakespeare"[2]

[1] "Henry Purcell: Towards a Tercentenary" (cited in Burden 1996: 1).

[2] As Rebecca Herissone explains, "the first substantial investigation of Purcell's posthumous fortunes, an essay that remains central to any assessment of his reception today, was Richard Luckett's 'Or rather Our Musical Shakespeare': Charles Burney's Purcell" of 1983 (Hogwood and Luckett: 59–77). Rebecca Herissone also quotes from Charles Burney's *History of Music* (1776–1789), one of the first published monuments of music history produced in Britain, who compares Purcell's legacy with other famous British artists or thinkers: "who is as much the pride of an Englishman in Music, as Shakspeare [*sic*] in

N. Cloarec (✉)
Univ Rennes, LIDILE-EA 3874, Rennes, France
e-mail: Nicole.Cloarec@univ-rennes1.fr

© The Author(s) 2018
D. Letort and B. Lebdai (eds.), *Women Activists and Civil Rights Leaders in Auto/Biographical Literature and Films*,
https://doi.org/10.1007/978-3-319-77081-9_13

207

to highlight his status as a national icon, it seems the musician shares with the Bard the paradox of being celebrated as one of the greatest and most famous English composers while actually very little is known about his life and character. We know when he died and where he is buried (in Westminster Abbey) but we don't know who paid for his memorial stone. Where he was born or even precisely when remains unclear.[3] We know he worked as a composer, organist, and singer in the service of the Chapel Royal at Westminster Abbey and that he ended up writing abundantly for the stage during the last five years of his life. We know he was a highly prolific composer, author of more than a thousand pieces in just 16 years, yet only 15 of them were actually signed, many of the music sources were printed or copied posthumously and the dates as well as the circumstances of composition related to some masterpieces like *Dido and Aeneas* are still being hotly debated among scholars. Last, Purcell did not leave any diary or correspondence and if he is seen by many as the first composer to have negotiated a major shift "from traditional patronage-based employment at court to the commercial life of the musical entrepreneur" (Herissone 2012: 308), one must bear in mind he was "writing at a time when there was no developed concept of the composer as artist, individual or genius" (Herissone 2012: 6), when music was "composed, used and discarded" (Weber 1992: 2).

How then to film the biography of such an enigmatic figure whose inner life and opinions remain a mystery, who, in other words, is known only through his work? This questioning is precisely what is at stake in Tony Palmer's *England, My England* (1995). Although there has now been a long tradition of biopics taking the form of elaborate puzzles where inner selves remain unfathomable enigmas, it seems rather more

---

productions for the stage, Milton in epic poetry, Lock in metaphysics, or Sir Isaac Newton in philosophy and mathematics" (Herissone 2012: 305, 331).

[3]For example, Bruce Wood starts his biography with the following: "The young Henry Purcell is a shadowy figure. Nearly all traces of his life during childhood have been obliterated by the passage of centuries since, and the first surviving documents to mention him by name date from 1673, when he was already a teenager. We do not even know exactly when he was born, for no record survives of either his birth or his baptism, and the only hard fact we have—from his memorial stone in Westminster Abbey—is that when he died, on November 21, 1695, he was in his thirty-seventh year" (Wood 2009: 1).

of a preposterous challenge to conceive of a biopic with very few actual biographical elements. But, instead of trying to fill up or conceal the gaps through fictional license, the film starts from the postulate of this absence and turns it into a self-reflexive quest. In keeping with the recent trend in contemporary biography,[4] the film thus shifts its focus from the biographical elements themselves to the dramatization of their pursuit. This will be the first of a series of displacements that all contribute to challenging the generic expectations of traditional biopics.

PORTRAYING THE COMPOSER

Although the opening scene is clearly set in seventeenth-century England, starting with Charles II's return in Britain and his Coronation, what first appears as traditional historical reenactment allowing "the spectator to imagine they are 'witnessing again' the events of the past"[5] is very soon disrupted by the use of a framing narrative set at the end of the 1960s. After only five minutes and a close shot of the King's face during his Coronation,[6] the next shot frames the same actor in a similar close shot but in front of a mirror and smoking a cigarette. The actor is actually in the dressing room of the Royal Court Theatre while performing George Bernard Shaw's play *In Good King Charles's Golden Days*.[7] As the play is clearly a box office failure, the actor suggests to the manager he writes a play about Purcell so they can still use the same sets and costumes. His quest thus involves scenes of dialogues with the manager and his girlfriend, visits to Westminster Abbey to see Purcell's tomb, to the Tower of London, to the National Maritime Museum in Greenwich, to the British Library where the actor peruses first *The London Gazette* of

[4] "The self-reflexive imperative in current biography underlies both the stream of first-person reflection on what to make of evidence and silence and the increasing tendency to include discussion of—and implicit dialogue with the reader about—authorial judgment and intention within a biography" (Walter 2004: 335).

[5] "The act of imaginative recreation that allows the spectator to imagine they are 'witnessing again' the events of the past" (Burgoyne 2008: 7).

[6] A first clue may be given as the close-up of the King's face shows some amused conniving concern when the ritual question is being asked "Any who may show good reason why Charles Stuart shall not be king of England, let him come forth and speak."

[7] The *mise en abyme* is made clear with the insert of the bill including the filmmaker's name as director of the play.

October 9, 1701 announcing a 20-guinea reward for whoever brings up the late Mr. Purcell's lost score of *The Fairy Queen,* then the manuscript itself while wondering at its blank pages. Historical information is also provided as, when after Mary's death is mentioned, the actor is reading statistical accounts as regards the health and prevalent diseases of the late seventeenth century.[8]

However, notwithstanding the manager's first reaction stating that since "nobody knows anything about him, that's what makes him an ideal subject for a play," and although Purcell died an untimely death at the early age of 36,[9] Purcell not only remains a shadowy figure throughout the film but he seems far removed from the ideal subject for a successful biography by today's standards. The composer is a far cry from the romantic figure of the tormented genius, misunderstood and ignored by his time.[10] On the contrary he is shown as a "natural" product of his time, which seems fairly apt for a court musician whose work was so closely linked to the commissions of the court and of the Church.[11] As a result, rather than the portrait of a man and his life, the film draws the portrait of a witness to a fascinating period whose turmoil and changes are shown to contribute to shaping his work. Rather than foregrounding an individual's story that is shown as the conduit of history, boiling down complex social processes to gestures of individual agency, the film

[8] "A statistical survey of the health of the late seventeenth century reveals that from every 100 births only one in three lived beyond the age of six. [...] Only one in ten lived until they were 70. The most common disease was rickets, resulting in deformed limbs and scrofula while spotted fever, pleurisy, pneumonia and above all smallpox killed two out of every five of the population."

[9] Some music scholars account for the melancholy and introvert tone of his music by stressing the recurrent bereavements Purcell had to face throughout his life, from the untimely death of his father when he was only five, soon followed by the plague, to the loss of four of his newly born children; but, there are also many celebratory, sanguine, or even ribald pieces.

[10] Dryden's voiceover: "From this blessed man, music just seems to flow: motets, anthems, songs, all manner of music for all manner of occasions."

[11] The parallel is set from the start as the voiceover relates: "At the end of Cromwell's time, in and around the year of our Lord 1660, two things miraculous came about which, as I shall relate, gave us great hope for the future of this island, this England. The first, the restoration of Charles Stuart to his throne of England after many long years of exile in Holland [...] and the second, the birth of Henry Purcell organist, composer of the Chapel Royal in the Great Abbey at Westminster. [...] together they changed our history for ever."

IN SEARCH OF PURCELL'S LEGACY   211

uses Purcell's life and music to dramatize the major political and social events of the time.[12]

While Purcell himself remains in the background as a mere witness to court events for nearly half the film,[13] his music comes center stage. From the start, his numerous court odes, anthems, and birthday songs accompany scenes evoking King Charles's return and Coronation—although in this case with flagrant anachronism—or later Mary's wedding and her landing in 1688. Martial and funeral marches are heard to illustrate the many turbulent events of a period marked by violence and upheaval. King Arthur's aria "The Cold Song" endows the Plague with a woeful throb, the opening of *Dido and Aeneas* gives the Great Frost of 1683/1684 a slow melancholy tone or Dido's famous lament "When I Am Laid in Earth" is used to mourn Purcell's own death.[14]

In this respect, Purcell's music becomes the true central character as the composer's life is not only superseded by the portrayal of the eventful period he lived in but also gives way to a reflection on his legacy. Indeed, the framing narrative provided by the actor's undertaking to write a play about the composer's life is doubled with constant metaleptic leaps. As in Karel Reisz's *The French Lieutenant's Woman* (1981), the same actors play different parts set in different periods of time but echoing each other. In addition to the actor playing King Charles, his mistress Barbara Palmer, Countess of Castlemaine,[15] interprets his divorced pregnant wife; Nell Gwynn is played by his current girlfriend; Shaftesbury (Murray Melvin) is also one of the assistants in the Royal Court Theatre and the manager (Bill Kenwright) is called Betterton, after Thomas Betterton, the most influential manager of the United Company which comprised the two main theaters in Restoration London.

---

[12] One major exception is the inclusion of *The Symphony of the Air* by William Walton, which he composed in 1969 in tribute to World War II air fighters. The "Battle in the Air" is used during the long scene of the Great Fire of London, whose chaos is conveyed by the dissonant chords of the musical piece.

[13] Purcell only appears briefly and episodically as a baby and a child until his first apparition as adult after 1 hour 8 minutes.

[14] In addition, the Abdelazer rondeau is played during court dancing, some catches are sung in taverns, and his dramatic work is performed in a large part of *King Arthur*.

[15] Barbara Palmer, 1st Duchess of Cleveland, Countess of Castlemaine, also known as Lady Castlemaine (1640–1709) was one of the most notorious of the many mistresses of King Charles II of England, who fathered her five children, all acknowledged and subsequently ennobled.

212   N. CLOAREC

MIRRORING THE BIOGRAPHEE AND THE BIOGRAPHER

Through elaborate sound bridges of dialogue and music or graphic matches, the film sets a series of echoes and contrasts between Purcell's time and the late 1960s. Heated discussions about financial difficulties between the actor and his manager are immediately followed by similar concerns which the Chief Minister imparts to the King. Likewise, the manager's eventual refusal to actually produce the play just precedes the Censor's visit to Purcell when he rails against his *King Arthur*.[16] There are parallels with other major historical events: the insert of some found footage of the American flag set on fire during one of the 1968 anti-Vietnam demonstrations dissolves into the outbreak of the Great Fire of London, reenactment of an anti-Popish procession merges into images of the Orange Order marching in Northern Ireland or again a short televised extract showing Iain Paisley's hateful ranting is immediately followed by a scene in the seventeenth-century English parliament which relates Titus Oates' spurious divulgation of a Popish plot against the King.[17]

Through this constant interweaving, the two periods are set to mirror each other, highlighting the "pastness" of the past as well as its legacy. In the same way, the first narrator, who turns out to be Dryden, close friend of Purcell who set many of his works to music, intermingles with the actor's discursive voice in a dialogic relationship. Just before the end, Dryden even addresses the camera, as if speaking to the centuries to come, stressing the everlasting similarities over the ages:

> No government has ever been or ever can be wherein timeservers and blockheads will be uppermost. The persons only are changed. The same juggling in the state, the same hypocrisy in religion, the same self-interest and mismanagement will remain—for ever.

The metaleptic device reaches its climax with the confrontation between biographer and biographee just before Purcell's death. After

---

[16] "It will not serve. [...] it has within it subversion and religion! And mention of the King's defeat at Mons which is not politic—nor is it true. Nor may you say he has a mistress." When Purcell argues "I say none of this. I simply set it. It is a work for the theatre, an opera!" he is answered "Opera is a danger you will do your best to avoid."

[17] "I, Titus Oates, tell you Lords there is a Popish plot in the land for the destruction of His Majesty King Charles… and that man, he, Lord Stafford, he took from me a commission that I was by Jesuits that he should act as Paymaster General of the Pope's army to ravage this land."

the two actors face each other in an impossible shot/counter shot, they meet in the actor's modern-day living room. In this scene, the actor who interprets Purcell is wearing modern clothing but still is speaking as Purcell. Here is the full dialogue:

Purcell: Still mediocrity is a great comforter, you'll see. I will become a grand object of public unconcern. My *Dido*? Not even performed. At least not in public. Since *Dioclesian*, some fifteen works for the stage in only four years. And the result? Penury. Begging for enough to … tell me is this ugly cheerless world in which we live supposed to be typical? Is this all?

Actor-biographer: Well at least you never assembled a lot of sloppy fads and served them up as innovations.

Purcell: I mourned the unknown, the loss of what went before, the deprivation of what, even as a child, seemed as tangible as death.

Actor-biographer: Have I looked for answers where there are none? Everyone demands answers, like happiness, as a right. How hopeless, how ironic.

Purcell: Ah! Irony! That English virtue that purifies our rowdy passion. No, hope comes within, my friend; when hope goes, we freeze. Hope falters but never fawns or crowds, never stands in line. Even in dread and noise it strains for coherence, for a snatch of harmony. An old trumpet played upon but not playing, sounding but only in my head. Alas coherence conceals as much as it reveals to the lost, like me, who contemplates the wreckage.

This meeting seals the defeat of the biographer's enterprise shown as an irredeemably incomplete puzzle where gaps prevail over completion, chaos over order. The dramatic *Mise en Abyme* of the play within the film is thus endowed with Shakespearean accent. Earlier on, the actor is seen waking up from a recurrent dream:

Last night I had the same dream I've been having all these years. I'm about to make my entrance on a stage. Behind the flats, the other actors are performing a play I know nothing about: a play about the short Life and tragic death of Henry Purcell, composer in Ordinary to the violins of

King Charles II. I play the King. My entrance is important, that I know. I stand there peering through the cracks in the scenery trying to find out what is going on. Eventually I decide I must have missed my entrance so I grab a door handle and push. Everything rattles. And suddenly I'm in a world where I can't see anything. I know the spotlight is on me. I don't know my moves, I don't know my first line but I make enormous efforts to speak, to say something. I open my mouth and drive all the strength I can find into my diaphragm but I make no sound. I try to force open my eyelids but I can't. I can feel the light but I can't see.

As later Dryden's voiceover recalls, life is but an "insubstantial pageant":

Our world was disintegrating. We moved as in a dream, shadows without substance. Thus did our life become. 'Tis all a cheat. Yet fooled with hope, men favour the deceit. Trust on, think tomorrow will repay. Tomorrow is falser than the former day. So when the last and dreadful hour this crumbling pageant shall devour, shall the trumpet still be heard on high? No the dead shall live; the living die while music shall untune the sky.

But what is even more striking is the logic of mirroring taken to an extreme whereby the pervasive feeling of failure and loss is suddenly transmitted to Purcell himself. And this crepuscular tone is actually accounted for by the presence of a third hidden party. Behind the actor's embittered, sometimes outrageously misogynistic and jingoistic ranting,[18] lies the unmistakable voice of playwright and screenwriter John Osborne, whom his biographer Luc Gilleman describes as the "man who all his life said the wrong things at the wrong time" (Gilleman 2002: vii). Purcell's biography becomes the hidden self-portrait of the writer. And this covert presence sheds new light on the choice of the embedded period: Restoration England with its flourishing art scene is set in parallel with the heydays of Osborne's stage production at the Royal Court Theatre.[19] (As an inside joke, the manager is actually interpreted by Bill Kenwright,

---

[18] During his visit at Westminster the actor rudely ignores a young foreigner who asks him with a strong Germanic accent if the tomb behind is Vellington's. When his ex-wife Barbara visits him to ask for money, she also mentions she has heard he was writing a play and asks whether there is "anything in it for me." She is answered: "I wouldn't think so. It's about genius."

[19] The heydays are 1956–1979. Osborne started working there as a jobbing actor in 1955.

who was then one of the leading producers of the West End and who also produced Osborne's last play *Déjà Vu*.)

Purcell's political time is thus oversimplistically glorified to underscore what Osborne considers today's despondent mediocrity. The actor becomes his spokesperson even though the film qualifies his perspective by also stressing his girlfriend's critical listening:

> What Charles wanted and what Purcell wrote about so gloriously was a country of tolerance, irony, kindliness. Not like today when the modesty of heroes is dispatched with derision and contempt and thus thrown up a generation for whom 'honour' is a forgotten, meaningless currency. May God rot the tyranny of equality, streamlining, classlessness and above all absurd irrelevant correctness. [...] we've become a nation of babbling backseat cab drivers.[20]

The very title of the film comes from one such griping diatribe, ranting against the European Economic Community: "England my England is shuffling about like an old tramp begging for a pair of boots at the tradesman's entrance of Europe." But it also recalls Osborne's infamous open letter published in 1961 in the socialist newspaper the *Tribune* entitled "Letter to My Fellow Countrymen" and often referred to as "Damn you, England."[21] In it Osborne vents his hateful grievance towards a country in which the angry young man who had once been hailed as a voice of the future has become a voice of the past, the young rebel a reactionary renegade. No wonder the manager finds the play unsuitable for production: "All this will have to go you know. No one will put up with all this violence, not on the telly anyway. No one will put up the money to make the thing."

In so doing, however, Osborne partly follows an old tradition whereby Purcell has been elevated to the status of national icon, "the pride of an Englishman in Music, as Shakspeare [*sic*] in productions for the stage, Milton in epic poetry, Lock in metaphysics, or

---

[20] Another similar diatribe later on goes: "What Charles wanted was for the Crowd itself to be extraordinary. Not like today when the monarchy isn't even the tarnished gold fillings in a mouthful of decay."

[21] The letter can be read at the following link: http://www.independent.co.uk/life-style/a-letter-to-my-fellow-countrymen-in-august-1961-the-cold-war-escalated-with-the-building-of-the-berlin-wall-and-the-proliferation-of-nuclear-weapons-seemed-certain-1367810.html (from *Tribune*, August 18, 1961).

Sir Isaac Newton in philosophy and mathematics" to quote from Charles Burney's *History of Music* (1776–1789), one of the first published monuments of music history produced in Britain (cited in Herissone 2012: 331). From the eighteenth century onwards, Purcell was often used for nationalistic purposes against what was perceived as "foreign" influences,[22] this culminating with the central part his figure played among the composers of the English Musical Renaissance of the late nineteenth and early twentieth centuries in their attempt to create a sense of English musical tradition.[23] And within this tradition the most notable stereotype associated with Purcell was the almost exclusive focus among the composer's work on his vocal output and particularly his dramatic music (Herissone 2012: 341), which the film largely perpetuates, as the most significant part of the musical pieces come from Purcell's dramatic work and *King Arthur* in particular.

But this emphasis also serves as Osborne's tribute to the stage and to illustrate his conception of his own dramatic art. Luc Gilleman comments on the cranky vituperations that so often characterize Osborne's works:

> Intense feeling, he hoped, would produce a style that, rather than coming in aid of meaning, would become meaning. […] but then the theatre, as Osborne points out, is "not a schoolroom." It is not a place for discussion and examination; if there are any lessons to be taught, they should be "lessons in feeling." (Gilleman 2002: 22)

These are the exact words that Captain Henry Cooke, Master of the children of the Royal Chapel, tells young Purcell during his music lesson: "This is a music factory. But make people feel, Master Purcell, give them lessons in feeling. Let 'em think afterwards." Significantly enough,

---

[22] How skewed this retrospective interpretation is can be seen in the fact that at the time Purcell was learning music, England was eager, after 12 years of Puritan rule, to embrace any cultural novelty coming from the Continent and his own music was as much shaped by foreign influences (mostly Italian and French) as by the old contrapuntal English tradition that he was taught by his master John Blow.

[23] Among the major English composers of the English Renaissance are Hubert Parry, Gustav Holst, and Ralph Vaughan Williams. A little later, Benjamin Britten and Michael Tippett also explicitly cited Purcell as a major influence on their works. See Rebecca Herissone "Performance History and Reception" (Herissone 341).

the scene is immediately followed by the present-day disgruntled actor bemoaning the inability of the British people to feel any more.[24]

A REQUIEM FILM

Through Osborne's prism, the film is thus both a tribute to Purcell's legacy[25] and the testament of a disillusioned old man who knew he was dying (and he actually died before the release of the film which is dedicated to him). As Allan Fish aptly remarks, it becomes "three requiems in one. A requiem not only to himself and his first love, the theatre, not only to Purcell and his too long neglected genius but to England itself."[26]

Nonetheless, Osborne's words do not cancel Purcell's music—nor Tony Palmer's filmic mastership. What starts as the quest for writing a biopic for the stage ends up a true dramatization of Purcell's music, epitomizing what Peter Ackroyd called "English music,"[27] by which he referred to the whole notion of English culture. As the music acquires historical and dramatic depth, it proves to be the true driving force of the narrative—linking together the different times, scenes of historical reconstitution with scenes of fictional license and a third layer of representation with scenes of documentary-like performances. In these the musicians and singers are filmed against a bare dark background, letting the background music enter center stage, since musicians and singers responsible for the musical score usually remain off screen.

What is more, while all of Purcell's musical pieces are conducted by John Eliot Gardiner, the film ends by a sort of coda that winds up the metaleptic *mise en abyme* of the whole film. In this ending a series of

[24] "Little danger of people feeling too much: not in England, not today, encircled as we are with a Cromwellian army of prigs, knighthood seekers and grubby timeservers."

[25] Just before the ending coda the narrator concludes: "He was a Colossus the boy. It flew up from him. Notes, everything—they'll not find the half of it. Did he not give to the Englishman his glorious, unquenchable music? There'll be none like him."

[26] Review by Allan Fish, July 24, 2012. https://wondersinthedark.wordpress.com/2012/07/24/england-my-england-1995-tv-tony-palmer/, accessed on March 2, 2017.

[27] *English Music* is the title of Peter Ackroyd's sixth novel, first published in 1992 by Hamish Hamilton, and which reviewer John Barrell described as "partly a narrative, partly a series of rhapsodies and meditations on the nature of English culture, written in the styles of various great authors" (Barrell 1992: 7).

brief shots that recap the film until the final bow of the actors on the stage is intertwined with actual footage from Tony Palmer's first music documentary of Benjamin Britten (*Benjamin Britten: A Time There Was...*, 1979) himself conducting his *Fugue from the Young Person's Guide to the Orchestra,* conceived as a tribute to Purcell, foregrounding both Purcell's musical legacy[28] and the filmmaker's own background. The film's approach to Purcell's life ends up in a portrayal of the composer depicted as a full participant in the rich and complex multimedia environment of Restoration England's cultural scene, highlighting the importance of the stage (both in past and modern times), but also of literature in all its guises (poetic, dramatic, musical), art, and architecture with the many recurring shots of magnificently adorned ceilings that open scenes throughout the film.

In the same way, Tony Palmer equally anchors his film within a filmic tradition. Whereas the very first shots of English landscape set in music recall Ken Russell's BBC documentary *Elgar* (1962), which has proved so influential in music documentaries, the closing credits pay tribute to the British documentary school which started in the 1930s to commit itself to documenting the British nation in all its diversity and landscapes, rural and industrial. Most importantly, though, Tony Palmer's film displays a stupendous array of light effects, celebrating the essence of cinematography. Thanks to the work of his cinematographer Nic Knowland, the feeling Osborne admired so in Purcell's music is thus conveyed through the extremely wide gamut of lighting: from the bland lights in modern times to the golden glow of Charles's reign, from elaborate chiaroscuro effects produced by candle sources to the numerous shafts of lateral lighting reminiscent of Dutch interior paintings, the numerous occurrences of backlighting, highlighting the ominous pulsating shadows of the Plague, or the eerie slow-motion shadow effects of the pageantry which illustrate the disintegration of the world following Queen Mary's death, to intense overexposure or again the pyrotechnical prowess that conveys the hellish furnace of the Great Fire, all resonate with Purcell's music. In this respect the film is a perfect illustration of Abel Gance's definition of cinema as "the music of light." Lighting is set into

---

[28]Another musical legacy is the electronic version of *Queen's Mary's Funeral March* arranged by Walter Carlos and used in Kubrick's *A Clockwork Orange* that accompanies the eerie slow-motion shadow effects of the pageantry that follows Mary's death.

IN SEARCH OF PURCELL'S LEGACY 219

symphonic drama, creating visual correspondences with Purcell's music while partaking of a celebration of the expressive powers of film.

Tony Palmer is a highly prolific director of music documentaries and historical dramas with a filmography that comprises over a hundred films ranging from a psychedelic portrait of Frank Zappa in *200 Motels* (1971) or documenting Leonard Cohen's tour in *Bird on a Wire* (1974), the TV series *Wagner* (1983) to portraits of performers like Maria Callas (1987) Yehudi Mehuhin (1991), Renée Fleming (2002), and composers like Gustav Holst, William Walton, Benjamin Britten, or Dimitri Shostakovich whose biography he adapted from Solomon Volkov's book in *Testimony* (1988).[29] The originality of *England, My England*, his biopic about Henry Purcell, lies in the complexity of its intermingled narrative threads, its self-reflexive dramatic devices, and the richness of its filmic textures. Through them, Purcell's music becomes the true central character of the narrative, an integral part of the expressive multimedia components of film.

WORKS CITED

Ackroyd, Peter. *English Music*. London: Penguin, 1992.
Barrell, John. "Make the Music Mute." *London Review of Books*, vol. 14, no. 13 (July 9, 1992): 7. http://www.lrb.co.uk/v14/n13/john-barrell/make-the-music-mute. Accessed on March 5, 2015.

---

[29] Tony Palmer realized a portrait of John Osborne himself a decade after his death. *John Osborne and the Gift of Friendship* (2006) includes many interviews of Osborne, his relatives, his collaborators, and friends as well as extracts of original stage performances of his most famous play. It is also worth noting that *England, My England* was Tony Palmer's second collaboration with Osborne after *God Rot Tunbridge Wells!* (1985) which is about German-born English composer George Frederick Handel who is introduced in old age, disgruntled, ranting and cursing, and looking back at his life. As Luc Gilleman remarks, "what this scene develops into is not docu-drama, however—no attempt to capture what the historic Handel might have been like, but, once more, a portrait of the loneliness of the artist—and that the artist, in the final instance, is always Osborne himself" (Osborne 1961: 175). Although the two films have many structural and formal echoes (including the quote "England, My England") and share the same cinematographer, the main difference is that Handel's voiceover is nearly omnipresent, sometimes even reducing scenes to pantomimes and characters to puppets. The overall aesthetics is more satirical and verging on the grotesque, using distorted wide angles, zooms, and fast forward in scenes recalling Tony Richardson's *Tom Jones* (1963).

Burden, Michael (ed.). *Performing the Music of Henry Purcell*. Oxford: Clarendon, 1996.

Burgoyne, Robert. *The Hollywood Historical Film*. Malden and Oxford: Blackwell, 2008.

Fish, Allan. "Review." July 24, 2012. https://wondersinthedark.wordpress.com/2012/07/24/england-my-england-1995-tv-tony-palmer/. Accessed on March 2, 2015.

Gilleman, Luc. *John Osborne, Vituperative Artist: A Reading of His Life and Work*. New York and London: Routledge, 2002.

Herissone, Rebecca. "Introduction." In Rebecca Herissone (ed.), *The Ashgate Research Companion to Henry Purcell*. Farnham, UK and Burlington, USA: Ashgate, 2012, 1–11.

Herissone, Rebecca (ed.). *The Ashgate Research Companion to Henry Purcell*. Farnham, UK and Burlington, USA: Ashgate, 2012.

Osborne, John. "Letter to My Fellow Countrymen." *Tribune*, August 18, 1961. http://www.independent.co.uk/life-style/a-letter-to-my-fellow-countrymen-in-august-1961-the-cold-war-escalated-with-the-building-of-the-berlin-wall-and-the-proliferation-of-nuclear-weapons-seemed-certain-1367810.html. Accessed on March 2, 2015.

Walter, James. "'The Solace of Doubt?' Biographical Methodology After the Short Twentieth Century." In Peter France and William St Clair (eds.), *Mapping Lives: The Uses of Biography*. New York: Oxford University Press, 2004, 321–335.

Weber, William. *The Rise of Musical Classics in Eighteenth-Century England: A Study in Canon, Ritual and Ideology*. Oxford: Clarendon, 1992.

Wood, Bruce. *Purcell: An Extraordinary Life*. Oxford: Oxford University Press, 2009.

PART IV

Postface

Does One Need to Be a Man
to Be a Great Man?

Nathalie Prince

Could great historical men be women? This is a puzzling question, which this book on different forms of biographical writings addresses between the lines. It is indeed a tricky question. The philosophical idea of a "great man" did not start with Machiavelli, but it was expressed in a symptomatic way in *The Prince* (Machiavelli 1952). Machiavelli writes that history or fortune is like a woman. What does it mean? First of all, contrary to men, women could not be *in* history or makers of history. History could be a woman, because it is beautiful and attractive, so beautiful, says the Florentine thinker, that the man of action may be paralyzed, as if struck down, by contemplation; it can be so attractive that he may feel stopped, frozen in a sort of expectation; unresolved and helpless, with his eyes wide open, he is unable to act or do anything. But history is a woman and it can be ill-treated, beaten, and dominated. Men of action should be able to move beyond a state of contemplation and remain cool in front of the beauty of history. He should seize history the way a woman should be seized, brutally and firmly, becoming her master

N. Prince (✉)
Le Mans Université, Le Mans, France
e-mail: Nathalie.Prince@univ-lemans.fr

© The Author(s) 2018
D. Letort and B. Lebdai (eds.), *Women Activists and Civil Rights Leaders in Auto/Biographical Literature and Films*,
https://doi.org/10.1007/978-3-319-77081-9_14

and submit her... this is why the "great man" in history can only be a man.

The image persists in Machiavelli's works and becomes more precise in one of his youth poems, through the allegory of the "occasion" in *Kairos*, that instant when time and action meet: before, it is too early and after, it is too late. Here again, one thinks of a woman; here again, she is sublime and fatale, but she is presented with originality: she has hair only at the front of her head. The back and the neck remain bald. Therefore if the man of action misses his chance, he will not be able to catch up with her, so he will be left with just two eyes to weep. Conversely, if the man of action wants to stick to "the effective reality of things," to history in progress, he must seize quickly the woman by her hair and drag her on the ground to him... Man's political capacity to control history is significantly called a *virtù* by Machiavelli. But this *virtù* is not the Greek *arété*, it is not at all our moral virtue, the "doing it right." Here, we are referring to the masculine *virtù*, etymologically from *vir*. For to dominate and defeat history, to leave one's mark and imprint, violence, nerve, and vice are needed. In brief, nothing feminine... I would underline that the historians of ideas all agree in recognizing Machiavelli's great modernity. Before him, the philosophies of history succumbed to fate. Fortune or history were unreadable, blind, and human actions were ineffective. That history becomes a woman, then it is a progress.

Under these conditions, it remains difficult to perceive how the "great men" of history could be women. Nevertheless, this book is concerned with "great women" such as Winnie Mandela, Ida B. Wells, or Michelle Obama... Is it possible to rethink history by giving women the place they deserve? Up to now, historians, poets, writers, even filmmakers, have convinced us that the "great women" of history were at best precious spouses and adorable mothers, wonderful lovers sometimes. It is true that women can provoke wars and wanderings; but then they are only present because they trigger Achilles' anger, Menelaus' jealousies, and Ulysses' love. They are Penelopes and Helens, they are also mothers and childminders, but in reality they are nothing more than stooges.

History and Gender

This book addresses the gender question (male/female) and the gender of history: it is first and foremost discussed through a generic approach. When biopics question the historical individual (female or male) his/her psychology, moments, affinities, they posit a meeting between the individual and history, the individual and the universal, the singular and the general. By nature, biopics tell individual history and personalize history. Here, there is no "cunning of reason" (Hegel 1979) and no "cunning by nature" (Kant 2009); no idealist dialectics, no materialist dialectics; no "end of History" (Fukuyama 1992), no providence or *fatum*. Human beings make history; the individual is its author. His/her emotions and his/her intentions explain everything. This is why biopics deviate to romance if one considers along with Walter Benjamin that romance glorifies the individual (Benjamin 1930). But then, does one make biopics to tell the story of a man or to tell history? But then, could not historical coherence be fictional?

Biopics henceforth build on two dialectical tensions: they always submit history to certain individuals, and at the same time they raise some individuals to a historical status. One can wonder (and this book has provided some answers) if, by making men (or women) great, by making their role in history great, by making historical characters great, is it not a way of shrinking history?

Answering these questions necessitates the work of historians, but not in isolation: the problematic of storytelling, of narrative instances, and the question of focalization have a role to play, if only because biographies and autobiographies mix truth and fiction, narration and reality, romance and history. There is no understanding of biopics without this multiplicity of viewpoints, which the Research Center 3L. AM encourages through its interdisciplinary research projects, notably within the study of identities and cultural memories, on individual and collective levels.

By focalizing on the historical figure, Delphine Letort and Benaouda Lebdai present an innovative research proposal on auto/biographies, carrying on their study into the construction of memory in the arts and in history.

WORKS CITED

Benjamin, Walter. "Crise du roman, À propos de Berlin Alexanderplatz de Döblin (1930)." *Œuvres II*, trans. R. Rochlitz, 189–197. Paris: Gallimard, 2000.
Benjamin, Walter. *Œuvres II*, trans. R. Rochlitz. Paris: Gallimard, 2000.

Fukuyama, Francis. *La Fin de l'histoire et du dernier home*. Paris: Flammarion, 1992.

Hegel, Georg Wihlhelm Friedrich. *Leçons sur la Philosophie de l'histoire* (posth. 1833), trans. J. Gibelin. Paris: J. Vrin, 1979.

Kant, Emmanuel. *Idée d'une Histoire universelle d'un point de vue cosmopolitique* (1784). Paris: Gallimard, 2009.

Machiavelli, Nicolas. *Le Prince* (*Il Principe ou De Principatibus*, 1532). *Œuvres complètes*. Paris: Gallimard, 1952.

INDEX

A

Activism, 3, 5, 34, 39, 45, 48, 49, 60, 68, 74, 77, 82, 94, 100, 105, 125, 198

African National Congress (ANC), 13, 18, 19, 26–29

Anti-apartheid, 13, 14, 21, 29, 30

Apartheid, 14–16, 18, 19, 21–24, 27, 28, 30, 31

Arab Spring, 5, 33

Arc, Joan of, 162–164

Asante, Amma, 7, 172, 178

The Audacity of Hope, 125

Auteur, 167, 191, 199

Authenticity, 1, 4, 6, 69, 70, 92, 102, 167, 195

Autobiographical pact, 15, 21, 69, 95

Autobiography, 1–4, 6, 13, 15–19, 21–24, 26–28, 30, 31, 46–48, 50, 52, 54, 56–58, 60, 61, 84, 93–97, 101–104, 109–121, 127, 142, 149, 172, 174

Autobiography of Malcolm X (The), 109

Autodiegetic, 17, 21, 110

Automedia, 68

B

Bakhtine, Mikhail, 124

Banner, Lois W., 124

Belle, 7, 50, 144, 172, 178–187

Bhabha, Homi, 3

Bingham, Dennis, 118, 153, 158, 164, 169, 189

Biographer, 94, 96, 134, 212–214

Biography, 3, 4, 47, 69, 105, 111, 121, 124, 125, 131, 132, 145, 154, 157, 159, 164, 169, 193, 203, 208–210, 214, 219

Biopic, 6, 7, 91, 98, 102, 103, 111, 112, 116, 121, 153–162, 164–169, 178, 189–191, 193, 195, 197, 198, 203, 209, 217, 219

Birth of a Nation (The), 92, 115

Black Nationalism, 114

Black Power, 2, 120

Blacks, 21, 112, 127, 129, 143

© The Editor(s) (if applicable) and The Author(s) 2018
D. Letort and B. Lebdai (eds.), *Women Activists and Civil Rights Leaders in Auto/Biographical Literature and Films*, https://doi.org/10.1007/978-3-319-77081-9

227

Black womanism, 74
Bourdieu, Pierre, 4
Brandfort, 23, 24
Breckinridge, Sophonisba, 5, 45–56, 58–61
Brown, Elaine, 2
Brown, Tom, 92, 155
Bruzzi, Stella, 194

C
Caine, Barbara, 3
Cairo, My City, Our Revolution, 5, 34
Celebrity, 155, 156, 166
Civil rights, 2–4, 8, 35, 37, 46, 54, 60, 92, 120, 129, 131, 134, 135, 194, 196
Civil rights activist, 56, 129
Civil War, 5, 51, 52, 54, 56, 58, 82, 91, 100, 130–132, 148, 176
Class, 6, 19, 27, 53, 54, 67, 68, 83, 86, 124, 129, 135, 174, 179, 185, 194
Clinton, Hillary, 72, 126
Colbert, David, 124
Crusade for Justice–The Autobiography of Ida B. Wells, 93, 95
Custen, George F., 91, 154

D
Davis, Angela, 2, 120
Deleuze, Gilles, 163
Documentary, 4, 5, 93, 98–100, 102–105, 157, 191, 193, 199, 217, 218
Douglass, Frederick, 92, 103
Dreams from My Father, 125, 135
Du Bois, W.E.B., 94, 104

E
Eakin, Sue, 141, 148, 149, 173
Egypt, 33–40
Emplotment, 3

F
Facebook, 65, 68–70, 76–78, 80, 82, 86, 166
Faludi, Susan, 82
Feminism, 5, 17, 46, 48, 49, 51, 69–78, 80, 82, 86, 94, 158
Fiction, 3, 34, 35, 74, 92, 102, 103, 134, 141, 142, 156, 197, 225
First Lady, 6, 124–126, 128, 130–133, 136
491 Days– Prisoner Number 1323/69, 15, 30
Friedman, Jeffrey, 156, 168

G
Garvey, Marcus, 114
Gbowee, Leymah, 82
Gender, 5, 8, 17, 28, 50, 72, 79, 80, 83, 93–96, 104, 105, 154, 161, 171, 179, 180, 185, 194, 224
Gengembre, Gérard, 4
Ginsberg, Allen, 168
Gone with the Wind, 91, 143
Government, 29, 36, 42, 55, 75, 82, 95, 125, 212
Grace and Grit (2013), 65
Greaves, William, 5, 92, 93, 98, 99, 105
Gunning, Tom, 163, 164

H
Haan, Binne de, 105
Hagiography, 149, 157, 190, 197

Haley, Alex, 6, 109, 111, 120
Hawking, Stephen, 165
Haynes, Todd, 156, 158, 167
Hero, 160, 166, 203
Historical leaders, 3, 4, 7
History, 3–5, 13–17, 19, 22, 39, 47, 54, 68–71, 73, 74, 82, 91–95, 98–100, 124, 125, 129–133, 136, 137, 140, 148, 153–155, 157, 158, 168, 169, 172, 173, 176–178, 182, 183, 185–187, 190–192, 197, 199, 207, 210, 216, 223–225
Howl, 116, 156, 168
Hutcheon, Linda, 162

I
Ida B. Wells–A Passion for Justice, 93, 98, 100
Imitation Game (The), 166
I'm Not There, 156, 158, 167, 189

J
Jesus movie, 7, 158
Jewison, Norman, 112

K
King, Martin L., 100, 120, 137

L
Lacanian, 190, 202
Lacan, Jacques, 200
Lean In, 65, 66, 68–70, 74, 76, 78–83, 85
Ledbetter, Lilly, 65, 67, 84, 85
Lee, Spike, 6, 92, 109, 110, 112–114, 116–121

Lejeune, Philippe, 1, 15, 16
LeRoy, Mervyn, 165
LGBT, 196–198, 203
Lincoln, 7, 91, 123, 159, 160, 168, 190, 193
Long Walk to Freedom, 19, 28, 31
Lyotard, Jean-François, 158

M
Madame Curie, 165
Malcolm X, 6, 92, 109–121, 137, 160
Mandela, Nelson, 4, 14, 15, 18, 19, 21, 23, 26–28, 30, 31, 120
Mandela (Madikizela), Winnie, 4, 13–17, 19–22, 24, 26–28, 30, 31, 161, 224
Marable, Manning, 111
McQueen, Steve, 6, 92, 141, 143–145, 149, 172
Méliès, George, 163, 164
Memoir, 1, 34, 68, 70, 71, 73, 75, 82, 85, 125
Michelle–A Biography, 124, 125
Michelle Obama–An American Story, 124, 131
Middle-class, 19, 27, 135, 174
Milk, 7, 189–191, 193, 194, 196–203
Milk, Harvey, 7, 190–196, 199, 200, 202, 203
Moulin, Joanny, 3, 105
Muhammad, Elijah, 111, 114, 118, 119
Mundy, Liza, 124, 130, 134
Music, 7, 69, 114, 117, 134, 145, 146, 167, 168, 202, 207, 208, 210–212, 214–219

N
Nation of Islam, 112, 114, 116

230 INDEX

Neale, Steven, 154
New Deal, 5, 46
Nichols, Bill, 103
Nonfiction, 92, 102, 103
Northup, Solomon, 6, 7, 139–141,
    144, 145, 148, 149, 172–174,
    176, 177

O
Obama, Barack, 123, 125–127, 130,
    135, 136
Obama, Michelle, 6, 124–128,
    130–133, 135–137, 224

P
Palmer, Tony, 7, 207, 208, 217–219
Part of My Soul Went with Him,
    13–17, 19, 22, 30
Perdomo, Emma, 83
Politics, 17–19, 27, 29, 38, 50, 57,
    68, 71–74, 93–95, 134, 158,
    162, 179, 180, 190, 191, 194,
    202
Postcolonial, 2, 3, 178, 183
Postfeminism, 72, 75
Psychology, 127, 225

Q
Queer, 7, 171, 187, 190, 191, 197,
    199, 203

R
Race, 54–59, 92–97, 100, 103, 105,
    114, 120, 124–127, 136, 154,
    179, 180, 182, 185
Racism, 60, 78, 82, 95, 103, 127,
    129, 130, 148, 171, 186

Renders, Hans, 105
Revolution, 5, 22, 28, 33–37, 39–42,
    66, 72, 77, 79
Robben Island, 14, 15, 26
Roberts, Martin, 75
Roots, 111, 125, 126, 155
Rose, Nikolas, 75

S
Said, Edward, 34
Sandberg, Sheryl, 5, 65, 66, 85
Segregation, 56, 57, 101, 130, 132
Sexism, 73, 77, 85
Shakur, Assata, 2
Slave, 6, 92, 100, 119, 130, 131,
    133, 136, 139–145, 147, 171,
    173–179, 182–187
Slavery, 7, 52, 100, 125, 131, 133,
    136, 139–141, 143–145, 148,
    149, 159, 171–173, 176, 178,
    180–182, 184–187
Soggot, David, 15
Soueif, Ahada, 5, 33, 35–43
South Africa, 14–17, 21, 22, 24, 29,
    31
Soweto, 14, 18, 21, 23, 26–28, 31,
    120
Starobinski, Jean, 1
Steve Jobs, 157, 165

T
Tahrir Square, 37
A Theory of Everything, 165, 166
Times of Harvey Milk (The), 193
Truth, 14, 16, 28, 31, 34, 35, 140–
    142, 149, 165, 174, 194, 225
12 Years a Slave, 6, 7, 92, 139–141,
    144, 145, 147, 149, 172–174,
    177, 178, 180, 182, 186, 187

U

U.S., 45, 46, 51, 68, 70–72, 78, 82, 86, 120, 127, 156, 172, 176, 178, 186, 190

Upper class, 103

V

Van Sant, Gus, 7, 190–193, 197, 198

Vidal, Belén, 92, 155

W

Walker, Alice, 73

Washington, Booker T., 93, 94, 99, 104

Wells, Ida B., 5, 93–99, 103, 105, 224

White, Hayden, 3

Whites, 16, 111, 127, 143, 181

Wilson, David, 6, 140, 141, 143, 149, 173

Woman activist, 5

Working-class, 67, 68, 86, 135

Z

Zanuck, Richard D., 165

Zuckerberg, Mark, 69

CPSIA information can be obtained
at www.ICGtesting.com
Printed in the USA
LVHW07*1919090518
576575LV00016B/196/P